LOVE IN THE TIME OF TYRANNY

A New Perspective on the Song of Songs

ANDREW LEVY

Dedicated to Hilary, Lilian, Rosie and Zack

And to the memory of Herbert Levy and Mike Solomon

La Nature est un temple où de vivants piliers
Laissent parfois sortir de confuses paroles

Nature is a temple where living pillars
Sometimes emit confusing words

Correspondances - Fleurs du mal

Charles Baudelaire

Contents

Part Three - The Song of Songs which is about Solomon

Conclusion

INTRODUCTION

An Upturned World in the Time of Tyranny

The editor unwrapped the papyrus in the antechamber of the house in Jerusalem. The commission had been to compose a love song surpassing any previously written. Unravelling before the editor's eyes on the table were layer upon layer of some of the finest erotic masterpieces that the region had produced. From Jerusalem itself, and the countryside surrounding it. But also from further afield - as far as Egypt in the South, and Lebanon in the North.

'How should I use these poems', the editor thought, 'when there is another burning message I also want to convey? Great love songs may reflect our highest emotions but they can also imply that all is well with the world. The world I live in is anything but. It is a world of hierarchy, where the palace dictates and the poor obey; where public affection is frowned upon; where wealthy men lead and women must follow. That world is an unjust world.

'I believe in a very different world - an upturned world - where the sort of oppressive power I know only too well is treated with the contempt it so richly deserves, and where its royal, human source is brought to book.'

After much consideration of the sublime material on the table, the editor picked up a pen and began the great editing process by adding in the following four words:

שִׁיר הַשִּׁירִים אֲשֶׁר לִשְׁלֹמֹה

'Shir ha-shirim asher li-shlomoh'
'The Song of Songs which is Solomon's'

The ravages of time prevent us knowing whether this portrayal of the creation of the first words of the finest love poem in the western canon bears any relation to reality. But, given the poem's message, it is entirely plausible and makes it as relevant today as it was when written over two millennia ago.

I have set out the words above as my attempt to understand how the Song of Songs came into existence. The fact that few commentators over the years would have described its formation in this fashion tells its own story. For a work which seems to be everybody's favourite Biblical book, the Song of Songs has been badly misunderstood over the centuries. Rarely has one book attracted such exuberant praise from so many strange bedfellows. One of the 'high priests' of the new Atheism expressed how much pleasure he derived from the English translation of the Song of Songs with which he was familiar from the King James version.[1] Rabbi Akiva in the second century CE famously remarked that the entire Bible may be holy but the Song of Songs was the holy of holies.[2] The early third century CE Christian scholar, Origen of Alexandria, stated that the Song of Songs 'speaks of this love with which the blessed soul is kindled and inflamed towards the word of God'.[3] Unsurprisingly, commentaries abound, written by scholars with the highest credentials.

This book, however, approaches the Song of Songs from a completely different angle. It seeks to answer a deceptively simple question. King Solomon appears in the Song of Songs a mere seven times. The Song of Songs is a poem about the erotic relationship between two lovers, neither of whom is King Solomon. What, then, has King Solomon got to do with the Song of Songs?

Solomon has had a remarkably good press over the years. His standing is that of the wisest of all kings whose wisdom and hubris were both exhibited with women. When two women claimed to be the mother of the same child, his powers of discernment could distinguish between the real mother and the impostor. However, his penchant for the fairer sex also brought about his downfall - an over-indulgence with a thousand wives who ultimately led him down the path to failure. But is that the full story? And how does it link to the Song of Songs?

The central contention of this book is that, while the Song of Songs is one of the greatest love poems in the whole of western literature, it is more than a love song. It also comprises an attack on the reputation of King Solomon and, thereby, his outlook on the world. Within the diverse parts making up its whole are clear elements of scorn for King Solomon, some of them direct, others subtle and more concealed.

---

[1] *'Forgive me, spirit of science'* New Statesman, 29 December 2010, Richard Dawkins.

[2] Mishnah Yadayim 3:5.

[3] Origen; *The Song of Songs: Commentary and Homilies*, Translated and annotated by R.P Lawson. London, Newmans Green, 1957, Prologue, 38.

This has been largely ignored for centuries and, with a few brief exceptions,[4] largely omitted from any discussion in modern commentaries on the Song of Songs, except for a few parenthetical comments. This book seeks to rectify that omission. It focuses on the interplay between the clear history we have of the life of Solomon in the books of Kings and Chronicles (which I will term, for convenience, the 'history books'), and the overt and covert references to Solomon in the Song of Songs. As we move through the history books and then the Song of Songs itself, a much more nuanced picture of King Solomon emerges.

In the history books, we will see that two competing portraits emerge of King Solomon. The first is the one on which his reputation is now built – that of the great and wise king who was beguiled by the charms of his women and, thereby, destroyed himself. But there is another portrait in the history books which I will consider in detail in this book. It shows a man who fails, on every count, to meet the requirements of a king, as set out in the book of Deuteronomy. It is the portrayal of a king who is predestined by God and birth to build the temple, yet ends up spending almost twice as long building his (much more grandiose) royal palace and, in the process, subjugating his own people. By the time of his death, long after the building project has been completed, the people still loathe him for the oppression he has wrought.

And Solomon's whole character may have resulted from his upbringing. His birth, and the traumatic events leading up to it, are fully recounted. However, the Bible's references to Solomon's youth are remarkably sparse (unlike the examples relating to his later life, referred to above, which are set out in great detail). But inferences from family events described in the book of Samuel, when he would have been a child (where his absence from the stories is striking), and his passivity at the time of his ascension to the throne, paint a picture of a child brought up in a dysfunctional family. His later cruelty is perhaps an unsurprising reaction to such a fraught upbringing.

The Song of Songs has a vast reception history. For Jews over the centuries, it has been a love song between God and Israel - and the terms of endearment in the poetry were largely interpreted accordingly. In somewhat similar vein, for Christians it has been understood as a love song, but between Christ and the Church. For modern academic writers, it is simply a secular love song, and nothing more, between a young man and a young woman, which weaves in older material to create the work

---

[4] Zakovitch, 10-11, Segal 151-4 (who focuses on the criticisms in the song of all ideas containing the root sh-l-m which comprises the root form of Solomon in Hebrew).

which has reached us. All these interpretations, while mutually contradictory, exhibit one common feature. Each seeks to reduce the Song of Songs to the theological or ideological position which it advocates.

It is the contention of this book that all such explanations, while varied in their conclusions, fail to do full justice to the Song of Songs. They tell us much more about their own underlying ideological predilections than they do about the Song of Songs. The argument of this book will *not* be that everything in the Song of Songs can be referred to the life of King Solomon - that would be to accept the sort of reductionism which this book specifically rejects. Rather, it is that the failure to appreciate the importance of King Solomon to the Song of Songs has led to significant misunderstandings of crucial parts of the poem. In redressing this absence and recalibrating our commentary, as it were, we will embark on a new interpretation and thereby strike a new balance. In so doing, it is to be hoped that the true power of the poetry and message of the Song of Songs can emerge and new conclusions can be drawn. That is not to say, however, that the whole of the Song of Songs can be fully interpreted or understood; it cannot, and this book does not claim to do so. There are still numerous gaps in our knowledge as to the exact meaning of many passages.

A fuller picture can only occur as a result of a process of interpretation. In embarking on this hermeneutical journey, the first stop will be the first verse of the Song of Songs. Traditional commentators, both Jewish and Christian, have argued that this verse ('the Song of Songs which is Solomon's') attributes authorship of the text to Solomon. Chapter 1 asks whether Solomonic authorship is possible and, if not, what we are to make of the enigmatic phrase 'which is Solomon's' (which hinges, in English grammatical terms, on the meaning of the apostrophe contained in the phrase). We shall see that the answer to this question is crucial to the rest of our journey.

Chapter 2 considers the earlier part of the life of Solomon. His birth is described in detail in the book of Samuel, whereas the Bible is entirely silent on his youth. What ramifications does this have? His story is picked up again in the book of Kings with his ascension to, and early years on, the throne. We will see that two stories are in fact being told; one of a wise king whose intellectual and emotional faculties are extraordinary and another, very different, story of a man who is destined for a dramatic fall from grace.

Chapter 3 considers Solomon's life from its defining moment – his building of the temple which became, and still remains in many ways, a central focus of Judaism.

The description of its construction, in the history books, might have been intended to exhibit the power and might of the great king; but, lurking near the surface and in full view of sensitive readers, is a story of slave labour, only too reminiscent for the Israelites of another time and another country. The Israelites might have been thinking of Egypt as that other time and country. The country, however, on which Solomon was fixated was Lebanon. It was from here that the materials originated which he used to build his temple and much more grandiose palace. Lebanon's relevance will only become fully apparent as we move on to the commentary on the Song of Songs.

With chapter 4 we end the description of the life of Solomon by briefly summarising the conclusions we can draw from analysing his biography as described in the history books.

Chapter 5 returns us to where we started – the opening line of the Song of Songs. Having determined the meaning of 'which is Solomon's' in chapter 1 of this book, chapter 5 looks at the words immediately preceding it. How are we to understand the phrase 'the Song of Songs'? It is capable of two meanings, both of which are considered in chapter 5. 'The Song of Songs' could indicate that it is the best song but it also might imply that it is a collection of songs. In different reception histories, these two meanings are crucial to its interpretation. For those approaching the text from the Jewish and Christian religious traditions, its outstanding quality ('the best song') seemed to entice them to read the Song of Songs wholly differently from its natural meaning. Whilst this may produce spiritual enlightenment, it rarely assists us in revealing the meaning of difficult passages.

For modern academic readers, the fact that the Song of Songs seemed to acknowledge in its title that it was a collection of songs only heightened their desire to reveal its parts. There are clear types of song making up the Song of Songs. It contains poems of dialogue between the lovers, soliloquies, erotically-laden physical descriptions of the lovers and even an apparent wedding scene. All such poems are known from other Middle Eastern cultures of the time. Dissecting the parts has been a regular feature of the interpretative process over the last two hundred years. Although this approach can uncover crucial information about the underlying material, especially in the light of new archeological evidence about the surrounding civilisations, it has often masked the need for an appreciation that the Song of Songs is more than the sum of its parts. Via a nineteenth-century musical analogy, chapter 5 seeks to remedy this.

These chapters mark a considerable detour from the text of the Song of Songs. They are, however, vital to answering the question, raised near the beginning of this introduction, concerning the connection between the life of King Solomon and the Song of Songs. They therefore form a necessary launchpad from which to embark on a detailed analysis of the text. Following on from these chapters is a commentary on the Song of Songs which, in turn, flows naturally from the chapters' dissection of the life of Solomon. An interpretation of the Song of Songs within the context of an analysis of the life of Solomon is very different from one lacking this crucial addition. The overt references to Solomon in the Song can be reinterpreted, and covert references to him can be understood.

What one discovers are two lovers who, apart from being deeply in love with each other, also believe in a very different world to the one they inhabit. The lovers never existed in reality; they are the mere playthings of the author and then of the editor. The editor's intention in fashioning the Song of Songs is crucial. That intention was to create much more than just a love story. The Song of Songs is also about the hierarchy and injustice at the heart of the establishment which the editor probably knew, and certainly knew of, in Jerusalem. It replaces that centre of power and oppression with a subtly egalitarian message which itself develops through the course of the poem. Both lovers learn from each other. They do so in order to build up a better description of the relationship which they desire and the sort of society which they (and by extension the editor) crave. That society is more just and more equal than the one that existed at the time.

Inevitably, a poetic text written in Biblical Hebrew involves nuance and wordplay which cannot be replicated, entirely or at all, in any translation. My translation seeks, as much as possible, to retain all such characteristics but, of course, fails to achieve its goal - as every translation inevitably must, especially one involving the interpretation of a finely-crafted poetic text, written well over two thousand years ago in a very different context. I have sought to explain both the difficulties and the delights of the Hebrew in the commentary.

We must embark on the first stage of our journey without further delay. This commences by seeking to understand who may have been claiming authorship of the Song of Songs. That, in turn, requires us to investigate the first verse of the Song of Songs in detail. What is the relationship between King Solomon and the Song of Songs? Scholars consider that the superscription was often the last thing to be added to a Biblical work (hence the imagined description of its creation at the beginning of this introduction). The use of superscriptions therefore takes on a great importance which we now consider in chapter 1.

PART ONE

לִשְׁלֹמֹה

SOLOMON'S

ONE

From the Top

Of one thing the Rabbis were certain. King Solomon wrote three books now canonised in the Bible; the Song of Songs, Proverbs and Ecclesiastes. Their disagreement lay in the order in which those books were written.[5] Rabbi Jonathan was of the view that Solomon must have written the Song of Songs in his youth because that is the time most appropriate to words of song. He would have written Proverbs in middle age when one thinks in proverbial form. Only in his dotage would Solomon have written Ecclesiastes because only then could he have written words of ephemerality (translating the term '*havalim*', a word central to the book of Ecclesiastes, as 'ephemerality'). Other Rabbis disagreed with this order but rarely doubted Solomonic authorship of all three books.

There is perhaps an irony in the fact that modern scholarship presents a complete mirror image of this unity in its rejection of Solomonic authorship of all three books. It does so on the basis of highly compelling evidence that some of the language in each book dates from a later period, and that each book contains internally inconsistent styles of writing. The Rabbis were probably wrong and modern scholarship is almost certainly correct; Solomon did not actually write any of the books.

Yet in order to understand what each book is about, we need to examine what assertions they make about their own authorship. The Rabbis thought that Solomon wrote each of the books because it appeared that each claimed Solomon wrote them. If the Rabbis were right (Solomon claimed authorship of each book) and modern scholarship is also correct (those claims of authorship are false), then each work is in fact pseudepigraphic: a work by a later author claiming authority by ascribing authorship to someone earlier (and in this case more prestigious).

Textual claims to Biblical authorship often rest on the first verse of the work. These have come to be known as 'superscriptions' which can sometimes serve other purposes but are mainly assertions of authorship. Each of the three books identified as having been written by Solomon has a first verse which contains a superscription. The book of Proverbs starts with the following superscript: 'The proverbs of

----

[5] Midrash Shir Hashirim 1.10.

Solomon, son of David, king of Israel'.[6]   Ecclesiastes opens: 'The words of Qohelet, the son of David, king in Jerusalem'.[7] The Song of Songs opens: 'The Song of Songs which is Solomon's'.[8] At this stage, we should note that this final superscription is more ambiguous than the others about authorship. It hinges on the meaning of the Hebrew particle '*li*' (translated by the possessive 'Solomon's' above). We will consider this in more detail later in this chapter. Our more immediate concern, however, is to consider how each of the three books treats the putative author, King Solomon, by considering, in turn, how the text itself refers to him.

The book of Proverbs

Following the opening superscription attributing authorship to Solomon, Chapters 1 to 9 of the book of Proverbs are seen by most commentators as one of the later parts of the book chronologically. Chapter 10 begins the part of the book regarded as the oldest and opens with another superscript 'The proverbs of Solomon' without needing again to refer to his lineage as the opening line of the book had previously done.[9] Scholars agree that the final chapters of the book are separate collections. Indeed, they appear to say so expressly. One collection in the book of Proverbs states: 'Also these are the proverbs of Solomon which the men of Hezekiah, the king of Judah, promoted'.[10] The final ones are even more explicitly independent: 'The words of Agur ben Yakeh, a speech of the man for Itiel'[11] and 'The words of King Lemuel, a prophecy with which his mother admonished him'.[12]

The Rabbis were keen to retain unitary authorship of the book of Proverbs and so sought to reconcile each of these references to Solomonic authorship. To the comment of one Rabbi, that Solomon had three names (Solomon, Yedidyah[13] and Qohelet[14]), another responds that he had four further names (Agur, Yakeh, Lemuel and Itiel) and in one fell swoop transfers authorship for all the apparently different authors in the book of Proverbs to Solomon.[15]

---

[6] Proverbs 1.1. All translations of the Hebrew Bible are mine unless otherwise stated.

[7] Ecclesiastes 1.1.

[8] Song of Songs 1.1.

[9] Proverbs 10.1.

[10] Proverbs 25.1. Translating '*he'etiku*' as 'promoted' which seems to be the meaning rather than 'copied' as favoured by the New JPS Translation.

[11] Proverbs 30.1.

[12] Proverbs 31.1. I take '*Massa*' as prophecy rather than 'King of Massa' as stated by the New JPS which goes against the trope.

[13] II Samuel 12.25.

[14] The Hebrew name for the author of Ecclesiastes.

[15] Midrash Shir Hashirim 1.10.

What cannot be in doubt is that an attempt was made later by the Rabbis to make Solomon the subject, as it were, of a series of proverbs and adages deriving probably from common folklore and, at one point at least, from Egyptian folk sayings.[16] The first person singular in the book of Proverbs is used of a father advising his son about how to lead a good life and to avoid its many potential pitfalls. The Rabbis infer that this father must be Solomon. Moreover, they have good grounds for doing so. Michael Fox points out[17] the degree to which so many of the proverbs are based on, and ideologically skewed towards, a royalist outlook. Yet paradoxically from a literary point of view, the book would work perfectly well without the references to Solomon. The proverbs stand or fall on their own terms. Solomonic authorship gives them authority but the book of Proverbs can be understood entirely independently of Solomon.

The book of Ecclesiastes

In the book of Ecclesiastes, on the other hand, the character Qohelet is involved very differently with the text. Qohelet is described as the son of David who was king over Jerusalem and so can readily be identified with King Solomon. Immediately following the superscript, the book opens with the words: 'Vapour of vapours, said Qohelet, vapour of vapours, everything is vapour'[18] (this is more familiar following the King James Bible translation as 'vanity of vanities...'). The book carries on for a few verses describing the repetitions which make the world and humans so ephemeral. Then it adds: 'I, Qohelet, was king over Israel in Jerusalem and I set my heart to inquire and to explore by means of wisdom all that occurs under the heavens'.[19]

With this introduction, the reader realises that the character, Qohelet, is to become centrally linked to the discussion. He is not merely a superscript addition by means of which a new meaning can be given to older poems and/or sayings. He sometimes speaks in the first person, and sometimes in the third person, but throughout we know that this is clearly his story. Near the end of the final chapter, chapter 12, a familiar message returns: 'And the dust will return to the earth as it was and the spirit will return to God who gave it. Vapour of vapours, said Qohelet, vapour of vapours,

---

[16] Proverbs 22.20 - 24.22.

[17] Michael Fox (2009), 500ff.

[18] Ecclesiastes 1.2. The word 'hevel' translated in the King James Bible as 'vanity' has many potential meanings. I previously translated it as 'ephemerality' in the context of the midrashic discussion in Midrash Shir Hashirim 1.10. Its prime meaning appears to be the ephemerality of breath - hence 'vapour'.

[19] Ecclesiastes 1.12 and 13a.

everything is vapour'.[20]   This has been described as the 'most memorable inclusio in the Bible'[21]; an inclusio means a wrapping of the text in repeated words at the beginning and conclusion in order to give the text a literary coherence. The text returns to where it came from at the very beginning, setting out in literary form the circularity of life which is at the heart of its message.

Thereafter the book carries on for another six verses.[22] Much ink has been spilled as to whether these six verses are integral to the book or a later addition. From a literary point of view, they make perfect sense. The inclusio means that Qohelet stops speaking at chapter 12 verse 8. In the next two verses, Qohelet is spoken of in the third person. This is no longer Qohelet describing himself, as he had done previously, even when he had spoken in the third person. He is clearly no longer speaking at all. It is a form of literary death. The six verses seem to be in two different styles. The first has been described by many commentators as an epilogue and the second as a postscript. I would prefer to see the first as a form of obituary. Qohelet is a character in this book and he has been killed off, as it were.

Proverbs and Ecclesiastes

As will be apparent, the use of the figure of Solomon/Qohelet in Proverbs and Ecclesiastes is very different. The literary centrality of Qohelet to the book of Ecclesiastes contrasts with the apparent irrelevance of Solomon to the book of Proverbs. Yet the stylistic difference masks a crucial similarity. In both books, Solomon/Qohelet is the subject and the author clearly wanted his work to be given a boost by means of a Solomonic authorial imprint, revealed in the first words of each work.

For the Rabbis, the same could be said of the Song of Songs. As stated previously, it opens with the Hebrew words 'Shir hashirim asher li-Shlomoh' - 'the Song of Songs which is Solomon's'. The Rabbis interpreted that as meaning that Solomon was the author. Our next task is to investigate whether the author of the Song of Songs intended the work (and indeed the superscription) to ascribe Solomonic authorship by using the format 'li-Shlomoh'. The answer to that question will help to reveal part of the meaning of one of the most enigmatic works in western literature.

---

[20] Ecclesiastes 12.7-8. The words translated as 'spirit' needs also to be understood as 'wind'.

[21] Michael Fox (1999), 332.

[22] Ecclesiastes 12.9-14.

Superscriptions

Superscriptions abound in the Bible. Many superscriptions are inserted in order to claim authorship but not all do so. Of the one hundred and fifty Psalms, one hundred and sixteen contain superscriptions. Sometimes they describe the type of Psalm (the words 'A song of ascents' appears before each of Psalms 120-134). They are sometimes longer and refer to an event in Biblical history; Psalm 34 for example begins with the superscript 'For David, when he feigned madness in front of Avimelech who expelled him and he left'. The Psalm which follows is in acrostic form and is a poem of praise of God. The superscript helps the reader to understand that this can occur even in a time of fear.

Many Psalms with superscripts refer to what might be seen as putative Davidic authorship. Some open with the superscript '*Mizmor le-David*' or '*Le-David mizmor*'. Crucial to such a claim of putative Davidic authorship of the Psalms is what the particle '*le*' means.[23] If it means 'of', then these phrases both mean something like 'David's Psalm' or 'A Psalm of David'. The problem with the particle '*le*' preceding a person's name is that it can mean different things in different contexts. One analysis[24] has shown that it can mean:

a) 'a work of X' (indicating X's authorship);

b) 'about X' (a work describing X);

c) 'for X's use' (X is a powerful person who can use the work as he thinks fit);

d) 'dedicated to X' (in other words clearly stating that it was not written by X);

e) 'belonging to X' (i.e. part of X's library as it were or of X's tradition); or

f) 'in the manner or style of X' (a later author deliberately writing in the style of X).

---

[23] '*le-*' and '*li-*' have the same meaning, the difference being a reflection of the different consonantal structure of the following word. Two of the Psalms are referred to as 'li-Shlomoh' (Psalms 72 and 127).

[24] L.A.F. LeMat, *Textual Criticism and Exegesis of Psalm 36*. (Utrecht, Holland: Kemink & Zoon 1957), 34.

The greater authority to be given to a work by writing the name of a famous king such as David as its first words must have been a great temptation for many of the authors of the Psalms. Most scholars agree that most of the superscriptions themselves are later additions to a psalm written at an earlier stage. Ultimately we do not know (and probably never will fully know) how and why Davidic authorship was ascribed to Psalms written after King David's time. Perhaps the richness and depth of the Biblical account of the life of King David allowed the author to pick events in that life which he could relate to in his personal prayer.

The Song of Songs with its phrase '*li-Shlomoh*' in the first verse also leads us to ask whether the author intended that curious, ambivalent phraseology to ascribe authorship to Solomon. Given the different meanings of the particle '*li-*', there are six possible options as to what is intended. It could mean:-

1. The Song of Songs by Solomon;

2. The Song of Songs about Solomon;

3. The Song of Songs to be used by Solomon;

4. The Song of Songs dedicated to Solomon;

5. The Song of Songs in the Solomonic tradition;

6. The Song of Songs in Solomonic style.

If we accept, as modern commentators do, that the Song of Songs was written after Solomon's time, then we must immediately eliminate the meanings in options 3 and 4 above. The work could not have been used by or dedicated to Solomon if written later. A dedication meaning could possibly be intended if the book had been written immediately after his death (in the way that many books today are dedicated to the memory of a recently deceased person) but that seems unlikely. In any event, the evidence pointing to later authorship points equally to the book not having been written in the immediate aftermath of Solomon's life but several centuries thereafter.

That leaves four possible options. Option 1 ascribes authorship of the work to Solomon even though it was written later. It is the option which ascribes the closest link with Solomon. Options 5 and 6 do something similar in that they assert that the work falls within his tradition or his style. Option 2 distances itself the most from Solomon. It does not claim autobiographical status; rather it concerns Solomon in much the same way that a work of Charles Dickens concerns David Copperfield or Oliver Twist. The opening line of the Song of Songs is certainly startling but which of the options available to us is the one which best reflects the author's intention in using the superscription '*li-Shlomoh*'?

The answer to that question must be based on a close analysis of the text of the Song of Songs itself. Within that context, we can come to a much more definitive answer.

Solomon in the Song of Songs

Solomon is a character who appears within the Song of Songs. This contrasts with the book of Proverbs, where the proverbs make sense perfectly well without the superscription reference to Solomon. Solomon is not really a character at all in the book of Proverbs. More of a comparison can be made to the book of Ecclesiastes where the character of Qohelet (i.e. Solomon) is central; here he appears either directly by his name or he speaks in the first person. In the Song of Songs, Solomon is also a character. There is, however, a fundamental difference in the nature of Solomon's character in the Song of Songs. The Song of Songs describes the love between a young man and a young woman. Solomon is mentioned seven times[25] in total in the book. Apart from the title, he appears in only three passages. These passages need to be studied briefly now to understand what role Solomon plays. They will play a central role later on as we use them to provide us with a fuller understanding of the work.

Solomon appears once in a passage near the beginning of the book. The lines are put into the mouth of the young female lover:

'Black am I and beautiful, O daughters of Jerusalem,
Like the tents of Qedar, like the curtains of Solomon.
Do not look upon me because I am dawn-darkened, that the sun has tanned me.
The sons of my mother became angry with me,
They placed me as a guard over the vineyard.
I have not guarded my own vineyard.'[26]

Solomon's appearance seems almost co-incidental at first and hardly central to the theme being played out. The young woman has already proclaimed in the opening lines of the book how wonderful her lover is and in these verses talks about the

---

[25] Song of Songs 1.1, 1.5, 3.7, 3.9, 3.11, 8.11, 8.12. There are allusions to him in puns in other passages which will be considered later in this book.
[26] Song of Songs 1.5-6.

problems she has in the treatment she receives from her brothers. The reference to Solomon's 'curtain' (translated by some as 'tapestry') is brief and apparently *en passant*. Some commentators do not see this reference to '*Shlomoh*' as being a correct understanding of the original text by the later Masoretic editors whose Hebrew version we now use. Their view is that '*Shlomoh*' ought to be re-vowelled as '*Salmah*', the name of a tribe which allows for a parallel between the 'tents of Qedar' and the 'curtains of Salmah'.

However, any such dismissal of the reference to Solomon as unimportant in this passage is incorrect. At the very end of the book, Solomon appears again in the final of his three 'scenes':

'Solomon had a vineyard in Baal-Hamon ['the Master of Plenty']
He gave the vineyard to the guards.
A man earns a thousand pieces of silver for his fruit.
My own vineyard is all mine in front of you,
The thousand is yours, Solomon,
And two hundred to those who guard his fruit.'[27]

As many commentators have noted, the reference here to Solomon is scornful or even mocking.[28] Many have also analysed the thousand pieces of silver and its potential meaning and the 'two hundred to those who guard his fruit'. Less commented upon has been the fact that there are clear parallels between this passage and the first passage in which the curtains of Solomon make an appearance. Both feature Solomon. Both include references to vineyards and watchmen. If the book of Ecclesiastes has the clearest inclusio near its beginning and its end, then this is a more subtle one. It is a framing more difficult to spot in that it does not repeat directly the identical words but it is more complete in that it includes not only the name of Solomon but also thematic links.

Crucially, in between these two passages framing the beginning and end of the Song of Songs is the only other passage making direct reference to Solomon. It does so three times. It is the longest such passage and gives a strong clue as to why the passage referring to Solomon at the end of the book is so critical:

---

[27] Song of Songs 8.11-12.
[28] Bloch, 220. Fox, (1985) 175. Zakovitch, 11 (Hebrew).

'Who is this coming up from the desert like pillars of smoke
Rendered more fragrant in myrrh and frankincense than all the powder of the
merchant?[29]
Look: Solomon's bed,
Sixty heroes surround it from the heroes of Israel.
All carrying a sword, trained in warfare,
Each man has a sword by his thigh, because of fear at night time.
King Solomon made himself a palanquin from the trees of Lebanon.
Its pillars he made from silver, its back from gold, its seat was purple,
In its midst it was inlaid with love.
Daughters of Jerusalem, go out and rejoice, daughters of Zion,
About King Solomon, about the crown
With which his mother crowned him,
On the day of his wedding, on the day of his heart's joy.'[30]

Again, this passage has been the subject of much interpretation. At first sight, it
appears to be a wedding ceremony and possibly a description of the procession. Any
attempt to place it in any historical context is likely to beg more questions than it
answers. The first word of verse 9 - '*apiriyon*' - translated here as 'palanquin', is
probably a loanword from Persian or Greek and appears nowhere else in the Bible.
No-one is sure what sort of structure it was. If it was some sort of sedan chair and
therefore the wedding ceremony is some sort of procession, then why does it have
pillars indicating something permanent? If, on the other hand, it is a permanent
structure, why are there men of war guarding it at night time when it is presumably
safely located in King Solomon's capital city Jerusalem?

The key to attempting to understand this passage, as so much else in the Song of
Songs, is not to take it literally as historical truth. The Song of Songs has a dream-
like nature and it constantly makes allusions to something or someone. Those
allusions are, however, often difficult to fathom and its enigmatic nature prevents
any interpretation being certain. Remaining tentative is a necessity when attempting
any analysis.

That said, there are enough clues, in what we have already seen, to draw certain
conclusions. Solomon's appearances in the Song of Songs are limited and fleeting.

---

[29] This verse is probably a separate poem but Solomon's apparent wedding ceremony is set within the
context of a (female) person coming up from the desert and as such I have chosen to present the
passage with the previous verse. Its link with the poem about Solomon will be discussed in the
commentary to this verse.
[30] Song of Songs 3:6-11.

He is not a major character. This distinguishes the book from Ecclesiastes where the figure of Solomon/Qohelet speaks regularly in the first person. In the Song of Songs, there are two main characters and they are the two lovers who largely talk to each other. Other characters intervene as they speak or reflect on the travails of love. Solomon is one of those other characters. From what we can see, he is scorned at the end of the Song of Songs. The wedding ceremony in the middle also seems highly unusual if understood as a poem in praise of the great and wise king. It might, at first glance, appear to be a beautiful description of Solomon's wedding but look closely and it is a parody of a wedding ceremony. It mocks what Landy describes as Solomon's 'self-glorification.....delusions of grandeur'.[31] Why describe a great king as having soldiers to guard him because of fear of the night? This might be true and a fair reflection of the need for security but why put it in a perfect report of a wedding ceremony? Why is there a reference to the crown with which Solomon's mother crowned him? Why could he not crown himself? There is clearly more to this passage than appears at first sight.

The superscription in the Song of Songs

We must now return to the issue of the superscription and what it means. In a book where the named character at the beginning of the book plays a fleeting role, it could have been the intention of the author to suggest that it was written by Solomon. The problem with this analysis is that we have seen that the references to Solomon, fleeting as they are, are almost entirely negative or mocking in character. It would be a brave author indeed who intended his work to be pseudepigraphic, implying Solomonic authorship, and then went on to create a song in which Solomon emerges a lampooned, minor character.

We can therefore eliminate option 1 from our menu of possible meanings of the superscription in the Song of Songs. The author did not intend the work to be seen as a work written by Solomon. Swiftly on its heels, we can also eliminate options 5 and 6. This work cannot, for similar reasons, have been seen as written in the Solomonic tradition or in the Solomonic style. It is far too critical for that.

Having previously eliminated options 3 ('used by Solomon') and 4 ('dedicated to Solomon'), the only option left is option 2. The author intended the Song of Songs to be about Solomon. In Proverbs and Ecclesiastes, Solomon is the subject. In the Song of Songs, Solomon is neither the subject nor the object - it is the lovers talking

---

[31] Landy (1983), 124, (2011), 119.

to each other who are both subject and object, depending on who is speaking. Solomon is, as it were, an indirect object.

At first glance, that appears a surprising meaning given that it indicates that the title of this love song is about a minor character who only appears fleetingly in it. Earlier, I compared the title of the Song of Songs to the way Charles Dickens named his books after their heroes. We can now see that that link is misplaced. A closer analogy, it seems to me, would be if Shakespeare had called one of his plays '*Tybalt*' rather than '*Romeo and Juliet*'. To resolve the dilemma that the Song of Songs is named after a minor character, some traditional readings have sometimes sought to identify the male lover with Solomon. This requires a reinterpretation of the text which is unsustainable.

In fact, the only meaning left is entirely appropriate if one looks more closely at the text. Is it merely a story of two lovers and their dreamlike calling to each other or is there something else going on concerning Solomon? Is it just a story of sweet nothings beautifully constructed or is there also a subtext which needs to be revealed? That is something I will seek to answer later in this book. At this stage, we need to consider the eponymous non-subject of our book. If the Song of Songs is about Solomon, who was King Solomon?

TWO

Dysfunction and Ascent

Solomon was an afterthought. His father was King David and he is the first major Israelite character in the Bible to have been born to a king. His mother was Bathsheba and this fact became a crucial factor in his ascension to the monarchy as we shall shortly see. His parents' adulterous union led to tragedy and he was born in its aftermath.

The book of Samuel is one of the finest pieces of literature that has come down to us from the ancient world. The narrative of the Hebrew Bible is almost always terse in style and in the David story we get one of its most exquisitely fashioned expositions. What characters say, and what they might be thinking, may be two wholly different things. In Erich Auerbach's memorable phrase, much of the action is 'fraught with background'.[32]

Solomon's birth

David's adultery with Bathsheba, and murder of Uriah, form a turning point in the David narrative.[33] David sees Bathsheba bathing on the roof and desires her. He sends a message to her and lies with her. She conceives. The problem however is that she is married to Uriah the Hittite, an army officer. It must be made to seem as if the child born of this adultery is actually a product of the marriage bed. So he gives Uriah, the professional soldier fighting in David's wars, an opportunity for leave to spend time with his wife. Uriah however refuses to go along with David's fiction.[34] David senses problems if Uriah stays alive and thus arranges for Uriah to be placed into the heat of battle where his death is inevitable. David effectively has killed him off.

Prior to this incident, David has been a strong character and leader who, through ruthless pursuit of his own ends, attained the throne and power. After it, he becomes

---

[32] Erich Auerbach: *Mimesis*, 12. Princeton, Princeton University Press, 1953.

[33] It is recounted at II Samuel 11.

[34] Whether Uriah knows exactly what is going on is not clear, as has been comprehensively demonstrated by Meir Sternberg. See Gaps, Ambiguity and the Reading Process 186-229 in *The Poetics of Biblical Narrative; Ideological Literature and the Drama of Reading*, Bloomington, Indiana University Press, 1987.

weak and easily manipulated by his children and others. His former absolute power turns into a series of episodes where he has to deal with rebel children. He no longer rules by means of his own wily political abilities but through the assistance of his generals to whom he becomes beholden.

David's nemesis is God. David quickly gathers Bathsheba into his household soon after her days of mourning for Uriah are over. He marries her and she gives birth to a son. In terminology which appears in similar fashion later in the book of Kings relating to David's descendants, the text then adds: 'But the thing that David had done angered the Lord.'[35]

God sends Nathan the prophet to admonish David. Nathan does so by means of a parable. When David recognises his own guilt through the message in the parable, Nathan's reply is interesting. It is commonly translated as 'The Lord has remitted your sin, you shall not die .... rather the son born to you shall certainly die'.[36] The translation of the Hebrew word '*he'evir*' as 'remitted' is one of a number of meanings of the word in Hebrew. In English, we sense the word 'remit' as meaning 'allay' or 'lighten'. The word does certainly have this meaning but crucially, in this context, its primary meaning is 'transfer'. God may have forgiven David but God has also transferred David's sin onto his newly-born son. The child is born and immediately becomes ill. David prays to God and fasts but to no avail. On the seventh day of his illness, the child dies.

David's reaction to this shocking tragedy is immediate. He goes to console Bathsheba. They have intercourse and produce another son whom God loved.[37] The son's name is '*Sh'lomoh*' - Solomon. The word means not only 'peace' but 'whole', 'full' and 'complete' and one can only assume that this was what his parents felt at finally giving birth to a healthy son. There is an interesting textual ambiguity as to which of his two parents decided to call their son Solomon. The Masoretic text as written down says 'and he called him Solomon' whereas a marginal note changes one of the letters so that it should be read as 'and she called him Solomon'.[38]

Solomon acquires another name, however. 'And [God] sent a message through Nathan the prophet and he called his name '*Yedidyah*', for the sake of God'.[39] The

---

[35] II Samuel 11.27.

[36] II Samuel 12.13-14.

[37] II Samuel 12.24. The word 'love' has a wonderful irony as the Bible never says that David loved any of his wives.

[38] Favouring 'and she called him Solomon' are the Syriac together with other masoretic manuscripts which may suggest that 'she called him Solomon' is the preferable reading.

[39] II Samuel 12.25.

name '*Yedidyah*' means 'beloved of God' or 'friend of God', reflecting that the text had previously said that God loved Solomon. The last two words in Hebrew '*ba'avur adonai*' have been translated as 'for the sake of God'. They are somewhat enigmatic and some have suggested the translation 'by the grace of God'.[40] Crucially however, the word '*ba'avur*' is the same root in Hebrew as the word '*he'evir*'. We now see that whereas David's sin is transferred to his first son who will die, God's love is transferred or passed on to Solomon, David's second son. To be born second and male is almost always to be granted favour in Biblical narratives.

Solomon's childhood - what we can infer

Given that Solomon is born with this portentous mark of favour, the Bible is remarkably silent on his early life. The Bible may have explicitly stated that God loves Solomon. At no point, however, does it describe David's relationship with his son. Following Solomon's birth scene, neither he nor Bathsheba is directly mentioned in the book of Samuel. They only reappear at the beginning of the book of Kings when David is an old man and about to die. We are left to imagine how they react to the events involved in David's fall from absolute power as described in the book of Samuel, the rape by David's son Amnon of his half-sister Tamar and the rebellion by another of his sons, Absalom.

In fact, one of the well-known moments in all these episodes is subtly linked to the events surrounding Solomon's birth and his elder brother's death. On hearing of the death of his rebellious son, Absalom, the text says: 'David was shaken. He went up to the parapet of the gate and wept, crying and saying as he went "My son, Absalom, my son, my son, Absalom. If only I had died instead of you, Absalom, my son, my son"'.[41] We recall that God transferred David's guilt onto his newly-born son who died as a result. In David's grief, he is reminded of that episode and wishes to reverse it. He wants to bear the ultimate price for his son's sin and die in his stead.

The silence about the relationship between Solomon and his father in the Bible can only lead us to speculate on the basis of what we are told. Nathan told David at the time of his adultery: 'And the sword will now never turn from your house since you despised me and took the wife of Uriah the Hittite to be a wife for you'.[42] It is hardly surprising therefore that, from the moment of Solomon's birth until David's death, the Bible describes David's family as dysfunctional. David is constantly facing

---

[40] See Alter: Ancient Israel 492-3.
[41] II Samuel 19.1 (in some translations II Samuel 18.33).
[42] II Samuel 12.10.

rebellion, much of it from family members. His failing powers and inability to lead require him to rely on plotting generals.

Solomon appears to grow up in a world of violence bereft of paternal love. The violence seems to have been preordained on Solomon as well as on David. When David is warned that it would be his descendant who would build God his temple, we are told by God: 'I will be to him like a father and he will be to me like a son who when he errs I will reproach with the rod of men and the afflictions of humans'.[43]

God may love Solomon but there is no evidence that his father does, or even has the inclination to do so. That gap in Solomon's upbringing must be a factor in our understanding of his actions as king. His wisdom may have been proverbial but, as we shall sec, it is accompanied by a cruel streak readily explicable from his childhood.

Given the number of events described by the Bible between the birth of Solomon and the description at the beginning of the book of Kings of the death of King David, we can assume that Solomon was a young adult at the time of the death of his father. Only when he becomes king does Solomon seem to assert himself. His path to the throne, though, is paved for him. It is made easy through the efforts of others.

Solomon's ascent to the throne

But for Bathsheba his mother and Nathan the prophet, Solomon would never have become king. The book of Kings opens[44] with King David being advanced in years. His eldest living son, Adonijah, the son of Chaggit 'was raising himself up saying "I will rule" and he made for himself a chariot and riders and fifty men running in front of him'.[45]

Adonijah got together members of the military and the priesthood but seems not to have been able to cover all bases since the text says that Nathan the prophet, the general Benaiah and others of David's fighting men were not aligned with Adonijah.

---

[43] II Samuel 7.14.

[44] There is a near consensus amongst scholars that the first two chapters of the book of Kings (describing the last days and death of King David) form part of the book of Samuel and were written by the same author. Certainly it retains the terseness of language and psychological insight of the book of Samuel. It also crucially contains Deuteronomic interpolations, discussed below, vital to understanding the relationship between the Solomon in the book of Kings and his depiction in the Song of Songs.

[45] I Kings 1.5.

The presumptive heir to the throne held a festive party to which he invited his family and the ruling classes, but pointedly the text adds: 'But he did not call on Nathan the prophet, Benaiah and his fighting men or Solomon'.[46]

Presumptive assertions of power, such as this, are of course extremely dangerous as rival claimants are notified as to exactly what the pretender's intentions are. Nathan goes straight to Bathsheba to warn her that Adonijah is ruling without David's knowledge. His advice to her is to go to David to inform the king of the position. Nathan also gives Bathsheba a short form of wording to use. He makes no mention of the festive party which Adonijah has organised.

In the Bible, when one person (A) tells another person (B) what to say to a third person (C), it is always worth comparing what A says to B with what B goes on to say to C. There are invariably differences and those differences are often highly telling.

Nathan's instruction to Bathsheba as to what to say is short. Bathsheba's conversation with David is much longer. Nathan may not have told her about the festive party but she mentions it to David as evidence of Adonijah's rebellion, indicating that she clearly knew more about the situation than we may first have thought.

She manipulates the limited information which she has been given by Nathan. However, she adds to it to make a much more powerful case against Adonijah and, thereby, puts her son in a much stronger position. First she repeats the comment which Nathan says she should tell the king: 'And she said to him: My lord, you promised by the Lord God to your maid servant that Solomon your son "will rule after me and he will sit on my throne"'.[47] There is no evidence of any such conversation in the Bible. Either we have not been told about it or it is a statement which Nathan and Bathsheba have concocted to manipulate an old and sick man. It is difficult to conceive that a declaration of such importance would have been omitted from the text, had it occurred.

She finally adds something entirely new: 'And my lord the king, the eyes of all Israel are on you to tell them who will sit on the throne of my lord the king after him. And it could be that when my lord the king lies with his fathers, I and my son Solomon could be treated as criminals'.[48] In other words she wants the whole situation to be

---

[46] I Kings 1.10.

[47] I Kings 1.17.

[48] I Kings 1.20-21.

made public. Solomon's position and indeed her own will only be safe through some sort of public declaration.

Nathan had presumably intended the truncated version of events he had given Bathsheba to be the prelude to the fuller version which he planned to give to the king. As Bathsheba is speaking, Nathan appears[49] and presents the fuller version of events of which we have been told.

David then calls Bathsheba back into his presence and repeats the promise which Nathan and Bathsheba have stated he had previously made. Again we have to look very carefully at the difference between the promise, as represented by Nathan to Bathsheba which she then told David, and what David actually promises. There is a revealing difference. David's version is as follows: 'And the king swore and said: "By the life of God who saved me from all evil, I swore to you by the Lord, the God of Israel saying that Solomon your son will rule after me and he will sit on my throne in my place and thus I proclaim today"'.[50] The crucial difference is the additional Hebrew word '*tachtai*' which I have here translated as 'in my place'. The Hebrew meaning of the word could also allow for a translation 'under me'. This has always, however, been rejected as not fitting the historical progression of son following father on the throne.

The problem with rejecting the translation 'under me', in this particular instance, is that there is ambiguity about exactly what Solomon's title is at this stage. David's order is that Solomon should immediately be crowned king - and that this should be done in public so that the kingdom is presented with a *fait accompli*. Solomon is to be made '*nagid*' - prince over Israel and Judah.

What are we to make of this apparent dual monarchy? It might be that it is all for show. King David wants it to be made abundantly apparent that Solomon is his successor. In this he is following Bathsheba's request to make things clear in the eyes of all Israel. Solomon rides out to a brook on the king's mule and is anointed there. And the people shout 'Long live King Solomon'. The text informs us that the sound is so great that the earth split open because of the noise.[51] Moreover, it has the desired effect on Adonijah and those he had invited to his own putative coronation feast. They each go their own way. The rebellion has been quelled and the succession has been established.

---

[49] At this point presumably Bathsheba withdraws, though the text does not say so explicitly. This is because at verse 28 King David calls for Bathsheba who then 'comes before the king'.
[50] I Kings 1.29-30. ('Proclaim' literally 'do').
[51] I Kings 1.32-40.

But this odd dual monarchy appears to have another purpose as well. There is an element of Solomon serving an apprenticeship in this arrangement. At this stage David does not seem to trust him.[52] We have so far been told nothing about the character of Solomon in either the second book of Samuel or here. He is an entirely passive figure in his own coronation and has yet to speak his first words in the Bible. He will exert enormous influence after his father dies. At this point, however, it is clear that he is not influencing events in any way. Rather, he is the beneficiary of the political manipulations occurring apparently between Adonijah and his priests and generals on the one hand and Nathan and his generals on the other.

Adonijah, seeing the way things are going, fears Solomon, grips the horns of the altar (i.e. he seeks sanctuary in a holy place) and asks for a commitment that he will not be killed by the newly-crowned king Solomon. King Solomon's reply is to say that if he behaves worthily he has nothing to fear. He then calls him out of his sanctuary and tells him to go home.[53] If Adonijah has any thoughts that he is now safe, he will be sorely disillusioned. Pretenders to the throne appear to live in a 'kill or be killed' world. Adonijah's fate is grim indeed, as we shall shortly find out.

More influential than anyone else in persuading David to make Solomon his chosen successor is Bathsheba. It is she who ensures that his coronation is public. She has masterfully manipulated the male figures in a patriarchal world to ensure that her son becomes king and thus her progeny will survive. At this stage, she appears to be the power behind Solomon's throne. The author of the Song of Songs, as we shall see later, knew it as well.

The commandment on kingship from father to son

When king David is about to die, he decides to instruct his son in the art of kingship. The first thing he says fits in with the impression we already have of David's relationship with Solomon - that David is not really sure that Solomon is strong enough to become king: 'I am about to go the way of all the earth; so be strong and you will become a man'.[54] While we have little evidence to go on, this comment is telling. In addition, Solomon will shortly tell God in a vision at the start of his sole occupation of the throne 'And now, o Lord my God, you crowned your servant in place of/under David my father, but I am a young lad without experience of the ways

---

[52] In this regard see I Chronicles 22.5 where David describes him as a gentle youth. This is discussed further in Chapter 3 below.
[53] I Kings 1.50-53
[54] I Kings 2.2.

of the world [literally I do not know about leaving and coming]'.[55]   The two comments together paint a picture of a father seeing his son as delicate and a son who describes himself as inexperienced.   Whether Solomon really is as weak as is presented is less the issue than that at this stage his father sees him as such.

What follows for a reader well-versed in the Bible is extremely unexpected and needs to be analysed closely.   On the surface, it appears to be merely a piece of advice from David to Solomon about the role he is about to take on as king:

'And you shall keep that which the Lord your God guards, to walk in his ways, to keep his statutes, commandments, judgments and precepts as written in the law of Moses in order that you should be wise in all you do and in everything to which you turn; in order that God establishes the word he spoke to me saying: "If your sons keep their way, to walk before me in truth with all their heart and all their soul, then no man of yours will be cut off from the throne of Israel"'.[56]

The verses are surprising not just for what they say but for their style.   They are clearly written in the style repeated again and again in the book of Deuteronomy. All modern scholars see them as a Deuteronomic interpolation into the story.   The book of Deuteronomy may well be the book referred to in II Kings 22.8 as the book of the law which Hilkiah is said to have found in the temple of the Lord.   From a historical perspective, the book of Deuteronomy appears to have been written later than other books in the Torah.   Much academic effort has gone into slicing up these and other texts and working out where they come from.

It seems to me more profitable to ask why an obviously different style of writing has been inserted at this stage into the story of King David telling King Solomon how to rule.   Robert Alter's literary approach provides a far more enlightening and persuasive reading as to why the text we possess has been sewn together in the manner it has than any number of other academics pouring over where the original cuts lay.

Robert Alter suggests[57] that the gist of the rest of David's deathbed pronouncement to Solomon (which involves David's request for Solomon to settle his old scores for him) was unbecoming to the Deuteronomistic editor.   I would like to suggest a

---

[55] I Kings 3.7. The words could also indicate lack of military prowess.
[56] I Kings 2.3-4.
[57] Alter: Ancient Israel 608.

different reason for its insertion which has little to do with David and much to do with Solomon.[58] It nevertheless reflects Alter's literary approach.

Solomon, the 'laws of the king' and the book of Deuteronomy

When David instructs his son, who is after all about to take on the full role of king, and in so doing uses the language of the book of Deuteronomy, the Deuteronomistic editor clearly required his readers to look at the book of Deuteronomy to see what it said about how a king should rule. There is a clear passage in the book of Deuteronomy about what a king should do and it needs to be quoted in full:

'If, when you come to the land which the Lord your God is giving you and you inherit it and dwell in it, you say "I will place a king over me like all the nations about me", you can place a king over you whom the Lord your God has chosen. You shall place a king from amongst your brothers; you cannot place over you a foreign man who is not your brother. Also he shall not increase possession of horses, nor send his people back to Egypt in order to possess more horses, as the Lord has said to you that you should not continue returning this way any more. And he shall not increase wives so that his heart does not turn; he shall not increase possession of gold and silver too much. And it shall be that when he sits on the throne of his kingdom that he shall write for himself a copy of this teaching in a scroll before the priests and the Levites. And it will be with him and he shall read from it all the days of his life in order that he learn to fear the Lord his God, to keep all the words of this law and these statutes in order to perform them. So that he does not elevate himself above his brothers or turn right or left from the commandment. In order that his days may be lengthened and those of his children on his throne in the midst of Israel'.[59]

If we break down this passage which is often known as the 'law of the king', we can see the characteristics perceived as royal vices. The text exhorts the people against appointing a king who indulges in 'excess' in the form of horses, wealth and wives. It also appears to link the desire for more horses with a return of the people to Egypt. Finally, he is required to write a copy of the scroll to increase his fear of the Lord. That, says the text, is the way in which a king can secure his and his descendants' future.

---

[58] On the links between Deuteronomy and Solomon, I am indebted to the excellent analysis by Goodman: 2014: 232-267 (Hebrew). His link between the 'law of the king' and Solomon allows for a fresh reading of the constant Deuteronomic interpolations in the story of Solomon in the book of Kings.
[59] Deuteronomy 17.14-20.

This intertextual link is absolutely crucial. The author or editor of I Kings 2, through the insertion of a passage about the new king's role and obligations, obviously written in a different Deuteronomic style, thereby reminded his readers of the law of the king in the book of Deuteronomy. In so doing, he asked them to follow through the story of Solomon to see whether this new king was able to live up to the exacting standards outlined in the book of Deuteronomy. We shall do so as well. As we shall see, King Solomon fails on every one of those requirements. Deuteronomic interpolations occur frequently in the book of Kings. This is the first and most striking. It interrupts the main narrative to which we now return.

King Solomon - securing the throne

On David's death, King Solomon lives in a precarious world. He is on the throne but his power base is not yet secure; ruthlessness is required to preserve his position. Opportunity presents itself in the form of Adonijah, venturing out of his home to visit the new queen mother. He asks but one thing; that Bathsheba should go to the new king and request that he be given Abishag the Shunamite as a wife. She had been King David's maid-servant with whom David had been unable to be intimate[60]. Bathsheba apparently sees this as just a lustful request from a former pretender to the throne. It may be that this is exactly what it is. When Bathsheba approaches Solomon with the question, he sees it entirely differently - as an attempt to reclaim the throne by someone older than himself and with arguably a better claim. After all, what could be a more brazen exhibition of kingship than taking the former king's mistress (asserting kingship by marrying the former queen; one is inevitably reminded of Claudius and Gertrude in *Hamlet*). Solomon is not sure of the throne yet and, in order to be secure, he needs to show the ruthlessness that his father had demonstrated in his youth. For Solomon, this is a 'kill or be killed' world and he arranges for one of his henchmen to ensure that it is Adonijah who dies and he who survives on the throne.[61]

The passage is remarkable for the apparent transformation it shows in the relationship between Bathsheba and her son. At the time when Solomon was in danger because of Adonijah, it was she who acted and prevented the catastrophe that she and her son would have suffered, had Adonijah's claim been successful. Solomon said nothing. Now she appears to take Adonijah's request at face value

---

[60] The apparently abrupt change of scene at I Kings 1.4-5, from King David's lack of intimacy with Abishag to Adonijah's first assertion of kingship, makes much more sense when we see it in the light of this link between Abishag and Adonijah. While we know about David's lack of intimacy, we are never told whether Adonijah knows of it when he makes his fateful request.

[61] I Kings 2.13-25.

and it is Solomon who sees it differently. If that is correct then the relationship between mother and son has changed entirely. I suspect, though, that another interpretation is much nearer the mark.

Robert Alter's intriguing suggestion[62] is that, far from Bathsheba being the manipulated mother, she knows exactly how her son will react to her 'one little question'[63] and therefore that she sees this as an opportunity to get rid of a potential competitor for her son. If Alter is right (and it is a highly persuasive reading, though not the only one in this marvellously - and one suspects deliberately - ambiguous text), then her powers of manipulation are strong indeed. She knows exactly how her son will react and she sees the chance to pounce on a potentially rival dynasty and, in so doing, end any claim it might have in one fell swoop.

Bathsheba fits a number of the stereotypes relating to women created by a patriarchal society. She is portrayed as the woman who, in her youth, enticed King David through her feminine charms and, in her old age, could see through the complexities of royal intrigue to promote her son. She disappears from the story but has made an enormous impression. It is she who changed the course of Israelite history through her resourcefulness.

King Solomon - the first years on the throne

Chapter 2 of the first book of Kings ends with the comment: 'and the kingdom was firmly set in Solomon's hand'.[64] Modern scholars have found the book division strange. The book of Kings begins with the story of King David's old age. His death is only described in chapter 2. Why have a division before the death of the first great Israelite king? Moreover, they have detected that the narrative style of deliberate ambiguity and terseness of the author of the books of Samuel continues for the first two chapters of Kings. Accordingly, both from a thematic and authorial point of view, the better division between the two books would have been between chapters 2 and 3 of the book of Kings and not where tradition has placed it.

There is much to be said for this argument when one is considering the life of King David. Against it, though, lies the life of Solomon. He may have been born in the book of Samuel but his whole active life can now been seen within the context of the book of Kings. Crucially also, the constant Deuteronomic comments on

---

[62] Alter: Ancient Israel: 612

[63] I Kings 2.20.

[64] I Kings 2.46.

Solomon, which appear throughout his life, would have missed the vital first reference in chapter 2 in which King David tells his son how he ought to act.

At first, everything goes well. Solomon marries Pharaoh's daughter.[65] Given the requirement to avoid 'returning to Egypt' in the law of the king, it is reassuring that he brings her to the city of David. His plan is to live there with her and to build his palace and the temple whilst residing in Jerusalem. The Hebrew word used for marriage is '*vayitchaten*' which has the sense of 'got himself married to' and has a clear implication of being a marriage for more than one purpose; the new JPS translation uses the phrase 'allied himself in marriage'. Robert Alter sees this as the first in a series of politically motivated unions[66] which Solomon would undertake over the next few years. However, given the traumatic relationship between Israel and Egypt, and the centrality of the exodus to the Israelite narrative of selfhood, it is difficult to see this as just one more alliance. Leaving Egypt, having nothing more to do with it, and serving God independently of Egypt are at the core of that narrative. Solomon's alliance appears to break a central taboo in Israelite society. For the moment, this marriage of convenience seems to pass off without comment. One wonders, however, whether this is a hint of trouble to come.

Solomon, having secured his alliance, now wants to secure God's promise to David that, whilst David would not build a temple to God, this task was to be fulfilled by his descendants.[67] Solomon needed to speak with God. The way to seek divine attention was to offer sacrifices. Although there was no central place for sacrifice yet, there were various high places deemed suitable for the task. Solomon went to Gibeon, described as the 'great high place'. There he sacrificed a thousand burnt offerings.[68] We should note at this stage that we have already seen the number 'one thousand' appear in relation to Solomon in the Song of Songs.[69] It will appear again later in his history.

Solomon's request to God comes in the form of a dream in Gibeon when he had just completed his sacrifices. It is admirable. We have already had cause to refer to his acknowledgement of his own inexperience in I Kings 3.7.[70] All he asks is that 'you

---

[65] I Kings 3.1.

[66] Alter: Ancient Israel, 618. The same verb is used to describe the prohibition on marrying those in the land of Israel in Deuteronomy 7.3.

[67] See II Samuel 7.

[68] I Kings 3.4.

[69] Song of Songs 8.11-12.

[70] See note 55 above.

give your servant a heart sensitive to judging your people, to distinguish between good and evil; for who can judge your numerous people'.[71]

We have no idea whether this display of modesty is false or genuine but it clearly works as a persuasive form of advocacy. Having eschewed all desire for power and wealth, Solomon receives a positive response from his own judge. He is granted the wisdom he requests. In modern day courts, it is very rare for a judge to grant a claimant a remedy beyond what he has requested in his pleadings. That is not the case when it comes to God in Solomon's dream. It appears as if, precisely because Solomon did not ask for power and wealth, God grants him these.[72] Let us not at this stage forget that too much power and wealth are exactly what the author of the book of Deuteronomy says the people should avoid in a monarch. Solomon has, as it were, to tread a very fine line between the divine promise of riches and the divine warning against excess.

As if on cue, it all comes with an obviously Deuteronomic warning at the end. Promises of good things to come in the book of Deuteronomy are often couched in contingent language. God will only grant you X if you perform your side of the bargain. God now makes Solomon such a contingent promise: 'And if you go in my ways, in order to keep my statutes and commandments as your father David did, then I will make you live long'.[73]

At this early stage in Solomon's reign, we know he has been promised power and wealth on the one hand, and wisdom on the other. We are about to see how these manifest themselves.

King Solomon's power and wealth

King Solomon's power and wealth are shown throughout his story but, at the beginning of his reign, the narrator is keen to show his domination of the region and the riches he was able to exhibit.

It has a purpose above and beyond the pure lust for self-aggrandisement. He reigned from the River Euphrates to the land of the Philistines and the border of Egypt. He ruled this area and he had peace with all the neighbouring territories, leading to peace within the borders of Judah and Israel as well so that each man felt secure under his

---

[71] I Kings 3.9.
[72] I Kings 3.11-13.
[73] I Kings 3.14.

proverbial vine and fig tree.[74] The implication of this last phrase is that he created the conditions in which the ideal, secure society could thrive. Only with such widespread peace could a king of Israel create the social conditions in which God's temple could be built. We will see that the Song of Songs implies criticism of the ideal society which the book of Kings suggests King Solomon had established.

In terms of wealth, we are told of forty thousand stalls for the horses for his chariots and twelve thousand charioteers each fully provided with the requisite amount of food.[75] At this stage this appears to be a formidable force but, as we shall see, it is just a prelude to King Solomon's increasing accumulation of material wealth.   By the time he has finished, we are told that silver was regarded in Jerusalem in the same nonchalant way one would think of stone.[76]

King Solomon's wisdom

Solomon's proverbial wisdom was of course legendary and it formed the basis for Israelite wisdom literature (such as the book of Proverbs and Ecclesiastes discussed in chapter 1 above). The book of Kings seeks to show how Solomon's wisdom manifested itself in two different ways.

First it shows his wisdom as a judge when the two prostitutes come to him arguing over who is the real mother of the live child they present to him. It is a well-known story. Solomon's threat to cut the baby in half reveals the real mother. Having heard the obvious anguish of a real mother, Solomon then renders a judgment, handing the baby to the woman who preferred the baby being handed over to her competitor rather than having the baby cut in half. Micah Goodman perceptively notes that this passage follows immediately after Solomon's own rhetorical success where he asked for little (wisdom) and received more (power and wealth in addition). Solomon also, on the standard reading, awarded the baby to the woman who asked for less.[77]

It may just be a corruption of the text but it is in fact not at all clear which of the two putative mothers the baby is actually handed to. Clearly it ought to be the mother

---

[74] I Kings 5.1 and 5.4-5 (using the Masoretic Hebrew chapter and verse numbers. Some alternative versions add the first fifteen verses of chapter 5 to the end of chapter 4. All further references to I Kings Chapter 5 refer to the Masoretic Hebrew version).

[75] I Kings 5.6-8.

[76] I Kings 10.27.

[77] Goodman: 255-6.

who cried out in mercy when the decision was made but the text merely says 'And the king responded, "Hand the live baby to her and do not kill him - she is his mother"'.[78] The question which we need to pose is who is the 'her/she' who is therefore 'his mother'. Obviously we expect it to be the mother who refused to have the baby cut into two but the text does not say this. If we therefore look at who is the last of the two women to have spoken (and therefore is more likely to be the 'her' being referred to), we are faced with the problem that the last speaker had been the woman who wanted the baby divided. Of course this might be a case of lack of clarity on the part of the writer but it might just be a hint that Solomon's wisdom was not quite as proverbial as some thought.

The second sign of Solomon's wisdom is more general. It is worth quoting in full:

'And God gave Solomon wisdom and very great discernment and a heart [i.e. understanding] as broad as the sand that is on the seashore. Solomon's wisdom was greater than the wisdom of all the ancient men of the East and than the wisdom of Egypt.   He was wiser than any other person - than Ethan the Ezrachite and Hayman and Kalkol and Darda, the sons of Machol, and his name was known in all the surrounding nations. He spoke three thousand proverbs, and wrote one thousand and five songs. He spoke about the trees, from the cedar which is in Lebanon to the hyssop which sprouts from the wall and he spoke about cattle, fowl, reptiles and fish. And people from all the different kingdoms came to hear the wisdom of Solomon as they had heard about his wisdom.'[79]

At first sight, this passage appears to set out the comprehensive nature of Solomon's wisdom. It describes the great breadth of Solomon's wisdom, first metaphorically in a geographical sense (he knew more than any other person in the world at the time), and second by his vast and extensive knowledge of nature. Having described all known types of animal, the text then tells us about Solomon's ability to speak about trees. They appear to have been chosen because one is vast (the cedar in Lebanon) and the other is tiny (a hyssop which sprouts from a wall). King Solomon knew about both the cedar and the hyssop.

As we read more of the story, we need to bear in mind these two examples because King Solomon's interest changes. He never loses his interest in the mighty cedar from Lebanon; it becomes a central part of his story - the building of the temple and his royal palace. By the time this mammoth project is finished, the Bible tells us

---

[78] I Kings 3.27.
[79] I Kings 5.9-14.

that cedars were as prevalent in Jerusalem as the sycamore tree in the plains near the sea.[80]

But as for the poor little hyssop; it never makes an appearance again. King Solomon is no longer interested in the tiny and unimportant. No temple or palace was ever built by means of the humble hyssop.

---

[80] I Kings 10.27.

THREE

Exploitation and Exhibitionism

The Temple

The origins of the temple in Jerusalem were humble. Its template was the '*mishkan*', the tabernacle which the children of Israel constructed in the wilderness shortly after leaving slavery in Egypt. The designs of both are described in great detail - the tabernacle in the book of Exodus, the temple in the first book of Kings. There are many points of similarity. However, there are also crucial differences, one of which is revealed at the outset of the description of each building's construction. When the tabernacle was built, we are told that 'God spoke to Moses saying: "Speak to the children of Israel so that they take an offering for me; from each person whose heart desires it, you shall take an offering .... And they shall make me a sanctuary so that I can live amongst them"'.[81] The offerings then described are all the materials required to build and fit out the tabernacle - and thereby a sanctuary appropriate for the God of the children of Israel. The clear message is that, by the process of voluntary contributions from the whole of the people, all can have a stake in the tabernacle's construction. One might not describe this as democracy, but it is certainly a prototype example of citizen participation.

The temple, by contrast, was not built by voluntary contributions; rather it was built as a result of an alliance between Solomon and Hiram, the king of Tyre. Solomon told Hiram that there were none amongst his people who could cut trees like the Sidonians (Sidon being the next major town north of Tyre on the Lebanese coast). The reality, one suspects, is that this request for assistance from the Sidonians had nothing to do with their expertise and everything to do with the fact that the tree which Solomon really desired did not exist in his own kingdom. He wanted the cedar tree which only grows in areas more than one thousand metres above sea level. The mountains of Lebanon are the only geographical area in the region which meet this requirement. The cedar tree, of course, still remains the symbol of modern-day Lebanon. Hiram promised to send him the cedar tree (in Hebrew '*erez*') and the cypress tree (in Hebrew '*b'rosh*'). He suggested that this be done by transporting the timber down from the mountains to the sea and thence by ship from Lebanon

----

[81] Exodus 25.1-2, 8.

along the Mediterranean coast, to be sent up to Jerusalem. In exchange, Solomon provided Hiram with annual provisions of food for his household.[82]

But there is more to this alliance than would appear at first glance. The text states that Solomon placed a '*mas*' on all Israel.[83] The meaning of the word '*mas*' is crucial. It is easy to misconstrue. The King James version of the Bible translates it as a 'levy'. In modern Hebrew, '*mas*' is the standard word for a 'tax'. It means neither of these things in this context. What Solomon is doing is compelling thirty thousand men from his kingdom to go to Lebanon for one month out of every three to bring back the cedar and cypress for his temple. Alter uses the term 'forced labor',[84] which is much nearer the mark.

The word '*mas*', used in conjunction with the Israelites, has a particular resonance. The very beginning of the book of Exodus states that a new Pharaoh arose who did not know Joseph and saw the children of Israel as a threat to his kingdom. He spoke to his people to show them how much of a threat these new immigrants could be. And then the text adds: 'And they put gang-masters over them in order to oppress them with their suffering'.[85] The word I have translated as 'gang' is the word '*mas*'[86] in the original text. It is used in the book of Exodus before we have even heard about the 'slavery' which was to come. The use of the same word to describe the manner in which the children of Israel were put into forced labour to go to Lebanon to fetch timber for the temple seems deliberate. As Micah Goodman puts it, there is a real sense of *déjà vu* for sensitive readers: 'It all reminds one of the days of slavery in Egypt. Except that this time the people do not need to return to Egypt; Egypt comes to them'.[87]

The negative textual link of the word '*mas*' to the worst example of Israelite suffering, and to the voluntary way in which the tabernacle was built, raises a fundamental question. The glorification of King Solomon, who created peace and a great kingdom, and who was wise beyond compare, is on the surface only. For Goodman's 'sensitive reader', there is something else going on. It is as if the writer of the text knew that there was another much more negative story to be told about King Solomon which could not be entirely suppressed. As we will see later, that story is hinted at in the Song of Songs. We now need to examine the historical basis

---

[82] I Kings 5.20-25.

[83] I Kings 5.27.

[84] Alter: Ancient Israel, 630.

[85] Exodus 1.11.

[86] The word appears as '*missim*' in the plural form.

[87] Goodman: 253 (Hebrew).

on which Solomon could claim the right to build the temple. That came as a result of God's promise to his father, King David.

David's son's temple

The tabernacle was a movable structure fitting for a nomadic people. It had been used as a symbol for war; the Ark of the Lord had even been taken at one stage by the Philistines.[88]   With the conquest of Jerusalem by King David, a new era beckoned. No longer would the temple be a movable fragile object. It needed to be something permanent in Jerusalem - at the very centre of Israelite power. David brought the Ark of the Lord into Jerusalem in an exuberant display of dancing.

Yet we are told that David sensed an embarrassment at the difference between his own accommodation and that of his God: 'And the king said to Nathan the prophet: "See now I live in a house of cedar but the ark of God lives in the midst of the curtain". And Nathan said to the king: "All that is within your heart, go and do, because the Lord is with you"'.[89]

There are two interesting issues to note in this passage. First, there is a reference to the fact that David lived in a house made of cedar. Like his son Solomon, David's cedar was brought to him by King Hiram of Tyre.[90]   So we now realise that Solomon's wisdom, in relation to the 'cedar that is in Lebanon',[91] could well have resulted not from any trip north to visit the splendid trees in their natural habitat, but from the fact that he grew up in a house built from cedar wood. Indeed in a passage in the book of Chronicles we are told that David possessed 'innumerable cedar logs because the Sidonites and Tyreans brought a great number of cedar logs to David'.[92]

Second, David's use of the word 'curtain' (Hebrew 'yer'iah') is unusual because, earlier, the Ark of the Lord had been described as being in a tent (Hebrew 'ohel').[93] Alter's suggestion is that curtain is the term being used to describe part of the whole.[94] Indeed one could add that the text links the words together in a way which was common in literature at the time. It could also be of assistance in seeking to understand the only disputed description of Solomon in the Song of Songs. As

---

[88] See I Samuel 5 and 6.
[89] II Samuel 7.2-3.
[90] II Samuel 5.11
[91] I Kings 5.13.
[92] I Chronicles 22.4.
[93] II Samuel 6.17.
[94] Alter: Ancient Israel, 462: 'The term is an obvious synecdoche for tent'.

described in chapter 1 above, the first reference to Solomon, after the superscription, refers to the young woman's blackness being 'like the tents of Qedar, like the curtains of Solomon'.[95] For the reasons set out in chapter 1, the reference to Solomon is unlikely to be an error as it fits into the structure of the Song of Songs. Given the references to 'Solomon', 'vineyards' and 'watchmen' at the beginning and end of the text, it enwraps the text thematically. One wonders whether the reference here to David's curtain is one which was known as an heirloom in his family, passed down to Solomon, and thereby referred to in the Song of Songs. This will be discussed further in the commentary to Song of Songs 1.5.

The '*bayit*'

The result of this discussion is that God appears to Nathan in a dream.[96] In it, God makes clear to Nathan that God wants to live in a '*bayit*'. The word '*bayit*', the basic meaning of which is 'house', has three other meanings. First, David uses the term as a synonym for his descendants[97] and it is adapted in this same way to mean a 'people' - i.e. the house of Israel. Second, it is the standard word for 'temple'. So that when we are told God says that God wants a '*bayit*' to live in, the reader should realise the ambiguity. We immediately link the word in our own anthropomorphic way to the human desire to have a home but we also remember that God dwelt in the tabernacle and wants to do the same in the temple.   Finally the word comes to mean 'palace'. This will become important shortly when we see that Solomon's grand design is not only for a temple but also for a royal palace. Whilst there are plenty of other Hebrew words for both 'temple' and 'palace', the text in the book of Kings, no doubt deliberately, chooses to use the same name for these two buildings.

The dream also stresses the importance of cedar wood. We learn not only that David and Solomon have a particular interest in houses made of this substance but so does God, who states that he has never previously expressed the desire to dwell in a 'house of cedars'.[98] It is not David, however, who will build this '*bayit*' for God but his descendant after him: 'he will build a house in my name and I will establish his royal throne for ever'.[99]

---

[95] Song of Songs 1.5.

[96] II Samuel 7.4-17.

[97] See Alter: Ancient Israel, 463.

[98] II Samuel 7.7.

[99] II Samuel 7.13.

The book of Chronicles

The book of Chronicles gives us another fascinating insight into the way this period of time was understood. Much of the book of Chronicles covers the same material as other sources we have, such as the books of Samuel and of Kings. We cannot be sure which was written first and it is entirely possible that the works are contemporary to each other. Where there are differences between the book of Chronicles and the other versions we have, then we have to consider why that may be.

The book of Chronicles goes into far more detail about this promise to build the temple and it is worth quoting in detail:

'And David spoke to Solomon saying "My son, it was really in my heart to build a temple in the name of the Lord my God. And the word of the Lord came unto me saying "'You have spilt much blood and you have fought many battles; you will not build a temple for my name as you have spilt much blood to the ground before me. Look a son will be born to you; he will be a man of rest and I will give him rest from all his enemies surrounding him; for Solomon will be his name and I will give Israel peace and quiet in his days. He will build a temple for my name; he will be a son for me and I will be a father for him and I will establish his royal throne over Israel for ever.'" Now my son, may the Lord be with you and make you succeed and you will build the temple for the Lord your God as he said to you. Only let God give you insight and understanding and may he command you over Israel to keep the law of the Lord your God. Thus will you succeed - if you keep observing the laws and statutes which the Lord commanded Moses concerning Israel; be strong and of courage - do not fear and do not be dismayed. Look, in my poverty, I have prepared for the house of God one hundred thousand gold talents and one thousand, thousand silver talents and so much copper and iron that it cannot be weighed as there is so much of it; and I have prepared wood and stone and you should add to it".'[100]

What is so revealing about this passage is that it contains such a detailed plan passed from David to Solomon about the oracle which David had received from God. The passage seems to say that, although David cannot build the temple because of a divine prohibition, he still wants to be in control of how it is built and so has stored up gold, silver, copper and iron for its use. Moreover, later on, David gives Solomon an even more detailed blueprint as to how these items are to be used in the temple.[101]

---

[100] I Chronicles 22.7-14.
[101] See I Chronicles 28.11-21.

None of this is mentioned in the book of Kings. All these metals were to be used in the construction of the temple as described in the book of Kings (and indeed later on in the second book of Chronicles) but no mention is made of the cedarwood which Solomon clearly sees as so fitting the construction of a '*bayit*'. As we will see, he does not just want to build a '*bayit*' fitting for God; he also wants to build a '*bayit*' fitting for a king. His own blueprint extends to building a palace with a Lebanon forest theme. We now turn to the two '*bayit*'s which Solomon built. And they involved the king's beloved cedars.

The '*bayit*' - the temple

Of course the temple was not just built out of cedar, but clearly its designer wanted it to have a really wooden feel - 'everything was cedar, no stone could be seen'.[102] So 'he built the walls of the temple from inside with cedar planks from the floor of the temple to the walls of the ceiling, overlaid it internally with wood; and he overlaid the floor of the temple with cypress planks'.[103] This apparently unassuming and uncontroversial comment about the detail of how the temple was built was used, as we shall see later, by the author of the Song of Songs to contrast the simplicity of the lovers with the wealth of Solomon.

Alter considers the dimensions of the temple as creating a 'relatively intimate structure' when compared to more recent grand buildings.[104] That is not surprising. The author of the description of the construction of the temple in the book of Kings is keen to ensure that it is compared not to something grand but to the building of the tabernacle. So it has all the hallmarks of the tabernacle style with references to the length, height and width of rooms, with all measurements set out in cubits. The temple also contained cherubs, as had the tabernacle (which itself may have been looking back to the cherubs which guarded the way of the tree of life outside the garden of Eden).[105]

At one point, when God speaks to Solomon, the style deliberately repeats what God had said about 'living' in the tabernacle:[106] 'And I will live in the midst of the children of Israel and I will not forsake my people Israel'.[107]

---

[102] I Kings 6.18.
[103] I Kings 6.15.
[104] Alter: Ancient Israel, 631.
[105] Genesis 3.24.
[106] See Exodus 25.8 for this comparison referred to at the beginning of this chapter.
[107] I Kings 6.13.

The context of this speech from God is interesting. Immediately prior to speaking about living in the midst of the children of Israel, God tells Solomon the following: 'This temple which you are building - if you walk in my statutes and keep my judgments and keep all the commandments to live by them, then I will keep my word with you which I spoke to David, your father.'[108]

These words are what all commentators understand to be a Deuteronomic interpolation. I do not believe we can simply leave it at that. It is another reminder of the undercurrent in the text that all is not well. The peace of the kingdom is contingent on Solomon observing the commandments. The commandments specifically pertaining to him as king have been referred to in the previous chapter and are based on the law of the king in Deuteronomy 17.14-20. At this moment of the expression of Solomon's greatest power, we are reminded indirectly that a king should not return the people to Egypt - 'you shall not carry on in that way any more'.[109] We realise that Solomon has already failed this part of the royal test by imposing a '*mas*' on the children of Israel - exactly what they suffered when they were in Egypt. Solomon is on royal probation.

Despite its relative intimacy, the building of the temple must have taken considerable organisational skill since it took seven years[110] to complete, notwithstanding the apparently limitless supply of men and timber which Solomon had arranged with King Hiram. The number seven has a symbolic value in the Bible. As the world was created in seven days, the number seven became a symbol of wholeness and perfection.

The '*bayit*' - the palace

We are told that immediately after finishing the temple, Solomon set about building his palace. We must not forget that the same word '*bayit*' is used in the original text to describe both constructions. One is required by God; the second is desired by Solomon. In a not very subtle segue, chapter 6 ends with the reader being told that it took Solomon seven years to complete the temple and we find out at the very beginning of chapter 7 that Solomon took thirteen years to complete the building of his royal palace.[111] Surely this contrast is deliberate. The perfection symbolised in the number seven of the length of time it took to build the temple is undermined by the period of time - almost twice as long - during which Solomon built his palace.

---

[108] I Kings 6.12.
[109] Deuteronomy 17.16.
[110] I Kings 6.38.
[111] I Kings 7.1.

Throughout its construction, the palace has a name - 'the palace of the forest of Lebanon'. As with the temple, its measurements are described in considerable detail. The temple was sixty cubits long by twenty cubits wide by thirty cubits high.[112] The palace was a hundred cubits long by fifty cubits wide by thirty cubits high.[113] This means that, although both were the same height, the area of the temple was 1,200 square cubits and the area of the palace was 5,000 square cubits - in other words, it was more than four times the size.

And the palace was awash with cedarwood. There were cedar columns and the beams on the columns were made out of cedar. Solomon's court room was entirely panelled in cedarwood, as was the house for his wife, Pharaoh's daughter.[114]

Hiram - the skilled craftsman

At this point in the Biblical text, we have a gap in the description of the building of the royal palace. King Solomon sends for Hiram of Tyre. The passage is very strange because we think we know already that the person being spoken about must be the king of Tyre referred to earlier. But apparently not. The person being described is a skilled craftsman who is 'the son of a widow of the tribe of Naphtali whose father was a coppersmith in Tyre'.[115]

Whether the person being described a) was actually the king of Tyre, or b) had the same name as the king of Tyre or c) has been misnamed by the text, are all interesting points from a superficial textual point of view. They miss the point, however, that this Hiram, whether royal or not, has a very specific role to fulfil. He is a skilled craftsman, as we are now told: 'and he was filled with technical wisdom, understanding and knowledge to do all the copper work and he came to king Solomon and did all his work'.[116]

At first, this just seems like a statement about an able craftsman. Yet if one looks closely, one sees that the wording deliberately imitates the wording describing Bezalel, the craftsman who built the tabernacle: 'And God spoke to Moses. See I have called on the name of Bezalel, the son of Uri, the son of Hur of the tribe of Judah. And I have filled him with the spirit of God, in technical wisdom,

---

[112] I Kings 6.2.
[113] I Kings 7.2.
[114] I Kings 7.3-12.
[115] I Kings 7.14a.
[116] I Kings 7.14b.

understanding and knowledge and in all manner of work. To conceive [technical] plans, to create in gold, silver and copper. To chisel stones for setting and to chisel wood - to do all manner of work'.[117]

What Bezalel is to Moses, so apparently Hiram is to Solomon. Yet, there are also crucial differences. Bezalel is brought in at an early stage in the building of the tabernacle, whereas Hiram is only summoned once the temple has been built. Hiram works alone to create the temple, whereas Bezalel is constantly described as working with 'all those endowed with technical wisdom'.[118] At this stage, one is again reminded of the difference in outlook; the tabernacle is a communal voluntary undertaking of a people who are creating a new reality under a divine blueprint. The temple, on the other hand, also has a divine blueprint, but it has been refracted through the prism of a royal hierarchical outlook. Most of those involved in the construction of the royal palace and temple are forced to undertake the work.

Hiram's additions to the temple involved creating two huge columns with capitals to be set upon them. These obviously imposing columns were inlaid with figures of lilies and pomegranates. Despite the depiction of fragile flowers, their purpose was clearly to create an impression of power. Each column was given a name '*yachin*' (he will establish) and '*boaz*' (power in him).[119] Various other parts of the temple were then constructed by Hiram: the tank of cast metal,[120] ten laver stands of bronze depicting lions, cattle and cherubs.

Once Hiram had completed this work, Solomon brought in the holy implements of his father David, including gold, silver and vessels. He then placed them in the treasury of the house of the Lord.[121]

A new permanent tabernacle

There is nothing coincidental in the links which one can draw with the tabernacle. The temple was intended to be the permanent successor to the tabernacle. Yet the text deliberately creates an extra link. In the same way as Solomon gathers up the children of Israel and the heads of the tribes to bring up the covenant of the Lord,[122] Moses also gathers up the congregation of the children of Israel to describe how to

---

[117] Exodus 31.1-5.

[118] Exodus 36.1.

[119] I Kings 7.15-22.

[120] I Kings 7.23 - thus the JPS translation. No-one is entirely sure what the Hebrew word '*yam*' means in this context.

[121] I Kings 7.51.

[122] I Kings 8.1.

build the tabernacle.[123]   The same verb in Hebrew (*haqhel*) is used, but whereas Moses undertakes this task at the beginning of the process, Solomon only does so once the temple has been completed.

The completion ceremony was intended to be a grand affair with sacrifices of sheep and cattle which were so numerous that they could not be counted.[124]   Yet it was also a reminder of the past in the wilderness. There was nothing in the Ark in the temple except the two tablets of stone which Moses had placed there when God made a covenant with the children of Israel at Horeb.[125]   And then, as if to stress that the temple was following in a direct chain of tradition from the tabernacle, the text tells us:

'And when the priests left the sanctuary, the cloud filled the house of the Lord. And the priests were not able to stand and serve because of the cloud since the glory of the Lord filled the house of the Lord'.[126]

This text is a deliberate imitation of the final words of the book of Exodus:

'And the cloud covered the tent of meeting and the glory of the Lord filled the tabernacle. And Moses was not able to go to the tent of meeting because the cloud dwelt on it and the glory of the Lord filled the tabernacle. And when the cloud was lifted from the tabernacle, the children of Israel travelled on all their journeys. But if the cloud was not lifted, they would not travel until the day [i.e. moment] it was lifted. Because the cloud of the Lord was over the tabernacle by day and fire was in it by night - in sight of all the house of Israel in all their journeys.'[127]

The word used in both texts for cloud is '*anan*' and clearly the priests' role in the temple is being compared to that of Moses in the tabernacle. The author of the book of Kings carries on the cloud imagery. Solomon then speaks and says[128] 'the Lord has chosen to abide in a thick cloud' (as per the New JPS translation) or 'the Lord meant to abide in thick fog' (Alter translation). The word translated as 'thick cloud' or 'thick fog' is '*arafel*'. This alternative word for dark cloud does not appear in the building of the tabernacle but it is a clear reference to the time immediately after the giving of the ten commandments on Mount Sinai, when we are told that 'The people

---

[123] Exodus 35.1.
[124] I Kings 8.5.
[125] I Kings 8.9.
[126] I Kings 8.10-11.
[127] Exodus 40.34-38.
[128] I Kings 8.12.

stood far off and Moses approached the dark cloud where God was'.[129] It is in this context that God tells Moses that he wants to have an earthen altar built. Solomon's comment picking up on the same word '*arafel*' is a clear indication that this temple is exactly the altar which God had wanted at Mount Sinai. He then describes it as the 'place where you shall dwell forever'[130] - again a quotation, as the 'place where you shall dwell' is amongst the final words of the triumphant Song of the Sea sung by Moses and the children of Israel once they had crossed the Red Sea.[131]

Grandeur or folly?

What are we to make of the description of this new building? The text is full of deliberately-fashioned quotes showing the connection between the fragile, wandering tabernacle and the strong permanent temple in which the sacrifices could continue. On this view, the temple was to be seen as a worthy successor to the tabernacle. One can read this text and marvel at what was achieved and, at times, that is the clear intention of the author. Solomon was at the height of his powers. Peace was established and the children of Israel had never experienced such success.

But the text reveals so many contradictions that an alternative reading is entirely possible - the temple and the palace were Solomon's vanity project. The comparison with the tabernacle on this reading reveals a self-aggrandisement on Solomon's part entirely missing from the construction of the tabernacle. When this is added to the Deuteronomic comments throughout the text, which remind us of the law of the king and the warnings contained therein as to what a king must avoid, we realise that this text can be read very differently from the standard way which sees this episode as glorious.

Solomon's next act is to pray in the newly instituted temple. The prayer is long and detailed and reminds us that God has fulfilled the promise which he made to David, that David's descendant would build the temple. The prayer then describes God's greatness and ventures to suggest that God may not really be able to 'dwell' on earth as God is too great even for the heavens to contain. The hope is that God will hear the people's prayer whenever they cry out and wherever they may be. This initiation ceremony has a purpose; it 'transforms a pile of lumber, stone, gold and cloth into a

---

[129] Exodus 20.18 (Exodus 20.21 in some translations).
[130] I Kings 8.13.
[131] Exodus 15.17.

temple'.[132]   The overall structure of this ceremony has been analysed by Cogan as being a standard one based on similar ceremonies in Mesopotamia.[133]   It consists of three parts. First, the temple is formally inaugurated through the introduction of the Ark; second, the king offers blessings for the assembled; and third, a celebration takes place. In Solomon's case, this celebration consists of offering up 22,000 cattle and 120,000 sheep.

Deuteronomic contingency at the height of triumph

At this moment of Solomon's greatest triumph, God appears again to Solomon in the same way that he had appeared to him in Gibeon (referred to in I Kings 3). We realise that the standard way in which Solomon has prayed to God will not work without accompanying action. God has put Solomon and his people on trial: 'If you go before me as David your father went before me with a pure heart and uprightly in order to do everything which I have commanded and you keep my laws and judgments, then I will establish your royal throne over Israel for ever, as I spoke to David your father when I said "No descendant of yours will be cut off from the throne of Israel".'[134]

This promise is not absolute. As we have seen before, a promise in Deuteronomic form always comes with a sting in the tail: 'But if you and your descendants turn away from me and do not keep my commandments and laws which I have given before you, and you go and serve other gods and worship them, then I will cut off Israel from the land which I gave them.   And as for the temple which I have consecrated to my name, I will send it away from my presence - and Israel will become a proverb and a byword amongst all the peoples. And this temple - which was exalted [135]- everyone passing by shall be appalled and whistle. And they will say "As a result of what did the Lord act thus to this temple and to this land?" And they will continue "Because they forsook the Lord, their God, who brought their fathers from the land of Egypt and took hold of other gods and worshipped and served them. That is why the Lord brought this evil onto them".'[136]

---

[132] John Walton: *The Lost World of Genesis One: Ancient Cosmology and the Origins Debate*. IVP Academic, Downers Grove, Illinois, 2010, 88. I am very grateful to Stephan Ford for referring me to this text.
[133] Cogan: *I Kings*, 291.
[134] I Kings 9.4-5.
[135] This is a somewhat forced translation following the Masoretic text; the Targum, Syriac and Vulgate, change the word 'exalted' to 'ruin' so that the text reads: 'And the temple will become a ruin'.
[136] I Kings 9.6-9.

The text never lets us feel satisfied. From a literary point of view, it clearly mirrors the warning which Solomon had been given just as he was about to embark on his reign.[137] We know that something is about to happen. Yet the text moves constantly from a degree of foreboding about the future to a sense that Solomon is the wisest man on earth, and that there is not a cloud in the sky. Clearly, text critics will argue that this is because the stitching is revealing itself in the different texts which have been combined to create the book of Kings we know. That may be correct, but it nevertheless must not obscure the fact that there is a theme running throughout the Hebrew Bible, of contingent happiness and prosperity dependent upon following God's commands. The book of Kings fits readily into this template. It is at this point of contingency that the Queen of Sheba appears on the scene.

The role of the Queen of Sheba in the temple

What function does the Queen of Sheba have in the story of King Solomon? A conventional answer is that she is a figure who provides a vehicle from which we can see Solomon's wisdom. Yet if that is her purpose, then the author has signally failed to achieve it. We are told that she came to test Solomon with riddles to which Solomon had answers. If the story wanted to show how wise Solomon was, then surely it could have given examples of Solomon's wisdom (in the same way as we see in the story of Samson)[138] but no such examples are supplied.

The purpose of the riddle sequence is not so that the reader can appreciate Solomon's wisdom (about which we have already been told) but rather for the reader to see that the Queen of Sheba is suitably impressed - and we are told that she is in no uncertain terms: 'And she told the king "The word which I heard in my land was true about your words and your wisdom. But I did not believe the words until I came and saw it with my own eyes and I had not been told the half of it. Your wisdom and wealth are even greater than the rumour I had heard'.[139]

It is what happens next which is crucial. The Queen of Sheba provides Solomon with a gift. Some of it is standard fare but crucially there is one extra item which has not been mentioned before: 'And she gave the king one hundred and twenty talents of gold and a great amount of spices and precious stone. Never again did such a great amount of spices come as the amount which the Queen of Sheba gave to King Solomon'.[140]

---

[137] See I Kings 2.3-4 and 3.14.
[138] Judges 14.12ff.
[139] I Kings 10.6-7.
[140] I Kings 10.10.

We are used to gold and precious stones which have become a staple part of the Solomonic household. However, as we can see in the quotation immediately above, the author specifically highlights the spices. It implies that spices were not a luxury easy to obtain in Israel. They had to be imported. This is borne out by other texts - such as the Ishmaelites in the Joseph story who were coming from Gilead bearing gum, balm and ladanum which they were intending to take down into Egypt.[141] The implication therefore is that these spices are not native to Israel (though there is doubt on this subject)[142] but rather were an import. There is no doubt, though, that merchants did trade in Israel and therefore that spices were available in one way or another.

At no point in the whole story of the building of the temple have we heard about spices. That is astonishing in its own way in that they played a crucial part in the tabernacle. This is recounted just before the description of the role of Bezalel and his skilled craftsman is set out. Yet in Solomon's building of a replica tabernacle - the temple - spices have not been mentioned[143] so we need now to turn to the role of spices in the tabernacle.

Spices in the tabernacle

The Queen of Sheba's gift to King Solomon is described using the generic Hebrew word for spices.[144] The description of the spices in the tabernacle is much more specific.[145] We are not sure of the meaning of each individually named spice but the section in which the spices are described is divided in the book of Exodus into two clear parts.[146] The detail analysed below is technical in nature but that detail is critical in order to understand some of the failings in Solomon's vision of the temple. He seems not to have been interested in that divinely laid-out detail. The Song of Songs (as we shall see later) may have been commenting on this. With that introduction, we now examine the requirements relating to the spices in the tabernacle.

---

[141] Genesis 37.25.
[142] When Jacob tells his sons later to bring gifts from the land of Israel to the new viceroy of Egypt (Joseph, unbeknown to them of course) the gifts include this same gum, balm and ladanum - see Genesis 43.11.
[143] The only previous reference which could negate this argument is to the Hebrew root for incense - q-t-r - in I Kings 9.25. It is in the context of a sacrifice made by Solomon. The text is corrupt but probably does not mean putting incense onto the sacrifice but, rather, (in the *Hiphil*) causing the sacrifice to go up in smoke. No spices are referred to in that passage.
[144] The Hebrew word is '*besamim*'.
[145] Exodus 30.22-38.
[146] Exodus 30.22-33 and Exodus 30.34-38.

In the first of the two parts, we are told that the Lord tells Moses to take the finest spices (in Hebrew '*besamim rosh*') for the purpose of creating anointing oil. These are then described. Three spices are to be taken. The largest in quantity is five hundred-weight of myrrh. The myrrh is qualified by an adjective in the Hebrew[147] which is difficult to translate. As a noun, it means 'sparrow' and 'freedom' and so here probably comes to mean 'free-standing myrrh' or 'free-flowing myrrh'. The other two spices are two hundred and fifty-weight each of aromatic cinnamon and aromatic cane. Added to this is five hundred-weight of non-aromatic cassia and some olive oil.

This mixture of myrrh, cinnamon, cane, (spices - '*besamim*'), cassia and olive oil (non-spices) is to be used solely as anointing oil for the purposes of the tabernacle to consecrate its vessels and the priests. The text makes abundantly clear it cannot be used for any other purpose: 'And you shall tell the children of Israel the following: "This shall be a holy anointing oil for me through your generations. It shall not be rubbed on a person's body and in its proportions you shall not make the like. It is holy and it shall be holy to you. Any man who re-creates it like this or who gives it to a lay person shall be cut off from his people".'[148]

In the second part, the Lord tells Moses to take four ingredients in equal measure. The first three are herbs[149] not spices - stacte, onycha and galbanum. The fourth ingredient is another spice - pure frankincense.[150] These are to be made into incense and ground down into powder. A similar injunction is then given about ensuring that a mixture made in these proportions is only to be used for consecrated purposes. The warning at the end of the first section prohibited re-creating it. The warning at the end of this section is even starker. Anyone who makes it or even smells[151] of it shall be cut off from his people.[152]

The spices are brought to the tabernacle together with a whole series of items which needed to be used in the tabernacle according to God's commandment to Moses. It was a communal effort as those who are 'wise' in technical skill now include the women who brought items which they had woven. It was the chieftains who brought

---

[147] The Hebrew word is '*dror*' - see Exodus 30.23.

[148] Exodus 30.31-33.

[149] The Hebrew word is '*samim*'.

[150] The frankincense is not described as a spice (which it clearly is) but is delineated separately from the herbs - see Exodus 30.34.

[151] There may be a wordplay in this section. The word in Exodus 30.33 which I have translated as 'recreate' has the Hebrew root *r-q-ch*; the word I have translated 'smell' has the root *r-y-ch*.

[152] Exodus 30.38.

the more costly items - and this included the spices. The whole picture painted is of a communal effort which is so successful that Moses has to tell the men and women to stop bringing any more as too much had been brought.[153] The communal nature of the fitting out of the tabernacle is entirely lacking in the description of the building of the temple.

There are a number of lingering questions which arise from the comparison of spices in the tabernacle and in the temple. We are not told what specific types of spices the Queen of Sheba brought to Solomon. We are told, however, that an amount this large had never been seen before. We also know that if Solomon had wanted to use them in the temple, then there are only four types of spice (described as the finest spices) - myrrh, cinnamon, cane and frankincense - which were permitted so long as they were used with other non-spice ingredients in the correct proportions.

We are not told what Solomon did with these spices. In all the grandeur of the newly-built temple, with its avowed intention of imitating the workings of the tabernacle, we are never told whether they were used. This seems an extremely surprising, and probably revealing, gap in the narrative. The implication is that Solomon, who had inaugurated the temple without any mention of spices, saw no reason to change that once the spices arrived from the Queen of Sheba. If he had decided to use the spices as prescribed in the book of Exodus, then surely the narrative would have told us so. By contrast, in the Song of Songs, when the male lover describes the spices on his lover's body, all these finest spices are included.[154]

So we are not told about the furnishing of the temple with spices which appears to have been of little or no interest to King Solomon. We are, however, told about the gathering of more wealth to King Solomon - and of course his fabled wisdom.

King Solomon's wealth and wisdom

The benefits of this meeting with the Queen of Sheba are now revealed to us in detail. King Solomon added almug wood, which he had received, to both the temple and the palace. That apart, we are not told of any of this new-found wealth making its way into the temple. He received 666 talents of gold each year plus further amounts as a result of the trade which appears to have opened up. He made shields with vast amounts of gold which he placed in his palace - the house of the forest of Lebanon.[155]

---

[153] Exodus 35.20-36.7.
[154] See commentary below on Song of Songs 4.13.
[155] I Kings 10.14-17.

Solomon's throne is now described. As one would expect, this ranks finer than any of the other items which Solomon has been able to build with the riches he has now acquired. It is also contains gold but it has two differences: 'And the king made a great throne of ivory and he overlaid it with refined gold'.[156] First the king is using ivory for his throne. There has been no reference to ivory previously. We can assume that it was only available as a result of the trade with merchants from well beyond the land of Israel.[157] Ivory must have been regarded as one of the most precious of all commodities. Second, the gold is described as being 'refined' ('*mufaz*' in the original Hebrew). The Hebrew root of this word is '*paz*' which appears rarely in the Bible and we can assume from this context and others that it is meant to indicate the very finest gold. As we shall see, the details of Solomon's throne become material which the female lover in the Song of Songs appropriates to describe her lover's physique.[158] There were six steps leading up to the throne with figures of lions lending the construction an appropriately regal tone.

The message is summarised as follows: 'Solomon's wealth and wisdom became greater than that of any other of the kings in the land. And all the earth sought out the presence of Solomon to hear the wisdom with which God had endowed him.'[159]

We are now presented with examples of Solomon's wealth. Solomon possessed one thousand four hundred chariots and twelve thousand horsemen. This literally changed values; people thought about silver and cedar wood differently. The text continues: 'the king rendered silver in Jerusalem as if it were stone, and cedars as if they were sycamores on the plain'.[160] This was achieved through trade made possible by Solomon's abundant wealth.

Solomon had a thousand wives

Solomon is famed for having had a thousand wives. In fact this needs to be inferred from the text. It states that he had seven hundred women (the word for women '*nashim*' doubles up for wives) and three hundred concubines, from which one can of course infer a thousand but the text never uses this number.[161] The point is that they were foreign and therefore, led his heart astray from serving God to serving their gods. The key word is 'heart'. In our time, the 'heart' is the seat of the

---

[156] I Kings 10.18.
[157] See the reference in I Kings 10.22 in this regard.
[158] See the commentary below on Song of Songs 5.14-15.
[159] I Kings 10.23-24.
[160] I Kings 10.27.
[161] I Kings 11.3.

emotions. In Biblical times, it was seen as the seat of understanding. Crucially, though, in the Solomon story, the word heart has been associated with wisdom - so for example, Solomon is described as having 'breadth of heart like the sand on the seashore'.[162] As if to emphasise the point, we are later told: 'At the time when Solomon was old, his wives turned his heart after other gods and his heart was not complete/at peace with the Lord his God, as the heart of David his father [had been]'.[163] This meant that he did 'evil in the eyes of God'[164] (a standard phrase used in the Bible to describe kings, and indeed others, who err). His wisdom deserted him.

He built altars to Chemosh, the 'abomination' of Moab, on the mountain facing Jerusalem and to Molech, the 'abomination' of the sons of Ammon, and similar acts for his other wives.[165] The choice of these two gods amongst all the possible examples is not of course co-incidental. The imprecation against the ways of the Ammonites and the Moabites is specifically referred to in the book of Deuteronomy: 'Neither an Ammonite nor a Moabite shall come into the congregation of the Lord even unto the tenth generation they shall not come into the congregation of the Lord in perpetuity'.[166] Yet again, we have a deliberate link showing us that what Solomon did was not only evil in the eyes of the Lord but the worst contravention of the Deuteronomic code, by invoking the Ammonites and the Moabites.

God says that the punishment for this offence is that the kingdom will be torn from Solomon's descendants and given to Solomon's servants. It will not happen in Solomon's day but afterwards and it will not relate to the whole of the kingdom - as Solomon's descendants will still rule one tribe 'for the sake of David your father and for the sake of Jerusalem which I have chosen'.[167] The conduit through whom God chooses to bring down this calamity on the house of Solomon is Jeroboam, whom the text describes as a capable man who had been put in charge of one of Solomon's corvees.[168] God speaks to Jeroboam, through the prophet Ahijah. Ahijah dramatically tears Jeroboam's cloak into twelve pieces, representing the twelve tribes and the division of the land into tribal areas, saying that God will give Jeroboam ten of these pieces but will leave one with Solomon's descendants

---

[162] I Kings 5.9.

[163] I Kings 11.4.

[164] I Kings 11.6.

[165] See I Kings 11.7-8.

[166] Deuteronomy 23.4. The words 'in perpetuity' - my translation of 'ad olam' - are regularly untranslated as they seem to contradict the rest of the statement. I prefer to leave the ambiguity in, though it presents problems.

[167] I Kings 11.11-13.

[168] I Kings 11.28.

including Jerusalem.[169]   God makes Jeroboam a promise but, in the way to which we are now accustomed, the promise is contingent: 'You will I take and you will rule over all that your soul desires and you will be king over Israel. And it shall be that if you listen to what I command you and you walk in my ways and do that which is right in my eyes to keep my statutes and commandments as did David my servant, then I will be with you and I will build for you a true house as I built for David and I will give you Israel. And I will afflict David's descendants because of this but not for ever.'[170]

The final thing we are told about Solomon's life is that he sought to kill Jeroboam, who escaped to Egypt. However, we are not told why as we have not been told of any enmity between Solomon and Jeroboam. Clearly, though, this must be linked to God's promise to reward Jeroboam and to punish Solomon's descendants. Solomon's death is described briefly. He had reigned for forty years - obviously intended as a perfect number mirroring the number of years the Israelites spent in the wilderness but also mirroring David's forty-year reign.[171]   Intriguingly the text says: 'and the other deeds of Solomon and all his deeds are written in the book of the deeds of Solomon.'[172] We do not know whether this is a literary flight of fancy or whether such a book about Solomon did indeed exist, and/or the extent to which it differed from the two accounts of the life of Solomon which have been handed down to us in the books of Kings and Chronicles.

Notwithstanding any gap in our knowledge about Solomon because of a potentially lost book, we have a welter of information on him. Much of what we think we know about him is often based on an idealised version of his life that does not mirror the full picture which I have sought to draw from the books of Kings and Chronicles. Before we return to the Song of Songs (where this picture will be crucial), we need to summarise the life of Solomon so that we can focus again on the Song of Songs.

---

[169] See I Kings 11.29-37.
[170] I Kings 11.37-39.
[171] I Kings 11.42 (Solomon reigning forty years). I Kings 2.11 (David also reigning forty years).
[172] I Kings 11.41.

FOUR

Fall or Continuation?

The narrative in I Kings 11, in which Solomon follows the ways of his foreign wives, is regularly spoken of as Solomon's fall. Robert Alter describes the opening of that chapter as marking 'a strong shift in the perception of Solomon. Up to this point, he had been portrayed as an ideally wise and fabulously wealthy king to whom God gave rousing promises and who built God's house in Jerusalem.'[173] Similarly, one of the leading modern Hebrew-language commentaries states: 'Chapter 11 which completes the chronicle of Solomon's kingdom stands in polar contrast to the previous chapters which described Solomon's life. Chapters 1-10 set out the positive approach of the editor who praises Solomon as having done right in the eyes of the Lord and who is described as a wise king, whose kingdom flourishes from an economic perspective and is strong from a political perspective.'[174]

I have to take issue with these comments.[175] They fail fully to take into account much of the analysis which we have undertaken in chapters 2 and 3 above concerning the centrality in the Solomon text of the Deuteronomic interpolations and the law of the king in the book of Deuteronomy.[176] Much of the text in the book of Kings does indeed display Solomon's wisdom and wealth,[177] but the constant reference to the contingency of such wealth leads one to question the degree to which we are meant to accept at face value all such claims to wisdom. It might be tempting on first reading to take the comments about wisdom as intended to be read straight, but the constant warnings do lead the sensitive reader already at this stage to wonder whether the text protests just a little too much, and to adopt a more subversive reading of these passages.

Moreover, the argument that there is a 'strong shift' or 'polar contrast' in the book of Kings between chapter 11 and its first ten chapters flies in the face of the material at the end of chapter 10 and the beginning of chapter 11. At the end of chapter 10, we are told that silver was like stones, and cedars like sycamores in Jerusalem and that Solomon purchased vast amounts of chariots and horses from Egypt. The

---

[173] Alter: Ancient Israel, 661.

[174] Garsiel: *Olam hatanach: Melachim Alef*, (The Biblical World: I Kings) 118.

[175] As had Alter himself previously - see Alter: Ancient Israel, 659, footnote 26.

[176] Deuteronomy 17.14-20.

[177] E.g. I Kings 5 *passim*.

beginning of chapter 11 then informs us of the vast number of wives whom Solomon possessed. If read separately, this misses the whole point of the link - namely that increasing silver, horses and wives is exactly what the law of the king in the book of Deuteronomy forbade.

If one reads the text straight through (as the text invites but as is rejected by many of the leading commentators), then marvelling at Solomon's acquisition of wealth comes with a sense of discomfort. It is one thing for a king to be wealthy, but to increase such wealth to excess will inevitably lead to downfall. One is half tempted to use the term '*hubris*' from Greek literature. It is useful because it highlights the fatal flaw in Solomon's make-up which we really notice from the moment that he constructs the temple and palace.

A naïve reading is currently much more popular than the subversive one I am suggesting. It sees King Solomon as the epitome of wisdom whose reign saw unprecedented peace, stability and economic expansion, the like of which was never seen before or since. Solomon was blessed and befriended by God and it was he who was chosen to build the temple. His downfall, on this reading, was a single aberration for which his descendants were punished.

It is very easy to dismiss this naïve reading as a misreading but I am not sure that it is. It appears to me that both this naïve reading and the more subversive one were intended by the editor of the text. It is perfectly possible to marvel at Solomon's wealth and wisdom, and to see them as intended to demonstrate that Solomon was exactly the right person to build the temple (which was, let us not forget, viewed as the very central ideal of the Israelites). On this reading, one has to ignore or downplay the constant warnings and view the fall as related largely or, indeed, wholly, to Solomon's fondness for foreign practices, led on by his wives.[178]

One senses that the editor wanted us to read the text naïvely but nevertheless left us many clues about another, much more subversive, reading which can be drawn out if we look closely. We need to consider, from all the information which we have received about Solomon, what that more subversive reading consists of.

---

[178] Most of the Solomon narrative is paralleled in the book of Chronicles. The biggest distinction is that there is no equivalent to I Kings 11 which contains the description of Solomon taking foreign wives. This should not be taken to mean that the book of Chronicles has sought to blot out entirely the subversive reading of the Solomon narrative. As will be seen below, it contains an extremely revealing comment about the popular perception of the reign of King Solomon.

The subversive reading of Solomon's life

1. Solomon was born as the second son of David and Bathsheba. Their marriage followed the aftermath of the murder of Bathsheba's former husband, Uriah. The first son died as a result of the murder which brought about their union. Solomon was given his name by one of his parents (the text is unclear which). It means 'whole', 'complete' or 'peace'. God gives him the name '*Yedidyah*' (loved by God).

2. We have no evidence of much of a relationship between King David and Solomon as a child, though we are told about many other incidents involving the relationship between David and his other children, from which we can infer that the relationship was largely dysfunctional.

3. David's view of his son seems largely suppressed. The only direct reference which we have is in the book of Chronicles in which David describes Solomon as a 'gentle youth'.

4. From the evidence which we have, David's view seems correct. At the time when the destiny of the throne is being decided, Solomon is entirely passive. It is Bathsheba his mother, with the assistance of Nathan the prophet, who persuades David that her son will become king.

5. David is not sure that Solomon has the ability to be king, and places him in an apprentice-like position. However, David needs the monarchy to be secured in Solomon's hands and ensures that Solomon's coronation takes place in public, whilst he himself is still alive.

6. David passes on a warning in Deuteronomic style about the need to obey the commandments - failure to do so will result in destruction. Given the context in which this warning is given, it inevitably reminds the reader of the warning about the law of the king contained in Deuteronomy 17.14-20. The warning appears so regularly that the reader becomes aware that Solomon is being portrayed as a fatally flawed character.

7. A fuller description is given in the book of Chronicles of a conversation between David and Solomon concerning the building of the temple.

8. Solomon sees off any rivals to the throne. It is highly likely that the text is hinting that the power behind the throne is Bathsheba. She ensures that there are no possible competitors to her son's claim to the throne.

9. Having secured the throne, Solomon now speaks to God. As he only asks for wisdom, God grants him wealth in addition to wisdom. Given our knowledge of the Deuteronomic imprecation against wealth, we realise that this is a double-edged sword and that Solomon is walking a narrow tightrope between sufficient and excessive wealth.

10. We are then shown examples of King Solomon's wealth and wisdom.

11. Solomon has a great knowledge of the cedar trees from Lebanon which were the basic wood used in the construction of his father's palace. He determines to use it as the foundation wood for his own building project. Serendipitously, God had told David that God also wanted to dwell in a cedarwood house.

12. Solomon spends half his reign on his great building project in the course of which almost twice as long is spent on the palace as it is on the temple commanded by God.

13. These two buildings are constructed using Israelite forced labour reminiscent of that imposed on them in Egypt. This is shown starkly by use of the same Hebrew word to describe the labour. The contrast is also clearly made with the tabernacle which was built with voluntary contributions.

14. The palace is over four times the area of the temple. It is named 'the palace of the forest of Lebanon', not surprising given its reliance on cedarwood from Lebanon.

15. Having constructed the temple, Solomon calls on the services of a skilled craftsman, Hiram of Tyre, to fit it properly. The intended parallel with the role of Bezalel as skilled craftsman in the building of the tabernacle breaks down for two reasons. First, Hiram is brought in after the temple has been built whereas Bezalel had been brought by God before the tabernacle had been constructed. Second, the building of the tabernacle is the combined effort of a number of skilled men and women who voluntarily donate their skills to the exercise, such that they have to be told to stop. No such mood exists in Solomon's autocratic regime where forced labour is the norm and Hiram is hired and works alone.

16. Solomon intends the completion ceremony for the temple to imitate the completion of the tabernacle but we are forced to read this with a degree of irony, given our knowledge of the differences. It is to be seen as Solomon's vanity project.

17. The Queen of Sheba has heard of Solomon's wisdom and is even more impressed with it in person than the rumours had led her to expect.

18. She gives Solomon many gifts including spices (in Hebrew '*besamim*').

19. Spices were an integral part of the tabernacle and detailed instructions had been given as to the correct proportions of the four spices used - myrrh, cinnamon, cane and frankincense. At no point has there previously been any mention of spices in the temple to parallel their crucial use in the tabernacle.

20. We are not told whether Solomon used the spices he received from the Queen of Sheba in the temple. Their omission is striking given their importance in the tabernacle and the detail afforded to them in the book of Exodus.

21. Solomon, having enriched himself, built a throne out of ivory and the finest gold.

22. Solomon increased his wealth, his horses and his wives. His wives inclined him to serve other gods and so, in increasing wealth, horses and wives, Solomon failed the threefold test in the law of the king in the book of Deuteronomy.

Solomon on this reading has to be read as a failure. There is one further comment which appears in both the books of Kings and Chronicles about what the popular perception of King Solomon was. It occurs after his death. Rehoboam, Solomon's son, is now king and Jeroboam and all of Israel come to him and say: 'Your father made our yoke heavy; now lighten the heavy work of your father and his heavy yoke that he gave us and we will serve you.'[179] This comment is revealing because it does not appear to be a Deuteronomistic slant on the life of Solomon but a comment from the people that they felt that Solomon had oppressed them.[180]   There appears

---

[179] I Kings 12.4 and II Chronicles 10.4.

[180] For a modern, fictional account of the subversive undercurrents in the Books of Samuel and Kings, see Yochi Brandes: *The Secret Book of Kings* (St Martin's Press, London 2016).

therefore to have been a tradition, suppressed but not excluded in the books of Kings and Chronicles, portraying Solomon in a very negative light.

We have focused on the life of Solomon for a considerable period of time. It is now time to return to the Song of Songs. We will not immediately examine it in the light of our conclusions about Solomon from our re-reading of the books of Kings and Chronicles, but Solomon's life will inevitably form a major part of our analysis as we proceed. At this stage, we should appreciate that the Song of Songs, in its trenchant criticism of Solomon, falls within the genre of subversive readings of the life of Solomon which we have uncovered. Yet its method of doing so is very different to that in the narrative books of Kings and Chronicles.

We therefore now need to look afresh at 'the Song of Songs which is about Solomon'. In chapter 1 above, we learnt why the superscription reference meant that the Song of Songs was intended to be *about* Solomon and not *by* him. Before we offer a commentary on the Song of Songs, we have one further area to consider; we need to ask what is meant by its opening phrase: 'the Song of Songs'? To that question there is a much more complicated answer than one might at first imagine.

FIVE

The Meaning of 'the Song of Songs'

In the previous three chapters of this book, we have focused on the figure of Solomon. He is the title character; indeed, while 'the Song of Songs' is the standard English title, the alternative title used by some is 'the Song of Solomon'. The Hebrew original reads: *'Shir Hashirim Asher Li'Shlomoh'*. As discussed in chapter 1 above, this best translates as 'The Song of Songs which is about Solomon'. Having considered Solomon in some detail already, we now revert to the first two Hebrew words of the title. What does *Shir Hashirim*, 'the Song of Songs', mean?

It is possible to explain this in two ways which are capable of sitting side-by-side very easily. The first is the traditional title though the second was probably intended just as much by its author. We shall now consider both meanings.

1. 'Simply the Best' - the first meaning of 'the Song of Songs'

The difficulty facing all readers of the Bible when approaching the Song of Songs is how to understand it, given that it is so different from any other book in the Bible. At its heart is a man's and a woman's description of their love for each other, often expressed in the most passionate of terms. It is couched in language which, at times, is open to numerous interpretations, leaving us bereft of a clear understanding as to what the text exactly means.

Yet the almost universal response over the centuries has been that the Song of Songs is a wonderful work, one of the great ancient works to have survived the ravages of time. The idea of something elevated or superlative has constantly entered discussion as to how we are to view it. This is no coincidence. It arises from the title of the work itself - the Song of Songs - which on this interpretation indicates that it is the finest work.

The Rabbinic reading - the finest work

The most well-known Rabbinic reading of the meaning of 'the Song of Songs' is in the context of whether the Song of Songs and other books could be considered part of the canon. A book which is part of the canon was seen as 'contaminating the hands'. 'Contamination' should not be seen in its modern pejorative sense. There is nothing negative intended here. Rather, the reading of a holy text rendered a person '*tamei*' (contaminated) because of its religious significance. A particular Rabbinic discussion about the Song of Songs proceeded on the basis that this was the question to be discussed:

'Rabbi Aqiva said perish the thought that any Jew might consider that the Song of Songs does not contaminate the hands. The whole world cannot be compared to the day when the Song of Songs was given to Israel - all the writings may be holy but the Song of Songs is the Holy of Holies.'[181]

What should one make of this comment? Many have thought that the openly passionate nature of the Song of Songs rendered the text controversial to the Rabbis. One cannot be sure of the Rabbis' motivation in including it in the canon but it is difficult to believe that they were embarrassed by the meaning of the text. That, it seems to me, is our own reaction to reading what is plainly an erotic text and thinking that the Rabbis must have seen it as we do, and allegorised it as a result.

In fact, that is exactly what the Rabbis did. Allegory abounds. God is probably[182] not mentioned at all in the Song of Songs. In the Rabbinic re-reading God is everywhere, as is Israel, and both are combined with a fierce awareness of the need to observe the Torah-based commandments. One cannot, however, assume that this allegorisation came about as a result of embarrassment. Those who seek to find vestiges of such embarrassment hidden within the Rabbinic corpus are likely to be disappointed. Rather, the Rabbis obviously delighted in it. They no doubt realised the beauty and literary merit of the Song of Songs and wished to preserve it. The whole text was viewed through the prism of Rabbinic ideology, which regarded the entire Bible as a journey towards redemption by following the God-given commandments. Almost every word in the Song of Songs was therefore allegorised to meet this need.

Much of the Biblical corpus fits easily into this Rabbinical ideology. There is a whole swathe of the Bible devoted to a narrative of what I have called contingent progress.[183] The children of Israel can enter the land of Israel in the book of Deuteronomy if they obey the commandments; a stable society will be produced contingent on the qualities of the leaders as seen in the books of Judges, Samuel and

---

[181] Mishnah Yadayim 3:5.

[182] The term 'probably' is used because of the word '*shalhevetyah*' in 8.6 where some read the last syllable as a reference to the divine name. Most probably however it is a suffix. See commentary to 8.6 below.

[183] Andrew Levy: *Ecclesiastes and Contemporary Argument*. European Judaism 17/2 158-164.

Kings; a just society will be produced if the people act in a morally upright fashion as seen in the writings of the prophets.

A poem devoted to the description of the love between a young man and a young woman fits uncomfortably into this normative narrative.[184] Yet Rabbinic remarks on the Song of Songs are unanimous in its praise. The Rabbis appear to have appreciated the work to such a degree that they felt the need to ensure its canonisation. They saw it as a superlative work. So they made it fit into their narrative. Rabbi Aqiva's comparison of the Song of Songs to the Holy of Holies interprets the title as indicating that it is the finest work.

Many dismiss the Rabbinic view as anachronistic and to be rejected out of hand. Often this is accompanied by a recognition that, if the Rabbis had not accepted the Song of Songs into the canon, its fate could have been like that of much of Sappho's erotically-charged, ancient Greek love poetry which is only available to us in fragmentary form.[185]

Yet to ignore the Rabbinic interpretation, allegorical as it is, because it has a different ideological outlook to our own, would be a mistake. The Rabbinic mind thought intertextually - it was fiercely aware of the link between different passages in the Bible and would make the comparison often on the basis of little direct connection. Sometimes that connection could be found because the word itself was the same or similar, sometimes the link was flimsier. Frequently we can reject their attempts to draw intertextual links if we want to understand the Song of Songs. So, for example, the man speaks to the woman and states: 'Your eyes are doves'.[186] One Rabbinic commentary on this links the terminology used to a text in Numbers 15.24 which also uses the word 'eyes' and says (based on the Aramaic translation) that these eyes are the Great and Small Sanhedrin.[187]

However, when the Song of Songs becomes more specific, the Rabbinic commentary sometimes provides insightful commentary on, for example, the role played by Solomon in the wedding scene (Song of Songs 3.7-11) referred to in chapter 1 above. We shall have occasion to consider it when we revisit that scene.

---

[184] Neither does the book of Ecclesiastes which also faced Rabbinic questions about whether or not it 'contaminated' the hands.
[185] Bloch: The Song of Songs, 32.
[186] Song of Songs 4.1.
[187] Midrash Shir Hashirim, Kasher, 177. Indeed the description of the woman's body in the Song of Songs 7.3ff is compared to the Sanhedrin - see BT Sanh 37a.

The Church reading - a monk's work

The Song of Songs' reception history is, of course, not only a Jewish one. The Church also saw the book's magnificent qualities. It allegorised the relationship between the two lovers largely as a relationship between Christ and the Church. As with the Rabbis, it interpreted the title, the 'Song of Songs', as indicating that it was the finest work. It did so, however, with a very different purpose.

Whilst Jerome, Origen and Augustine wrote on the Song of Songs, it was the Cistercian monk, Bernard of Clairvaux, who wrote most extensively on the opening section we are now considering. He composed eighty-six sermons on the first two chapters of the Song of Songs, presumably shortly before his death because he never wrote about the remainder of the Song of Songs. His first sermon was devoted to the title of the book. He posed the question why was the book not just a 'Song' but the 'Song of Songs'. He contrasted it to the other 'songs' referred to in the Bible, none of which repeat the word 'song' as our text does. On all such other occasions (the songs of Moses, Deborah, Judith or Hannah) he thought that the person singing the song was inspired to sing as a result of events. The Song of Songs by contrast, on Bernard's view, was not written because King Solomon needed a particular benefit:

'We must now conclude then it was a special divine impulse that inspired these songs of his that now celebrate the praises of Christ and his Church, the gift of holy love, the sacrament of endless union with God.'[188]

On that basis, the Song of Songs' divine purpose was an entirely appropriate one for the monastery. It excelled all other songs such as the psalms. It stood at a point where all the other songs culminated.[189] For this reason, it was not a work for all monks:

'The novices, the immature, those but recently converted from a worldly life, do not normally sing this song or hear it sung. Only the mind disciplined by persevering study, only the man whose efforts have borne fruit under God's inspiration, the man whose years, as it were, make him ripe for marriage - years measured out not in time but in merits - only he is truly prepared for nuptial union with the divine partner.'[190]

---

[188] Bernard of Clairvaux 86 Sermons: Sermon 1 paragraph 8 www.duke.edu>texts>clairvaux (accessed 08.10.2017).
[189] Ibid Sermon 1 paragraphs 10 and 11.
[190] Ibid Sermon 1 paragraph 12.

We can see from this description that the Song was regarded not just as being a work describing union with God but also as a work whose dissemination was to be limited. Whilst psalms were (and still often are) part of the daily ritual in the monastery, the Song of Songs clearly was not. It was associated in the monastic mind with the elite. The title of the work, interpreted as 'the finest work', easily fits into that outlook. It could only be for the initiated.

Martin Luther's Reformation in the early sixteenth century aimed at getting rid of the power of the church and its monks. According to Luther, the way to salvation was via grace and scripture directly, without any intercessor (*'sola scriptura'*). It therefore became important that a good translation of the Bible should be available for the masses. Luther provided the most famous translation of the Bible into German. It is a version treated with almost as much reverence and respect in German-speaking countries as the King James version of the Bible is given in English-speaking countries. Luther based the title of the book in German on its first two Hebrew words. He called it *'Das Hohelied'* which literally means 'the High Song'. The intention can easily been seen as a hidden superlative - i.e. 'the Highest Song', a further example of the value accorded to the work.

This translation of the words *'Shir Hashirim'* as 'Song of Songs' or 'the Highest Song' has always been associated with the notion that its meaning is something like 'the best song'. This sits comfortably with Hebrew usage where phrases such as the 'Holy of Holies' (referred to above by Rabbi Aqiva), the King of Kings, vapour of vapours (commonly translated as vanity of vanities in Ecclesiastes) abound. It is possible that this is the meaning intended by the author. Yet it is entirely conceivable that the phrase also has another meaning - this time based not on a value judgement about the Song's literary merit but on the structure of the work.

2. 'A song containing songs' - the second meaning of 'the Song of Songs'

Commentators have debated the structure as well as the meaning of the song for many centuries. Is it one poem or a series of possibly independent poems gathered together to form some sort of collection? On this second, alternative reading of the title, the Song of Songs is also understood to be one song or poem. However, this reading implies that this one poem comprises earlier shorter poems which may or may not have been independent of each other but which, when read together, create one larger, coherent poem - hence the Song of Songs. The Aramaic translation of the Song of Songs expands on the first two opening words of the Song of Songs in Hebrew, to indicate that they mean 'songs and praises which Solomon, the king of

Israel said with the holy spirit before God, the master of the world'.[191] The implication of this observation is that the Song of Songs was seen as being made up of independent poems. As we will see, when examining the Song in detail, there are poems comprising dialogues between the lovers, angst-filled soliloquies, descriptions of the bodies of each of the lovers and wedding scenes.

Yet any perception of the Song of Songs as consisting entirely of separate poems comes up against obvious thematic and vocabulary links shared throughout the work as a whole. This creates a tension between these two ways of understanding the poem. How can independently composed poems nevertheless be viewed as forming a unity?

We shall return to the Song of Songs but only after a detour into the publishing patterns of some of the finest musical works composed in German in the early nineteenth century. They provide a surprisingly fruitful analogy and a series of potential answers to the question posed above.

A foray into early nineteenth-century romanticism

When the German poet, Heinrich Heine (1797-1856), later in his life, wanted to publish a new edition in 1837 of some of his earlier poetry, he called it 'Buch der Lieder' (Book of Songs). It contained some of his finest poetry and, in the introduction, he termed it an anthology - 'Gedichtesammlung'[192] (literally 'poetic collection'). An anthology is defined by the Chambers English Dictionary as 'a choice collection of writings, (esp poems) ...'.[193] An anthology thereby means the best poems. This does not imply that there is necessarily any connection between them. Heine's intention was clear; to produce, for a willing public, the finest poems from his output over the years, regardless of thematic connection. Their only link was that he had written each of them.

It is fascinating to compare and contrast Heine's thought process to that of the great Lieder writer Franz Schubert (1797-1828) when composing his great song cycles, Die Schöne Müllerin (the beautiful maid of the mill) and Die Winterreise (the winter's journey). In these song cycles, there is an obvious thematic link between the individual poems, making the whole something different to, and more than, its parts. This is hardly surprising given that the texts which Schubert chose to set had been intended by the poet, Wilhelm Müller, to be an interlinked cycle of poems in

---

[191] Targum to Song of Songs 1:1. Kasher, 2.
[192] Buch der Lieder, Vorrede (Introduction) Heine, 1837, Paris.
[193] Chambers Dictionary 11th Edition 2008.

which different poems and themes nevertheless reflect an overall unity. Unarguably, this sense of a whole to the poems is enhanced by Schubert's exquisite musical setting, which adds to their coherence.

When it comes to determining whether the Song of Songs comes within the Heine analogy or the Schubert analogy set out above, it is clear that the Song of Songs falls fairly and squarely within the Schubert analogy. The Song of Songs may be a series of poems but it is clearly not an anthology; it has a coherence to it which allows one to read it as a whole.

Perhaps, though, the closest analogy which we need to draw is to another of Schubert's song cycles. Schubert's third (and final) great song cycle written shortly before his death is, therefore unsurprisingly, called '*Schwanengesang*' (Swansong). In contrast to his other two song cycles, Schubert chose not to use an existing cycle of poems. Instead, he selected poems from three contemporary poets, Ludwig Rellstab, Heinrich Heine and Johann Gabriel Seidl whose single poetic contribution provides the text for the final song. Obviously, the poems had not been intended by their authors to be read together. Yet when we hear them now, they clearly have a coherence - they 'fit together' in our own minds as one musical whole comprising individual, differently-intended parts.

There is an irony to the unity we perceive in *Schwanengesang*. These were probably the last songs which Schubert wrote, shortly before his death on 19 November 1828. He did not have time to specify exactly how they ought to be set out and there are indications that he may have wanted them published separately. This applies especially to *Die Taubenpost* (Pigeon Post), his final song written in October 1828, based on the words of Seidl (of course the only song in *Schwanengesang* by Seidl). It is a wistful tale of a lover who uses a pigeon to send messages of longing to his beloved. The simple melody sung by the singer is accompanied by a syncopated piano part, indicating restlessness, and a rolling figure in the treble almost certainly intended to indicate musical interludes from the pigeon!

On its own, *Die Taubenpost* sounds like so many of Schubert's songs - a wistful yearning after love, requited or otherwise. Yet it is rarely, if ever, heard on its own. In the *Schwanengesang* song cycle, it follows one of the most powerful songs Schubert ever wrote. That song is *Der Doppelgänger* (the Double) which is a setting of Heine's poem about a man seeing his double at the house where his lover, many years previously, used to live. The man attacks the double for mocking him. Schubert's interpretation is so powerful because, whilst the singer chants the words of misery, he is accompanied by a piano score which contains a series of chords ranging from pianissimo to fortissimo and back again, ending with a series of modulations into a quiet ending of despair. We sense that the man, in seeing his own double, is actually describing his own premonitions of death. We are heightened in this by the knowledge that Schubert wrote the piece in August 1828, only a few months before his own.

The wistful, apparently simple, *Taubenpost*, describing the yearning of a lover, fits perfectly our sense of the ending of an interlinked song cycle after the tension of *der Doppelgänger*. The singer stops singing, the pianist no longer trills the motif of the pigeon, and all we are left with is that restless accompaniment which now seems peaceful, comprising a very simple syncopated D major (dominant) and G major (tonic) melody, to end the song and, as it were, the song cycle and, thereby, as we know, the whole of Schubert's work.

The Song of Songs as *Schwanengesang*

We previously asked, in the context of the Song of Songs, how independently-composed poems can come to be seen as forming a unity. This foray into early nineteenth-century German romanticism has enhanced our understanding of what is meant by a Song of Songs as it has provided us with useful analogies and comparisons. We can now clearly reject a comparison with Heine's collection of independent songs as an anthology in *Buch der Lieder*. Heine's rearrangement and title was not intended to indicate unity. The Song of Songs is not an anthology as we will see even more clearly when we examine the unity running through the Song of Songs in the commentary section below.

Yet the example of Schubert's song cycles still leaves us with two separate models. The first one is that of his first two song cycles, *Die Schöne Müllerin* and *Die Winterreise*, in which the individual poems were written with the intent of being linked together, both by the poet and the composer. Unity is clear therefore as the aim of both artists. If the analogy is to be made with this model, then the Song of Songs was written by one person and, even though it contains disparate poems on the subject of love, was intended to be seen as a single whole by its author. That is an entirely plausible analogy to make with the Song of Songs. Many consider that the various scenes in the Song of Songs were written by one person; there are certainly thematic links between several poems which I have already highlighted in chapter 1 and will consider in more detail below. Others, though, reject the idea of single authorship on the basis of disparate styles and abrupt changes of subject matter between poems. Ultimately the truth may be lost in the mists of time and one cannot be sure whether one person wrote the whole song. However, the implication that a song cannot be unified if it was originally written by different authors is one which must be rejected. The Schubert song cycle analogy helps us understand this. It also presents us with another possibility.

Schwanengesang reveals a different, more complicated, model of unity. Here it is not the original poet who intended the whole to be a single unit. Rellstab, Heine or Seidl could not have known how Schubert would use their original work. It could be argued that the unity of *Schwanengesang* was created by Schubert in his deliberate linking of these originally independent works. The distinct literary styles of different poets could be contrasted to Schubert's musical interpretation of the poems in his own individual style. That is certainly the case with the poems of Rellstab and Heine which Schubert intended to form one unified song cycle. In other words, on this analogy, the poems in the Song of Songs could have been written by different authors but brought together. We know however that the word '*shir*' means both 'poem' and 'song' in Hebrew and, on this interpretation, separate poems were gathered together by a musician to be performed as one unified song - a Biblical-era Schubert, as it were.

The *Taubenpost* song at the end of *Schwanengesang*, with words by Seidl, presents us with a further analogy. We have no evidence that Schubert had intended this song to comprise part of his song cycle, but a later editor may well have determined that it was an appropriate song to be included. If this supposition is correct, then we now have a song cycle which we accept as being entirely unified, even though neither poets nor composer had intended it to be such. The Song of Songs analogy is clear. A later editor created a unity out of the work of earlier poets, and from the oral traditions as to how those poems ought to be sung.

Unity within multiple authorship

Much has been written on the Song of Songs but I doubt that an analogy with Schubert's *Schwanengesang* has ever been made before. However, this is certainly not the first time that a comparison has been made between the Song of Songs and songs in German. Michael Fox compares the Song of Songs to the medieval Germanic folk song tradition of '*Zersingen*'[194] whereby a song would change in its performance; through this process 'transmitters became authors in their own right'. Fox believes that one must see the Song of Songs as a unity but he in no way considers that this impedes multiple authorship.

---

[194] Fox, 1985, 222. See also Bloch, 18 for an *en passant* reference to 'the narrative thread in a Schubert song cycle'.

The idea of a unity, notwithstanding multiple original authorship, is a very satisfying way of explaining the Song of Songs. Both Michael Fox and Marvin Pope have written extensively about the work's links with the love songs of other Middle Eastern cultures. Comparison between, say, the Song of Songs and ancient Egyptian love songs clearly reveals a link; so far, however, we have not seen any evidence that there was any direct borrowing of material. This can be contrasted with one particular section of the book of Proverbs which the German Egyptologist, Adolph Erman, discovered in the 1920s was in fact a translation of the Egyptian Pharaoh Amenope's thirty chapters,[195] often faithfully following the original.

On this basis, the best we can say is that the Song of Songs is a collection of poems which may have been independent of each other at one stage but clearly at a later stage were linked together in artful fashion. Whether that joining together was a one-off event or occurred on more than one occasion is not clear to us.

We may however be helped in our understanding by the references to Solomon in the Song of Songs. As was discussed in chapter 1 above, Solomon's name appears in the superscription and then in three further different sections of the Song of Songs.[196] Most love songs do not have a political purpose to them and much of the material within the Song of Songs seems, at first glance, to fit into this category of erotic love poetry. Yet we cannot ignore these direct references to Solomon. They appear to be comments about him, at best unfavourable, at worst derogatory. It seems clear that deliberately veiled references to Solomon also appear in other, apparently independent, sections of the Song of Songs but that his influence does not pervade the whole of the Song of Songs. Indeed, there are parts of the Song of Songs in which Solomon does not appear at all, either overtly or covertly. If much of the rest of the Song of Songs is simply a selection of love poems, then the theory of originally multiple authorship helps us understand why something so different has been interpolated into works otherwise sitting easily within the Middle Eastern love poem tradition. On this basis, it might well be that the final editor stitched together disparate individual poems, possibly by different authors, into one whole.

The fact that the separate parts work so well together is probably testament to the skill of the editor who wove the original material into the established norms of literary form of the day. One of those norms is the way in which Biblical poetry functioned as a form to which I now turn.

---

[195] Proverbs 22.17 - 24.22.
[196] 1.1, 1.5, 3.7-10, 8.11-12.

A word about parallelism and Biblical poetry

The Biblical poetry we are about to consider does not work in the same way as poetry in most western languages. It adopts what has come to be known as parallelism, a form without great use in western literature. We are used to rhyme, alliteration and metre being the most common way to create poetry. In Hebrew, given that roughly half of all nouns end '-*ah*' in the singular and almost all nouns end either '-*im*' or '-*ot*' in the plural, rhyme was far too easy a method of writing for the result to be called 'poetry'.

The first person to have coined the term 'parallelism' in relation to Hebrew poetry appears to have been the eighteenth century Bishop Robert Lowth.[197] The basic way of creating a parallel is of course to have two different phrases giving synonymous ideas in different words ('When Israel left Egypt, the house of Jacob left a foreign people' to use an example from Psalm 114.1). This synonymous form of parallelism had been recognised for a long time. Lowth realised, however, that there were three types of parallelism which could be distinguished in Biblical poetry - synonymous, antithetic and synthetic. In other words, verses may not just say the same thing but they could also create contrast or resolution as well. Whilst the discussion of the nature and dynamics of Biblical parallelism has moved on considerably in the last two hundred and fifty years (see in particular in this regard Adele Berlin in a seminal work published in 1985 entitled '*The Dynamics of Biblical Parallelism*'),[198] this threefold analysis of parallelism will be sufficient for our purposes as we note the way in which the poet weaves the material together in the Song of Songs.

Concluding remarks

We have now considered Solomon's life in more detail than one would normally do when reading the Song of Songs and we need to look again at those four places referencing Solomon, but this time within the context of the rest of the Song of Songs. As we will see, it will give us cause to think about how the whole of the Song of Songs has been written.

That whole has secrets which need to be prised out. A saying attributed to (but probably not in fact by) the tenth-century Jewish scholar Saadya Gaon states:

---

[197] Lowth 1754, *Praelectiones Academicae de Sacra Poesi Hebraeorum* (On the Sacred Poetry of the Hebrews).
[198] Adele Berlin, 2008 (revised edition), *The Dynamics of Biblical Parallelism*, William B. Eerdmans, Grand Rapids.

'Know, my brother, that you will find great diversity of opinions as regards the interpretation of the Song of Songs, and it must be confessed that there is a reason for it since the Song is like a lock, the key of which has been lost'.[199]

The key may have been lost, but should that really stop us seeking to prise the lock open?

---

[199] Quoted in Kingsmill, 12.

PART TWO

שִׁיר הַשִּׁירִים

THE SONG OF SONGS

SONG OF SONGS 1.1 - 2.7

Song, Scent and Cedars

א שִׁיר הַשִּׁירִים אֲשֶׁר לִשְׁלֹמֹה:

1.1. The Song of Songs which is about Solomon.

The opening verse of the Song of Songs is a superscription which was probably added at the final stage of the editing process. It consists of four words in Hebrew ('*Shir Hashirim asher Li'shlomoh*'). The first two words ('the Song of Songs') and the last word ('about Solomon') have been discussed in great detail above. As I have argued, they go to the heart of the text.

The word '*asher*', meaning merely 'which', might not normally be worthy of comment. However, this is the only time it appears in the Song of Songs. On the many other occasions when the writer wishes to use 'which', the Hebrew term used is '*she-*'. This term is only associated with later Biblical Hebrew, a sign that the Song of Songs is a relatively late Hebrew work (educated guesses place this work somewhere between the sixth and third century BCE, but there is no absolute scholarly consensus).

So why does the superscription use the term '*asher*', associated with an older period of Biblical Hebrew? There are two possible explanations. The first is that the sentence itself was written at an earlier period. This is highly unlikely because it would then relate to a series of poems which, given their late language, had yet to be composed either at all or, at the very least, in their final form. The second, more likely, explanation is that it was written once all the poems had been gathered together as a cycle and an antiquated word was chosen as a deliberate attempt to focus readers on a former time, when Solomon was king.

ב יִשָּׁקֵנִי מִנְּשִׁיקוֹת פִּיהוּ
כִּי־טוֹבִים דֹּדֶיךָ מִיָּיִן:
ג לְרֵיחַ שְׁמָנֶיךָ טוֹבִים
שֶׁמֶן תּוּרַק שְׁמֶךָ עַל־כֵּן עֲלָמוֹת אֲהֵבוּךָ:
ד מָשְׁכֵנִי אַחֲרֶיךָ נָּרוּצָה
הֱבִיאַנִי הַמֶּלֶךְ חֲדָרָיו

נָגִ֫ילָה וְנִשְׂמְחָה֙ בָּ֔ךְ
נַזְכִּ֤ירָה דֹדֶ֙יךָ֙ מִיַּ֔יִן
מֵישָׁרִ֖ים אֲהֵב֑וּךָ:

She speaks to him:

1.2. May he kiss me with his mouth's kisses:
For your caresses are better than wine.
     1.3. Your oils smell wonderful.
'Poured oil' is your name,
     that is why girls love you.
1.4 Draw me after you, let us run,
     the king brought me to his rooms.
We will be glad and rejoice in you.
     We recollect your caresses above wine.
       They love you straight away.

1.2

The opening words set the scene for an outpouring of passion between the two lovers. There are any number of difficulties in understanding in the Song of Songs, and one of those appears in verse 2. The female lover starts by speaking about her lover in the third person repeating the word for kiss[200] but then continues by addressing him directly in the second person. The translation here suggests that the opening might be her internal monologue which breaks to the surface as she then voices her feelings to her lover.

One fascinating modern commentary[201] asks us to elide versus 1 and 2. On that basis, 'may he kiss me' clearly refers to 'Solomon'. The female lover then proceeds to address her lover directly in the second person. This is an intriguing suggestion. It implies that the memory of Solomon is an aphrodisiac for the lovers, as it were, so that their dialogue can continue. Given the scorn with which Solomon is addressed by the end of the Song of Songs, this interpretation does present challenges. Perhaps this, and the fairly neutral reference to Solomon's curtains in 1:5 (discussed below), are an indication of a development towards the negative

---

[200] In one Midrash, the Rabbis link the Hebrew word for kiss '*neshikah*' to the word for desire '*teshukah*' which appears later in the Song of Songs (7.11), (*Shir Hashirim Rabbah*. Kasher, page 15). This point is considered in more detail in the commentary to 7.11 below.
[201] Gurevitch, 43.

endpoint portrayal as the lovers realise that what they bring to each other is far better than anything King Solomon could provide.

One word which presents difficulties is the Hebrew '*dod*'. It is the word which appears most frequently in the Song of Songs and is usually translated as 'love'. Often I will do the same. However, the standard word for love, '*ahavah*', appears almost as frequently and so the word '*dod*' can mean other love-like things as well. In the book of Samuel, Nathan's chosen name for Solomon was '*Yedidyah*'[202] which derives from the same root meaning 'loved'. David's name derives from the same root. A similar root '*dad*' means 'breast' and there is always this possibility in translating it. Here, I have chosen J.P. Fokkelman's translation of 'caresses'[203] because it appears best to parallel the previous reference to 'kisses'.

1.3

The word translated 'poured' is problematic and some have suggested that it may be a particular type of oil. However, the gist is clear - the reference to the man's sensuousness now adds his aroma to his touch referred to in verse 2. All five senses will be mentioned in the Song of Songs, all are beautifully described but smell, as we shall see, is developed in a far more complex way than the other four senses.

1.4

Who is the king referred to near the beginning of this verse? Some have sought to identify him with King Solomon. But that would require the male lover to be King Solomon which is inconceivable given the later scorn in which King Solomon is held in the Song of Songs. The 'king' here is clearly the term the woman uses to describe her lover. He brings her to his 'rooms' as if he were a 'king' with a whole series of private chambers, available for his (and now her) private pleasure. It would, however, be a mistake to ignore the fact that the female lover refers to her beloved as her 'king' immediately after (1.1) and immediately before (1.5) references to Solomon. Although one can dismiss the notion that the king is Solomon, the text strongly hints that the lover is being not so much identified with him as compared with him. As we shall see, the comparison is not being made to say that the lover is as good as Solomon; rather that he is far, far better.

---

[202] II Samuel 12.25.
[203] Jan Fokkelman, *Cavalcade*, 13.

She then says 'we will be glad and rejoice in you'. This is almost certainly a deliberate allusion to and misquote of psalm 118.24 which says 'This is the day which the Lord made, we will be glad and rejoice in Him'.[204] To many modern religious thinkers, the idea that the Bible could take a reference to God and transform it into part of a very earthy praise of one's lover might appear sacrilegious. That appears, however, to be exactly what the author of the Song of Songs has chosen to do.[205] To many secular thinkers, on the other hand, this might be an opportunity to rejoice in one of the few books in the Bible which is no longer in thrall to theological thinking.

Both approaches would be wrong. The Song of Songs is a transformative work. The fact that it probably does not use the name of God does not mean that it is 'secular' in our modern understanding. The word 'secular' has no real meaning in the ancient Middle-Eastern world. Everyone was, in one way or another, linked to a world in which God exists. The Song of Songs does not reject theological ideas which it inherited; rather it uses them in different ways. If the Psalmist can praise God in a certain manner, then it is entirely appropriate to allow the woman to describe her lover in a similar fashion, using a similar word construction. We should neither miss this reference altogether nor, in any way, be shocked by it.

The psalm seems, literally, to be a reminder for the author of the Song of Songs because, immediately after the psalm is quoted, the final two phrases of this poem start with the word 'remind' ('*nazkirah*') and then repeat two phrases stated earlier but in separate contexts - the references to caresses being better than wine and the maidens loving you.

Verses two to four appear to comprise the first poem in the Song of Songs. The female lover will carry on speaking in verse five but will introduce a new theme. What have we been able to learn so far? Immediate passion, sensuous language and a willingness to use and transform older forms for the purpose of describing the beloved. All these characteristics permeate the whole of the Song of Songs.

שְׁחוֹרָה אֲנִי וְנָאוָה בְּנוֹת יְרוּשָׁלָ͏ִם ה

---

[204] Given that 'day' is masculine like 'the Lord', the word translated 'Him' in this sentence could mean 'we will be glad and rejoice in the day' but the references surrounding this sentence in Psalm 118 clearly indicate that the much more likely reference is to 'the Lord'.

[205] One Rabbinic midrash states that the 'you' referred to is the Torah. The logic for this is that the Hebrew word for 'in you' is '*bach*' which in the alpha-numeric gematria system adds up to twenty-two which in turn corresponds to the 22 letters of the Hebrew alphabet by means of which the Torah was written. *Shir Hashirim Rabbah*, Kasher 33.

כְּאָהֳלֵי קֵדָר כִּירִיעוֹת שְׁלֹמֹה:
ו אַל־תִּרְאוּנִי שֶׁאֲנִי שְׁחַרְחֹרֶת שֶׁשְּׁזָפַתְנִי הַשָּׁמֶשׁ
בְּנֵי אִמִּי נִחֲרוּ־בִי שָׂמֻנִי נֹטֵרָה אֶת־הַכְּרָמִים
כַּרְמִי שֶׁלִּי לֹא נָטָרְתִּי:

She speaks to him:

**1.5. Black am I and beautiful, o daughters of Jerusalem,
     like the tents of Qedar, like Solomon's curtains.**
**1.6. Do not look at me as if I am dawn-darkened, as if I am sun tanned.
     My mother's sons' anger boiled over at me. They placed me as a guard
     over the vineyards.
         I have not guarded my own vineyard.**

1.5 and 1.6.

These verses have already been discussed in chapter 1 above, given the reference to
Solomon. The female lover describes herself as black. The word for black in
Hebrew ('*shachor*') is linked to the word for 'dawn' ('*shachar*'). I have translated
as 'dawn-darkened' the word in 1.6 which could have been rendered as 'dark-
skinned' which plays on the black/dawn imagery. The passage is not necessarily a
comment on ethnicity but about the fact that the female lover works in the open and
therefore is sun-tanned. As in many non-modern societies, a sun tan was a sign not,
as now, of opulence but rather of lowly status - and clearly the female lover's
comment is an attempt to say that he should look beyond skin colour.

She does so by means of a comparison - to the tents of Qedar and to Solomon's
curtains. Both have previous reference points in the Bible though neither directly
refers, as she does, to colour. Dark, however, is implied from the name of the tribe
Qedar which means 'dark-coloured'. Jeremiah in a series of curses against various
of Israel's neighbours refers to both tents and curtains. He says the following
concerning Qedar:

'About Qedar and the kingdom of Chatzor which Nebuchadnezzar smote, thus says
the Lord. Arise, go up to Qedar and plunder the Qedemites. They will take their
tents and their flock, they will carry away their curtains and all their vessels and their
camels and proclaim terror all about them.'[206]

---

[206] Jeremiah 49.28-29.

Furthermore, the ark of God was located in a tent which (as previously discussed in chapter 3) was also described, in the book of Samuel, as being behind a curtain.[207] The context was a discussion between David and Nathan before Solomon was born. The reference in the Song of Songs to 'Solomon's curtain' is difficult to understand. While the description of the tabernacle in the book of Exodus is full of references to curtains, there is no reference in the book of Kings to the temple containing them.

So what are we to make of this obscure reference? Robert Alter[208] rejects entirely the attempt by some modern scholars to re-vowel Solomon in this verse as '*Salmah*' - like Qedar, a Middle Eastern tribe. On this basis, the text would read 'like the tents of Qedar, like the curtains of Salmah'. Alter rather reads the text as a paradox - I may be as dark as a nomad's (i.e. Qedar's) tent but as lovely as the curtains of a king - the implication being that Solomon's curtains were intricate and complex in their beauty.

I would suggest another possibility. This is that both the tents of Qedar and the curtain which Solomon inherited from David were simple affairs. The woman describes herself in similar terms. This reading has attractions because it carries on her previous comment that she is black and beautiful - the tents of Qedar and Solomon's curtains give her two further examples of blackness, simplicity and beauty. The difficulty with this reading is that we are not told about Solomon's curtains anywhere else and, if it is correct, the female lover is making the comparison to Solomon whilst actually referring to a curtain inherited from David or to a separate curtain about which we have not otherwise heard.

Whichever of these two readings is chosen, an unnecessary reworking of the text is avoided. I also mentioned in chapter 1 that a reference to 'Solomon', 'guards' and 'my vineyard' appears at the end of the Song of Songs (8.11-12). If the reference to Solomon in verse 5 is allowed to stand, then both passages contain these three references and one has a powerful and beautiful inclusio.

There is an irony to the anger in verse 6 exhibited by the female lover at her mother's sons' attitude to her. Those described must be her brothers or her half-brothers. In chapter 8, she expresses the frustration that her lover could not be seen as like a brother to her by others because then she could be intimate with him in public. In this passage, she says that she has not guarded her own vineyard; this is likely to be a reference to her exerting sexual choices against her brothers' wishes. Brothers can

---

[207] II Samuel 7.2.
[208] Alter, 2015, 9.

be supportive but they can be dangerous as well, as the author would have known from the story of Amnon and Tamar where a half-brother rapes his sister.[209] We will have cause to see this dichotomy, in striking and shocking form, later on in the Song of Songs.[210]

These verses are addressed to the 'daughters of Jerusalem' who appear here on seven occasions, mostly in the context of a repeated adjuration. Their role will be considered in more detail in chapter 7 below. She now turns to her lover and addresses him.

ז הַגִּ֣ידָה לִּ֗י שֶׁאָהֲבָה֙ נַפְשִׁ֔י

אֵיכָ֣ה תִרְעֶ֔ה אֵיכָ֖ה תַּרְבִּ֣יץ בַּֽצָּהֳרָ֑יִם

שַׁלָּמָ֤ה אֶֽהְיֶה֙ כְּעֹ֣טְיָ֔ה עַ֖ל עֶדְרֵ֥י חֲבֵרֶֽיךָ׃

ח אִם־לֹ֤א תֵדְעִי֙ לָ֔ךְ הַיָּפָ֖ה בַּנָּשִׁ֑ים

צְאִי־לָ֗ךְ בְּעִקְבֵי֙ הַצֹּ֔אן

וּרְעִי֙ אֶת־גְּדִיֹּתַ֔יִךְ

עַ֖ל מִשְׁכְּנ֥וֹת הָרֹעִֽים׃

She speaks to him:

1.7. Tell me, soulmate of mine,

> **how will you pasture, how will you graze, how will you lie down at noontime.**

> > **Why should I be like a wanderer over your friends' flocks?**

He responds to her:

1.8. If you do not know yourself, most beautiful of women,

> **follow the traces of the flock for yourself**

and graze your kids

> **by the shepherds' bothies.**

The imagery in these two verses is that of shepherds, leading many to interpret the whole of the Song of Songs as some sort of pastoral idyll. As I have suggested in chapter 5 above, the Song is incapable of one clear-cut meaning. Whilst we will see shepherd imagery often, such imagery is too episodic in nature to reduce the whole poem to a shepherd's narrative.

---

[209] II Samuel 13.
[210] See commentary on 4.9 below.

Besides, these two verses can be easily read as lovers' banter. She asks him 'why shouldn't I leave you and look after the other shepherds' flocks?'. His reply is effectively 'be my guest'. In other contexts, one might take this literally as an invitation, which has been accepted, to break up the relationship. In our context, where we are to see a series of further erotic episodes, at this stage the gentle terminology should surely be seen as a tantalising mutual tease.

Verse 8 is the first time that the male lover speaks. As we will see, the male lover takes time to find his voice. What he will say is often a reflection of what she has told him. He will later speak frequently but not as often as the female lover, making this the only book in the Bible where more of the dialogue is spoken by female rather than male characters.

ט לְסֻסָתִי בְּרִכְבֵי פַרְעֹה
דִּמִּיתִיךְ רַעְיָתִי:
י נָאווּ לְחָיַיִךְ בַּתֹּרִים
צַוָּארֵךְ בַּחֲרוּזִים:
יא תּוֹרֵי זָהָב נַעֲשֶׂה־לָּךְ
עִם נְקֻדּוֹת הַכָּסֶף:

He speaks to her:

1.9 To a mare amongst Pharaoh's chariots,
          I have compared you, my beloved.
1.10 Your cheeks are beautiful in earrings,
          your neck in beads;
1.11 Let us make gold earrings for you
          with silver filigree.

If the male lover's response to his lover's banter is (in verse 8) at first reciprocated, then the banter does not last long. He stops playing 'hard to get' and carries on what Exum calls a 'dialogue about love'.[211] Now his description of her is meant to indicate the confusion of sexual frisson that she engenders in male company. Pharaoh's chariots were pulled by stallions. So one beautiful mare would create quite a stir.[212]

---

[211] Exum, 97.
[212] Keel, 56.

Much of the beauty of the Song of Songs is its wordplay and use of homonyms - where the same word means different things in different contexts. So the word for 'earrings' in verses 10 and 11 above (in Hebrew '*tor*') is the same word used to designate the 'turtle dove' we will see in 2.12.

More importantly, there are only two uses of gold and silver together in the Song of Songs. The first is here, where the male lover praises his beloved's gold and silver earrings. The other is the reference to the palanquin which Solomon built in 3.10 where we are told that 'its pillars he made from silver, its back from gold'. These two references to the finest metals are probably another indication of comparison and contrast between the lovers and Solomon. In other words, Solomon may have built himself temples and palaces from the finest materials but the female lover deserves something just as good. We will consider this further at the commentary to 3.10. As we are about to see, she responds to this compliment and comparison by imagining him in regal fashion.

יב עַד־שֶׁהַמֶּ֫לֶךְ֙ בִּמְסִבּ֔וֹ
נִרְדִּ֖י נָתַ֥ן רֵיחֽוֹ׃
יג צְר֨וֹר הַמֹּ֤ר ׀ דּוֹדִי֙ לִ֔י
בֵּ֥ין שָׁדַ֖י יָלִֽין׃
יד אֶשְׁכֹּ֨ל הַכֹּ֤פֶר ׀ דּוֹדִי֙ לִ֔י
בְּכַרְמֵ֖י עֵ֥ין גֶּֽדִי׃

She speaks to him:

1.12 Whilst the king is on his divan,
my nard has brought forth its fragrance.
1.13 A bundle of myrrh is my beloved for me;
he will rest between my breasts.
1.14 A cluster of henna is my beloved -
in the vineyards of Ein Gedi.

Her response to him is not only royal but also involves scent, both his and hers. The Song of Songs opens with her description of his aroma. She now continues by describing the nard (spikenard) she has put on and the myrrh and henna which she can smell on him. Read in isolation, this seems to be just a description of the two lovers. Things are, however, rarely as simple as they seem in the Song of Songs. The passage here is imitated and modified at 7.12-13 (it may or may not be mere coincidence that this parallel passage appears at a similar distance from the end of the Song of Songs as our passage does to the beginning of the Song). The comparison and contrast will be made at that stage in the commentary.

As Alter has pointed out,[213] there is an ambiguity in verse 14 as to whether the description of the cluster of henna, like the beloved, resembles the vineyards of Ein Gedi or whether the vineyards of Ein Gedi are the location of the lovers' meeting. The masoretic text divides verse 14 in exactly the same way in which it has divided verse 13, implying that the lovers are at Ein Gedi. My translation reflects this but it seems to me a fruitless task seeking to attempt to work out the author's original intention.   In any case, a choice is not necessary; both images ought to stand together. If the location of the beloved is in Ein Gedi, then he is with her at that location resting between her breasts. Verse 1.13 and 1.14 parallel each other; the myrrh parallels the henna and the breasts parallel Ein Gedi.

We should however realise that this passage opens with the implication that the lovers are indoors (the 'king' is on his divan) but ends with, at the very least, a hint that the lovers are in fact outside in a vineyard. It therefore implies that our initial assumption of a domestic location is incorrect. The image of a type of bed combined with the outdoors continues in the next part of the dialogue.

טו הִנָּ֤ךְ יָפָה֙ רַעְיָתִ֔י
הִנָּ֥ךְ יָפָ֖ה עֵינַ֥יִךְ יוֹנִֽים׃
טז הִנְּךָ֤ יָפֶה֙ דוֹדִי֙ אַ֣ף נָעִ֔ים
אַף־עַרְשֵׂ֖נוּ רַעֲנָנָֽה׃
יז קֹר֤וֹת בָּתֵּ֙ינוּ֙ אֲרָזִ֔ים
רחיטנו (רַהִיטֵ֖נוּ) בְּרוֹתִֽים׃

He speaks to her:

1.15 Look how beautiful you are my beloved;
         look how beautiful, your eyes are doves.

She responds to him:
1.16 Look how beautiful you are my love, even handsome,
         even our couch is luxuriant;
1.17 The beams of our houses are cedars,
         our rafters are cypresses.

---

[213] Alter, 2015, 12.

Dove-like eyes are a theme reappearing in the Song of Songs. He also describes her eyes as dove-like later, again whilst speaking to her (4.1). She will then go on to describe his eyes in the same manner but not directly to him; rather to her female friends (5.12). It appears to be one of their favourite terms of endearment as they both describe each other as 'my dove, my perfect one' (see 5.2 and 6.9).[214]

It is she who appears more interested in where their lovemaking takes place. As referred to earlier, there is an ambiguity in verse 14 as to whether she is speaking about somewhere geographical, when she refers to Ein Gedi. She now talks about the location of the couch which is described as luxuriant.

It is the final sentence (1.17) of this praise of lovemaking which reveals even more ambiguity. Taken at face value, the sentence appears clear. We have been led from assuming an indoor location to a realisation that the opposite is the case. The lovers are outdoors amongst the cedars and the cypresses, enjoying their love '*al fresco*', as if their 'house' comprised the trees surrounding them. This is the sort of imagery which we could expect in poetry from any society, concerning the need for young lovers to escape the restrictions of home and venture into the nearby forests.

There is, however, one large problem with this image. The problem has been hinted at in much of the material I have presented prior to the discussion of the Song of Songs. We know both from the Bible and from external sources that cedars did not grow in the land of Israel.[215] So, when the author of the Song of Songs put this image of the lovers making their home amongst the cedars and cypresses, the author could not have been signifying a literal meaning. Nor, importantly, would the author's readers have thought it should be taken literally.

The image of a cedar in Biblical thought is that it either grows in Lebanon or is used in the temple. We know from chapter 3 above that David first brought cedars into Jerusalem for use in his own buildings but that it was Solomon who imported the trees to such an extent that cedars were commonplace - regarded as like sycamores

---

[214] She responds to his description of her beauty with a similar comment in 1.16 adding that he is 'even handsome'. There is an (almost certainly unintended) pun here. The Hebrew word translated as 'even' is '*af*'. This word is a homonym for 'nose' ('*af*' is masculine and therefore agrees with '*na'im*' [handsome]) meaning that the secondary meaning of this phrase is that she may have dove's eyes but his beauty derives from his handsome nose which links back to the spices referred to previously. Later in the Song of Songs he will describe her body and use the words 'eyes' and then 'nose' (see 7.5) as is done (in, one suspects, unintended fashion) here.

[215] See chapter 3 above.

on the plain.[216]   The image is seen, more positively, in a psalm: 'A righteous person shall blossom like a palm tree, shall flourish like a cedar tree in Lebanon. Planted in the house of the Lord, they shall blossom in the courtyards of God'.[217]

The image of cedars and cypresses referred to together must connote the temple. As we saw earlier, the only two woods with which the temple was built were cedars and cypresses: 'he built the walls of the temple from inside with cedar planks from the floor of the temple to the walls of the ceiling, overlaid it internally with wood; and he overlaid the floor of the temple with cypress planks'.[218] Isaiah refers to the idea that it was God (and not King Sennacherib who wanted to claim the honour) who climbed to 'the height of the mountain in the midst of Lebanon and cut down the highest of its cedars and the choicest of its cypresses'.[219]

Isaiah's reference is useful for two reasons. First, it reinforces the understanding of cedars and cypresses as being located in Lebanon. Second, it implies, by the rebuke of Sennacherib for asserting that it was he and not God who felled the trees in Lebanon that this project had a divine purpose - namely to be transported to be used in the temple in Jerusalem.

These trees, like many others, were scarce and Deutero-Isaiah also saw a Messianic aspect to where they might be able to flourish: 'I will place cedar in the wilderness, acacia and oleasters, I will place cypress in the desert with box tree and elm together. So that people will see, know, take note and realise together that the hand of God has done this and the Holy One of Israel has created it'.[220]

We need to look at these other references to cedars and cypresses to see what we can make of their reference in the Song of Songs. Clearly the trees were numerous in Lebanon but did not exist in Israel. It was only God who could make the desert bloom with these and other trees. Indeed, it was God who, through David and Solomon, had made Jerusalem overflow with cedar timber for use in the temple and the royal palace.

We have already seen in verse 4 that the Song of Songs has used a reference in the book of Psalms to God in the temple ('we will be glad and rejoice in Him') and

---

[216] I Kings 10.27.

[217] Psalm 92.13-14.

[218] I Kings 6.15.

[219] Isaiah 37.24.

[220] Isaiah 41.19-20. I am reliant on the JPS version for translation of some of the names of the trees in verse 19 which are obscure.

transformed it to a lover's reference ('we will be glad and rejoice in you'). Something very similar appears to be happening here. The female lover seems to be saying: if Solomon can celebrate God in the 'houses' of his temple and palace made out of cedar and cypress, then I can enjoy my lover in our imagined outdoor 'houses' made of the same woods.[221]

Yet, given the scorn with which Solomon is directly treated in the Song of Songs (as considered in chapter 1 above), is it not also possible to view this verse as much more critical? It is as if the lovers are saying: 'Solomon's houses took twenty years to build. He may have enjoyed the company of a thousand women but he never enjoyed real love. We two lovers can enjoy the sensual pleasures each affords the other without the status symbol of having a built a temple and a palace. Our houses may be simple but we have escaped the clutches of the town; real freedom comes from our mutual love.' As we shall see, escaping from the stifling nature of the city is a theme running throughout the Song of Songs.

Once we take this as the meaning of this verse, it also permits us to highlight the false dichotomy by which the Song of Songs has been understood for too long. The religious tradition has allegorised the beauty of the poem and has transformed the sensual for its own purposes to something very different. The modern tradition has read the sensual back into it, but has largely failed to build into its interpretation the fact that the Song of Songs was not written in a textual or historical vacuum. The text tells us that the poem is about Solomon. Once we appreciate that the male lover cannot in fact be Solomon, we should be on notice that Solomon does indeed appear - but only indirectly as he does in this verse. He, or events in his life, will appear again in the Song of Songs.

א אֲנִי֙ חֲבַצֶּ֣לֶת הַשָּׁר֔וֹן
שֽׁוֹשַׁנַּ֖ת הָעֲמָקִֽים׃
ב כְּשֽׁוֹשַׁנָּה֙ בֵּ֣ין הַחוֹחִ֔ים
כֵּ֥ן רַעְיָתִ֖י בֵּ֥ין הַבָּנֽוֹת׃
ג כְּתַפּ֙וּחַ֙ בַּעֲצֵ֣י הַיַּ֔עַר
כֵּ֥ן דּוֹדִ֖י בֵּ֣ין הַבָּנִ֑ים
בְּצִלּוֹ֙ חִמַּ֣דְתִּי וְיָשַׁ֔בְתִּי
וּפִרְי֖וֹ מָת֥וֹק לְחִכִּֽי׃
ד הֱבִיאַ֙נִי֙ אֶל־בֵּ֣ית הַיַּ֔יִן

---

[221] Attempts have been made to argue that the Hebrew word for 'houses' is incorrect and ought to be changed to 'house'. These attempts at emendation are of course entirely unnecessary when one appreciates the actual intent of this verse and its link to the royal temple and palace (both described as 'houses').

וְדִגְלוֹ עָלַי אַהֲבָה:
ה סַמְּכוּנִי בָּאֲשִׁישׁוֹת
רַפְּדוּנִי בַּתַּפּוּחִים
כִּי־חוֹלַת אַהֲבָה אָנִי:

She speaks to him:

2.1 I am a rose of the Sharon,
           a lily of the valleys.

He responds to her:

2.2 Like a lily amongst the thorns,
           thus is my beloved amongst the daughters.

She responds to him:

2.3 Like an apple in the trees of the forest,
           thus is my love amongst the sons.
       In its shade, I have yearned to sit
           and its fruit is sweet to my palate.
2.4 He brought me to the house of wine
           and his banner over me is love.
2.5 Support me with raisin cakes,
           uphold me with apples
               because lovesick am I.

2.1 and 2.2.

This passage takes on what appears to be an entirely new theme from that in the previous dialogue. Yet, despite this, there is a literary link. His term of endearment for her in both is '*ra'yati*' (translated here as 'my beloved') whereas hers to him is '*dodi*' ('my love'). More importantly, we have just been introduced to the rare cedar and cypress in whose shade the lovers lay. Now the lovers further develop the verdant theme by describing themselves as various plants or fruits. Whilst the lily, the rose and the apple may be more common than the cedar and the cypress, they are given special status because they belong to, and can be identified with, the lover.

She describes herself as a lily and a rose abundant in the Sharon and the valleys. This of course allows him to pay her the compliment of saying that her beauty is entirely different from the other young women who are but thorns when compared to her. His one line response to her in verse 2 has become one of the best known lines in the Song of Songs. Yet her response to his metaphor is much more detailed.

2.3 - 2.5.

She compares him to a fruit amongst the trees of the forest. I have used the standard translation 'apple' for the fruit, though this cannot be correct as apples did not exist in the Middle East at the time. Many suggestions have been made for better translations (such as apricot[222] or quince[223]). All are educated guesswork, however, and I have left the traditional reading, since for most English speakers an apple has the common quality intended by the metaphor.

The second part of verse 3 is deliberately ambiguous in the original text. It could mean that the female lover yearns to sit either in the apple tree's shade or in her lover's shade; thereafter, it could either be the apple tree's fruit which is sweet to her palate or her lover's fruit. The writer allows us to read both versions. As we will realise from reading the next verse, the second, more erotically-charged, sensuous reading is the one which the writer develops.

The first part of verse 4 ('he brought me to the house of wine') recollects 1.4 where she says (using the same Hebrew verb in the same form) 'the king brought me to his rooms; we will be glad and rejoice in you'. If the comparison is deliberate, then the rules of Biblical Hebrew parallelism suggest we ought to compare 'the house of wine' to 'his rooms' and then possibly the continuation of verse 2.4 ('his banner over me was love') with the continuation of verse 1.4 ('we will be glad and rejoice in you').

The raisin cake (in Hebrew '*ashisha*') with which she wishes to be supported in verse 5 has an interesting back history. It is very rarely used in the Bible but it is one of the items which King David handed out to his people when he came into the city of Jerusalem with the Ark of the Lord.[224] There is a wonderful irony in the choice of this cake in the context of love and lovesickness. Immediately before David hands out the raisin cake, the text describes that his wife Michal (the former King Saul's daughter) sees David leaping and whirling, as she sees it inappropriately, with the Ark of the Lord. She despises him for it.[225] Then David,

[222] Bloch, 149
[223] Alter, 2015, 14
[224] II Samuel 6.19.
[225] II Samuel 6.16.

having handed out the raisin cake, returns to his wife who confronts him with his behaviour. He entirely rejects her criticism and the text chillingly ends by saying: 'And Michal daughter of Saul had no child until the day of her death'.[226]

There is an irony to this intertextual link in the context of a love poem. In this Song of Songs passage describing the raisin cake, there are two references to the word '*ahavah*' (2.4 and 2.5); Michal is the only person in the Bible described as having loved David, using the same word '*ahav*'.[227] Perhaps no link was intended but, if it was, then the food associated with an act of shame and loss of love in the story of David becomes a food that the woman wishes to use to abandon herself in her love and declare herself lovesick in the Song of Songs.

These five verses form one episode. Whilst she continues to speak in the next verse, for a number of reasons the author or editor clearly intended a pause at the end of verse 5. One of these is that verses 1 to 5 are clearly delineated by starting and ending with the word 'I' ('*ani*') - as reflected in the translation. As with the whole of the Song of Songs, she speaks most of the lines and indeed in these five verses, whilst his comment in verse 2 is beautiful, it is she who takes his comment (a rose amongst the thorns) and expands it to produce her own metaphor using the apple.

ו שְׂמֹאלוֹ תַּחַת לְרֹאשִׁי
וִימִינוֹ תְּחַבְּקֵנִי׃
ז הִשְׁבַּעְתִּי אֶתְכֶם בְּנוֹת יְרוּשָׁלַםֹ
בִּצְבָאוֹת אוֹ בְּאַיְלוֹת הַשָּׂדֶה
אִם־תָּעִירוּ ׀ וְאִם־תְּעוֹרְרוּ אֶת־הָאַהֲבָה
עַד שֶׁתֶּחְפָּץ׃

She speaks of him:

**2.6 His left hand is under my head
          and his right hand embraces me.**

She speaks/[anonymous voice?]:

**2.7 I have made you swear, oh daughters of Jerusalem
          by the gazelles, or by the hinds of the field,**

---

[226] II Samuel 6.20-23.
[227] I Samuel 18.20. In this passage, Michal is clearly a pawn in a political game between Saul and David. The contrast with the autonomous female lover in the Song of Songs is striking.

not to rouse or arouse love
until it is ready.

These two verses appear together again in similar, but not identical, form in verses 8.3 and 8.4. Verse 2.7 additionally appears in identical form at 3.5. Both seem to be verses separating different parts of the text. Unsurprisingly, many commentators have seen verse 2.7 as having a chorus-like quality and so have assumed that it would have been performed by a chorus. It is also entirely possible that the female lover is speaking herself to the daughters of Jerusalem (which on balance I prefer for the reasons set out below).

Verse 2.6 beautifully sums up the rich metaphors which the woman has just bestowed on her male lover. A left hand on my head and a right hand embracing me, in a Klimt-like kiss. She is no longer speaking to him. Rather, she is speaking about him - so, presumably, this verse could be construed as her internal monologue.

Verse 2.7 is unusual in that most verses in the Song of Songs are one or other of the lovers speaking to the other or speaking about each other. This verse does neither. It appears to be general in nature. It could be seen as the woman, having spoken to and then embraced her lover, turning to other daughters of Jerusalem to set out the general lessons arising from her experience of love. The Hebrew grammatical form of the verse indicates that it is in the form of an oath. Oaths were of course a staple part of the Biblical system and they were normally taken by invoking the name of God. So being made to swear by two different forms of deer appears, at first glance, striking.

There are, however, a number of points which need to be made about the names of the 'gazelles' (in Hebrew 'tse'vaot') and the 'hinds' (in Hebrew 'aye'lot'). From this it will become clear that things are not quite as they appear to be. First, in verse 2.9 in two verses' time, the female lover will compare her lover to both these animals. So clearly the oath is meant to indicate animals of great importance to her (which is why I prefer the reading that it is she who speaks these words). Verse 7, which has a chorus-like feel to it, marks the end of one poem and the beginning of another. The repetition of the gazelles and the hinds stresses the importance of these animals in the linking of the various poems in the Song of Songs. Though there may originally have been disparate poems which make up the Song of Songs, they have been woven together to fashion a whole. One of the ways in which this has been done is to create these word-links between different parts of the text.

Second, many commentators have realised that these two names sound remarkably similar to names for God. *Tse'vaot* is a homonym for 'armies' or 'hosts'. God is described as 'the Lord of Hosts'. The hinds in this verse are 'hinds of the field' or, in Hebrew, *'aye'lot hasadeh'*. The word *'aye'lot'* resembles the Hebrew word for God *'el'* and the word *'hasadeh'*, in Hebrew though much less so in English transliteration, resembles *'shadai'* meaning 'almighty' - together forming the phrase 'God almighty'. Both phrases therefore appear to hint at a divine oath. Michael Fox argues that these are circumlocutions for God and that 'the author uses these animal names to avoid divine names in a secular context'.[228]

I am not sure that 'secular context' has any real meaning in the Biblical world.[229] The word 'secular' was coined in the nineteenth century. Though the idea goes back to Greek thought, there is no Biblical secular tradition. So when the author of the Song of Songs uses animal names, which resemble divine names, in an oath, it is anachronistic to see this as a secularisation. In more standard oaths, a person invokes God before reciting the oath and setting out the wish or conviction which is backed up by the force of the oath. By invoking animals, with God-like names, the author glorifies the natural world and clearly encounters God in it. This is, of course, not some proto-Spinozist tract about God being identical to nature. Rather, we should see it as a celebration of the divine by wordplay in, what is after all, a literary text.

Concluding remarks on 1.1 - 2.7

So what are we to make of these opening verses?

They consist of a dialogue between the lovers. The dialogue was a common form in which love poems in the ancient Middle East were written (and indeed still are written all over the world). Yet nothing is entirely conventional in the Song of Songs. The word 'dialogue' used by many commentators to describe these verses has a somewhat hollow ring. Of the twenty-four verses in this section only eight are spoken by the male lover. Hers is the dominant voice throughout the poem. This is seen at its starkest in these verses at the outset. If this is a dialogue, then at this stage it is a very uneven one. In so many books in the Bible, the female characters speak little and, when they do, they rarely lead. In the Song of Songs, our opening verses suggest the exact opposite. It is the male lover who is reticent. He reacts to her. The voice we largely hear is that of his female lover and it is she who is educating him in the role of lovemaking - an influence which will pervade the rest of the poem.

---

[228] Fox 1985, 110.
[229] See commentary to 1.4 above.

And where is Solomon in all this? Someone (probably the song's editor) chose to place him in the very first verse to alert the reader that this song is about Solomon. The female lover straight away refers to her lover as her 'king' – who, as explained above, cannot actually be King Solomon himself. It is, however, an obvious reference to Solomon, indicating that she is appropriating the royal name to her red- (not blue-) blooded, lover. Immediately thereafter, she makes an explicit reference in 1.4 to Solomon's curtains. This time the reference links the curtains to her, probably indicating a simplicity in line with Solomon's curtains inherited from his father king David.

These references to Solomon do not appear negative at all – direct pejorative comments about Solomon will only occur later in the poem. However, a hidden reference to Solomon is clearly intended in verse 1.17 in the mention of the cedar and cypress being the 'houses' where the lovers have their couch. This is obviously a literary artifice as no such forest was in fact available to the lovers in Israel. It can only be a hint at the other 'houses' made out of these two woods – namely the temple and the royal palace. As such, it invites comparisons between the lovers' dwelling created in nature, and God's dwelling created by Solomon. At this stage, no directly negative comment is made about the dwelling created by Solomon but the lovers' dwelling is described in the most positive way possible.

Our passage ends with an oath, invoking animals with probably deliberate allusions in their names to some of the names of God. We are thereby alerted to the fact that we are dealing with an entirely different way of looking at the world, at God and at nature than the normative vision present in most other books in the Bible. We are beginning to realise that, although the Song of Songs is a love song, it is also a lot more than that.

SONG OF SONGS 2.8 - 3.5

Interrupted Idyll

ח קוֹל דּוֹדִי
הִנֵּה־זֶה בָּא
מְדַלֵּג עַל־הֶהָרִים
מְקַפֵּץ עַל־הַגְּבָעוֹת:
ט דּוֹמֶה דוֹדִי לִצְבִי
אוֹ לְעֹפֶר הָאַיָּלִים
הִנֵּה־זֶה עוֹמֵד אַחַר כָּתְלֵנוּ
מַשְׁגִּיחַ מִן־הַחַלֹּנוֹת
מֵצִיץ מִן־הַחֲרַכִּים:

2.8 - 2.9

She speaks

2.8 Listen out, my lover;
  look, he is coming;
Striding on the mountains,
  leaping on the hills.
2.9 My lover is like a gazelle
  or a deer amongst the hinds;
Look, he is standing behind our wall;
  gazing in through the windows,
    peering in through the lattices.

The division of the poem into Biblical verses sometimes masks more than it reveals. The two verses being analysed here are a speech she makes, in which she actually presents three ideas. First, the lover is coming from the mountains (2.8). He is then compared to a gazelle or a deer - the immediate reaction being of course that gazelles and deers, like the lover, are capable of striding out on the mountains and leaping over the hills (2.9a). Finally, the lover has arrived and is standing by the wall gazing in (2.9b).

The central of these three ideas therefore is the comparison of the lover to a gazelle or deer. I have explained its immediate context but, if we look only a little further afield, we will see that the gazelle and deer formed part of the natural oath which she made to the daughters of Jerusalem (2.7) not to wake or arouse love until it was ready. The implication of the repetition here is that she certainly thinks she is ready!

But we cannot only draw the conclusions from a previous section as to the meaning of words. The author has chosen to reuse them here - in a different context. As can be clearly seen from the delineation above, they are placed between a passage containing four phrases (2.8) and then a passage containing three phrases (2.9b).[230] Both need to be analysed and then compared. As we will see, this section is full of parallelisms. They need to be unravelled.

Verse 2.8 starts with sound and vision. First we hear the lover. The Hebrew is ambiguous. Do we hear the sound of his arrival far away or do we hear his voice speaking in the distance (the Hebrew word '*qol*' serves both purposes and so either or both could be intended - 'the voice of my lover' would have been a perfectly acceptable translation). We then see the lover (the word I have translated 'look' is '*hinei*' in Hebrew, regularly translated as 'behold'). The 'listen' and 'look' immediately notify us of parallels. This is but the first of many. Following swiftly on, the sound and vision are set out in detail - he is striding on the mountains and leaping on the hills - in the clearest of parallels.

It is within this context that the gazelle and deer, originally described in the oath in 2.7, make their reappearances. We now see that the gazelle and deer perform an entirely different function from that which they offered in relation to the oath. They allow the parallelism just described in 2.8 to be furthered by means of the description of two such obviously similar animals which can be compared to the lover.

2.9b, in describing what happens when the lover arrives, first sets out where he is. He is standing behind our wall. But what fascinates is the vision. 2.9b starts with the word '*hinei*' indicating that the female lover is visually perceiving her lover. This parallels her lover who is also looking - and does so by means of his own parallelism - gazing in through the windows and peering in through the lattices.

To sum up this section of parallels, we can see that, at its core, it parallels gazelle/deer (2.9a). Prior to that it parallels listen/look and striding on mountains/leaping on hills (2.8). Thereafter, it parallels his looking/her looking and gazing in through windows/peering in through lattices.

---

[230] Biblical scholars would analyse the 'four phrases' as two bi-cola and the 'three phrases' as a tri-colon. This terminology is very useful for the parallelism which I describe.

However, the poet is much more sophisticated than mere line parallelism implies. There is what I am going to term a vision meta-parallel in our passage. The passage starts with listening and vision (2.8a) ('Listen out … look'). The vision at the end (2.9b) ('look') is clearly intended to parallel the vision at the beginning. Had the analysis stopped at this juncture, a problem would remain. In order to complete the meta-parallel, the sound of the lover ('listen out') at the beginning is required at the end. It is absent. The genius of the poet is that it has not been forgotten - merely tantalisingly delayed. In verse 2.10, the lover will speak. However, as I discuss below, this may just be her internal monologue as she sets out his words. The sound is therefore, finally, beautifully paralleled but she is the only one who can hear.

2.10 - 2.13

י עָנָה דוֹדִי וְאָמַר לִי
קוּמִי לָךְ רַעְיָתִי
יָפָתִי וּלְכִי־לָךְ:
יא כִּי־הִנֵּה הַסְּתָו עָבָר
הַגֶּשֶׁם חָלַף הָלַךְ לוֹ:
יב הַנִּצָּנִים נִרְאוּ בָאָרֶץ
עֵת הַזָּמִיר הִגִּיעַ
וְקוֹל הַתּוֹר נִשְׁמַע בְּאַרְצֵנוּ:
יג הַתְּאֵנָה חָנְטָה פַגֶּיהָ
וְהַגְּפָנִים ׀ סְמָדַר נָתְנוּ רֵיחַ
קוּמִי לְכִי (לָךְ) רַעְיָתִי
יָפָתִי וּלְכִי־לָךְ:

She says:
2.10 My lover answered and said to me:

He speaks to her probably in her internal monologue:

Rise up, my beloved,
       my beauty and come away
2.11 Because the winter is over,
       the rain has passed, has gone away.
2.12 The buds can be seen in the land,
       the time of pruning has arrived
           and the voice of the turtle dove is heard in our land.

2.13 The fig tree puts forth its fruit,
      and the vines are giving off blossom scent.
Rise up, my beloved,
      my beauty and come away.

The inclusio of the words 'Rise up……..and come away' before and after verses
2.11 - 2.13 indicates that this is intended as a separate section.

Does he say these words to her or does she imagine them? The text did not have to
say that she mentions that he responded ('my lover answered and said to me'); it
could just have allowed him to speak; the change in gender in Hebrew in the first
word ('*qumi*' - 'rise up') makes clear that he is now speaking. The fact that the text
introduces what he says with her comment implies that she could be inferring his
answer or, even, making it up. It seems to me that the narrative interjection in 2.10
is a telling indicator that this is indeed what has happened. Of course, as with so
much, we cannot be sure and therefore we do not have an answer to the question
posed at the beginning of this paragraph. We are left with that ambiguity.[231]

What I have translated as 'rise up' and 'come away'[232] is literally 'rise to yourself'
and 'go to yourself'. In 1.8 we saw further examples of 'to yourself' following the
verbs 'know' and 'leave'. What makes the phrase 'go to yourself/come away' (in
Hebrew '*le'chi lach*') remarkable is that it is the feminine form of what God told
Abram: 'And God spoke to Abram saying: "Come away (in Hebrew '*lech lecha*')
from your land, your birthplace and the house of your father, to the land that I will
show you".'[233]

The parallel is striking and telling. Abram went to the land (in Hebrew '*eretz*') to
serve God in accordance with God's command. The same word for land is used
twice here in the Song of Songs in 2.12. These are the only two occasions on which
the word 'land' is used in the Song of Songs. This conjunction of the words 'land'
and 'come away' might be coincidental but the word 'land' could have been inserted
in numerous other places in the Song of Songs. That the author chose not to do so

---

[231] The Hebrew phraseology used in her description '*anah...ve'amar*' is a relatively frequent one meaning
'he responded'. In the book of Deuteronomy it is used for the purpose of what the philosopher J.L. Austin
called a 'performative utterance' (see Deuteronomy 21.7ff and 26.5ff) whereby a specific form of words
must be used in order to be efficacious. Performative utterances are largely limited in their use to legal or
quasi-legal settings of one sort or another. It certainly does not feel a natural use of words in the context
of a love poem but one wonders possibly whether the words 'rise up, my beloved, my beauty and come
away' had some sort of performative meaning now lost to us.

[232] Following Bloch, 59

[233] Genesis 12.1.

may be significant, indicating the lovers are imitating Abram by going onto the land. Of course the significance of going onto the land is a different one in the two different contexts - thereby transforming the original meaning of the phrase in appropriating it.

The beauty of the image of spring being the time to come away is heightened by some of the language. The word translated as 'pruning' in verse 12 has another meaning, every bit as appropriate. Rather than this being the time of 'pruning', it could be the time of 'singing'. The double meaning is so apt given that, immediately preceding the phrase, there is a reference to the buds being seen (meaning that 'pruning' would seem the preferable understanding); immediately thereafter is a reference to the sound of the turtle dove (meaning that 'singing' would seem the preferable understanding). The need to translate renders ambiguity difficult to convey. When that is compounded by insistence that one's translation is 'correct', the translator has surely missed the point. The image of both natural fecundity and birdsong is surely his enticement to her to 'come away'.

The Hebrew word translated as 'turtle dove' ('*tor*') is, as previously stated, a homonym for earrings (see comment above in relation to 1.10). Given that he had used the same word to describe her cheeks (as 'beautiful in earrings'), the implication might be that the turtle dove is also to be read as a hidden reference to the female lover.

יד יוֹנָתִ֞י בְּחַגְוֵ֣י הַסֶּ֗לַע
בְּסֵ֙תֶר֙ הַמַּדְרֵגָ֔ה
הַרְאִ֙ינִי֙ אֶת־מַרְאַ֔יִךְ
הַשְׁמִיעִ֖נִי אֶת־קוֹלֵ֑ךְ
כִּי־קוֹלֵ֥ךְ עָרֵ֖ב
וּמַרְאֵ֥יךְ נָאוֶֽה׃

He speaks to her

2.14 My dove is in the crags of the rock,
     in the crevice of the cliff.
Let me see glimpses of you,
     let me hear your voice,
Because your voice is sweet
     and a glimpse of you is lovely.

He previously described her eyes as doves (1.15). He now uses this term as a pet name for her as a whole. His description will revert throughout between a) her eyes, and b) all of her, being compared to a dove. Moreover, the imagery of a bird (the turtle dove in 2.12) we have just heard could, in stream of consciousness-like fashion, lead him to describe her whole self as a dove.

The word translated 'glimpse' is a noun from the standard word for 'see'. The idea of the woman being hidden dove-like in the rocks and cliffs presents the sense of a tantalising, momentary glimpse of the lover in the rocks whilst she sings. He uses the word for voice (*qol*) which was last used by her when describing the sound of the lover coming towards her in 2:8. The chiastic[234] structure (glimpses - voice - voice - glimpse) beautifully sets out in poetic form the sensually heightened awareness of her presence.

טו אֶחֱזוּ־לָנוּ֙ שֻׁעָלִים
שֻׁעָלִים קְטַנִּים
מְחַבְּלִים כְּרָמִים
וּכְרָמֵינוּ סְמָדַר:

She speaks?

2.15 Catch for us foxes,
little foxes
are ruining vineyards;
and our vineyards are in blossom.

This verse has puzzled commentators. Who is speaking (there are no signs of the speaker's gender in the text). What does it mean? The only clue is that the word 'blossom' (Hebrew '*smadar*') has already appeared in 2.13 as a description of the smell coming from the vines themselves. So there is a sense that, in some way, it is an addition to the original description of the spring budding.

Unfortunately, however, it also appears negative in its description of foxes ruining the vineyard. The idyllic rural scene seems to have stopped abruptly and the first real note of tension has appeared. Peace will only return when the foxes have been caught. The clue to the insertion of this verse may lie in the Hebrew word for 'catch' ('*achaz*'). As we will shortly see, the female lover once she has 'caught' her male lover is not prepared to let him go (3.4).

---

[234] *Chiasmus* from the Greek meaning an x-shaped structure.

On that basis, let us tentatively suggest that this verse is spoken by the female lover. It is used as a phrase to set the scene for the tension which is about to occur in the night scene at the beginning of chapter 3.

טז דּוֹדִי לִי וַאֲנִי לֹו
הָרֹעֶה בַּשׁוֹשַׁנִּים:
יז עַד שֶׁיָּפוּחַ הַיּוֹם
וְנָסוּ הַצְּלָלִים
סֹב דְּמֵה־לְךָ דוֹדִי לִצְבִי
אוֹ לְעֹפֶר הָאַיָּלִים
עַל־הָרֵי בָתֶר:

She speaks to him

2.16 My lover is mine and I am his
who pastures amongst the lilies.
2.17 Before the day breathes
and the shadows have fled,
Turn, make yourself, my love, like a gazelle
or a deer amongst the hinds
on the cleft mountains.

In some ways, within the context of where it lies within the poem, these two verses are even more enigmatic than the previous verse. Is this a return to the idyllic norm? If that were the correct interpretation, these verses would indicate a playful encounter of the lovers in which she asks him to depart in deer-like fashion before the morning. It may, on the other hand, be a continuation of the tension. On this alternative reading, she is warning him that the lovers' tryst must break up because of some (unspecified) danger.

I prefer the former view. The verse is repeated in very similar form as the very final words of the Song of Songs (8.14). As we will see when looking at that passage, it has a mysterious air at the end of the poem but no real hint of tension. The main change in the final verse of the Song of Songs is that the 'cleft mountains' become 'spice mountains'. The phrase 'cleft mountains' is particular to our context of course. It also links back to the crags of the rock and the crevice of the cliff which the male lover had described as the location of his 'dove' (2.14).

א עַל־מִשְׁכָּבִי֙ בַּלֵּיל֔וֹת
בִּקַּ֕שְׁתִּי אֵ֥ת שֶׁאָהֲבָ֖ה נַפְשִׁ֑י
בִּקַּשְׁתִּ֖יו
וְלֹ֥א מְצָאתִֽיו׃
ב אָק֨וּמָה נָּ֜א וַאֲסוֹבְבָ֣ה בָעִ֗יר
בַּשְּׁוָקִים֙ וּבָ֣רְחֹב֔וֹת
אֲבַקְשָׁ֕ה
אֵ֥ת שֶׁאָהֲבָ֖ה נַפְשִׁ֑י
בִּקַּשְׁתִּ֖יו
וְלֹ֥א מְצָאתִֽיו׃
ג מְצָא֙וּנִי֙ הַשֹּׁ֣מְרִ֔ים הַסֹּבְבִ֖ים בָּעִ֑יר
אֵ֛ת שֶׁאָהֲבָ֥ה נַפְשִׁ֖י רְאִיתֶֽם׃
ד כִּמְעַט֙ שֶׁעָבַ֣רְתִּי מֵהֶ֔ם
עַ֣ד שֶֽׁמָּצָ֔אתִי אֵ֥ת שֶׁאָהֲבָ֖ה נַפְשִׁ֑י
אֲחַזְתִּיו֙
וְלֹ֣א אַרְפֶּ֔נּוּ
עַד־שֶׁ֤הֲבֵיאתִיו֙ אֶל־בֵּ֣ית אִמִּ֔י
וְאֶל־חֶ֖דֶר הוֹרָתִֽי׃

3.1 - 3.4

She speaks

3.1 On my couch at night,
    I sought my soulmate;
I sought him
    but did not find him.
3.2 Let me get up and roam in the town,
    in the markets and the squares.
Let me seek
    my soulmate;
I sought him
    but did not find him.
3.3 The guards who roam the city found me;
    "Have you seen my soulmate?"
3.4 I had scarcely passed them
    when I found my soulmate;
I caught hold of him
    and would not let him go
until I had brought him to my mother's house,
    to my parent's chamber.

The earlier images of glimpsing and teasing are transformed here into something much darker. She is on her couch at night. This begs the question where is the couch? Previously, the image of a couch or divan (both using different Hebrew words to the one used here) have implied that the lovers have been outside and enjoying their bed in nature (see 1.12-17). The imagery here suggests something very different. She is in her bed which must be in town, given the rest of the passage. She is yearning for her soulmate. Many have suggested that this is a dream. It certainly has a dream-like quality. Ultimately, though, its sense of longing for the lover renders it somewhat irrelevant as to whether she is expressing a dream or not. The repeated use of words such as 'find' and 'seeking/sought' (four times), 'soulmate' (in Hebrew this is a phrase repeated four times), 'roaming' and 'city' (twice) indicate an intensity, not associated with her lover, and a danger, both of which have so far largely been absent from the Song of Songs.

There is a clear reason for this. She gets up from her couch and roams the streets. In the patriarchal society in which she lived, roaming the streets at night was not only a dangerous thing to do (as implied in the text above), it was also regarded with deep suspicion.

The female lover and the 'strange woman' in the book of Proverbs

A clear example of this suspicion can be seen in the book of Proverbs. This book, whilst often disparate in nature and content, has, as its primary aim, the education of a son by his father as to the right course of action. In chapter 7 of the book of Proverbs, we are introduced to the 'strange woman'. Various interpretations have been made as to who she is, ranging from prostitute to older married woman attempting to lure away an innocent young man. Whichever it is, the father warns his son that if he wanders about the streets, he could encounter her:

'And here is a woman, come to meet him, in the clothes of a prostitute, keeping her intentions hidden. She is loud and wayward. Her feet are never at home. Sometimes on the streets, sometimes in the squares, she lurks in every corner. She seized hold of him and kissed him.'[235]

What is so remarkable about this passage in the book of Proverbs is how similar it is, thematically, to the passage in the Song of Songs we are considering. In both passages, the woman leaves her home and goes into the town appearing in various

---

[235] Proverbs 7.10-13.

places ('markets' and 'squares' in the Song of Songs, 'streets' and 'squares' in Proverbs). In both passages she finds a man, catches hold of him and either kisses him or does not let him go. Later the 'strange woman' will invite the naïve young man to her house[236] while her husband is away; the female lover in the Song of Songs will not cease until she has brought her lover back to her mother's house.

Yet to compare the two passages also surely requires us to contrast them. Once this is done, the difference becomes just as stark as the thematic similarities. In the passage from the book of Proverbs, the 'foreign woman' is clearly the 'other', the dangerous *femme fatale* of the male imagination. The passage from the Song of Songs, on the other hand, reflects the woman's own experience, from her own perspective. It shows her despair at having lost her lover and her passionate desire to be reunited with him, to the extent of taking the dangerous step of going out at night. As we will see later in the Song of Songs (5.7), this can have the effect of the lone woman being assaulted or possibly even raped. Yet she appears prepared to take the risk for the sake of her love.

The remarkable thematic similarity of these two sections, together with the contrasting messages, suggests that the passage in the Song of Songs may have been written with knowledge of, or in response to, the passage in the book of Proverbs. It has transformed archetypal patriarchy in the book of Proverbs into our empathy for the *cri de coeur* of a woman in love in the Song of Songs.

The town as metaphor

This is the first time that the Song of Songs has implied that the location of the action is in the town. Previous references to items commonly associated with the town such as 'chambers' and 'houses' have come to be seen by the reader, in context, as in fact metaphors used by the lovers in their rural idylls for their meeting places. Here, by contrast, it is clear that the female lover is in the town. Twice she uses the phrase 'I sought him but could not find him', the first time she does so on her couch in the town, the second time in her unsuccessful attempt to find him in the markets and the squares. Only once she ventures beyond the guards and the town does she find her soulmate.

It is also the first time that the town is given a negative image. Increasingly, as the Song of Songs progresses, we will realise that the imagery we had seen of 'come away' (2.13) is not just a comment between lovers. The need to escape the stifling

---

[236] Proverbs 7.18.

oppression of the town becomes a running theme throughout the poem. Speaking about the Song of Songs, Sophie Thöne says that 'it follows that nature and culture form an additional contrast'.[237] This image of town and country being in opposition to each other is an important point to take from Thöne's remark. The love that the lovers feel for each other is often expressed by reference to location; they will want to go to a garden, they will want to escape. They will describe each other in terms of the names of towns. But we have been warned that the point of this love story is not, by contrast to more normative texts, to see the woman in the town as dangerous; rather, its message is that there is something about the town which it wishes to eschew entirely.[238]

ה הִשְׁבַּ֨עְתִּי אֶתְכֶ֜ם בְּנ֤וֹת יְרוּשָׁלַ֙͏ִם֙
בִּצְבָא֔וֹת א֖וֹ בְּאַיְל֣וֹת הַשָּׂדֶ֑ה
אִם־תָּעִ֧ירוּ ׀ וְֽאִם־תְּע֥וֹרְר֛וּ
אֶת־הָאַהֲבָ֖ה עַ֥ד שֶׁתֶּחְפָּֽץ׃

She speaks/[anonymous voice?]:

3.5 I have made you swear, oh daughters of Jerusalem
by the gazelles, or by the hinds of the field,
not to rouse or arouse
love until it is ready.

The female lover (or possibly anonymous voice), which spoke at 2.7, repeats exactly the same words here. The contexts are different however. In the first case, his left hand was under her head and he was embracing her. Here it is she who has taken the initiative and brought him to her mother's house. I would suggest it is most likely that, here, the female lover is speaking and giving a warning about the dangers of early love, given the delays to which she has been subject in finally being in union with her lover.

Concluding remarks on 2.8 - 3.5

What can we say about the Song of Songs so far? That it is a love song between a young man and a young woman is obvious. It is clearly episodic in nature and its meaning is often hard to fathom. Yet it is rooted in its own place and time. In terms

---

[237] *'Natur und Kultur binden folglich ein weiteres Gegensatzpaar'* (My translation in the text above). Sophie Thöne: *Liebe zwischen Stadt und Feld: Raum und Geschlecht im Hohelied* (Exegesis in unserer Zeit 22: LIT 2012) 419. Quoted in James, 89.

[238] I return to this area in the final part (see chapters 6 and 7 of this book below).

of place, it refers specifically to locations within ancient Israel. It does so frequently and this will increase, as we shall see. In terms of time, two lovers stating their heartfelt desire for each other is of course a timeless emotion. Yet the way in which they do so is not. Here the literary means by which they express those desires and emotions is rooted in the forms of the period in which it was created.

To say that a work of art is deeply beholden to its age often implies to many that it is conservative in nature. Yet, when comparing the Song of Songs to other books in the Bible (as the comparison to the book of Proverbs in the passage just analysed makes clear), it is obvious that the Song of Songs is radically different. It is no paradox to say that a work very much of its time can, concurrently, exhibit radical features. Indeed, as the philosopher Alasdair MacIntyre has argued, that is exactly how new ideas develop. They cannot develop in a vacuum; rather, they develop from within their own societies:

'For all reasoning takes place within the context of some traditional mode of thought, transcending through criticism and invention the limitations of what had hitherto been reasoned in that tradition'.[239]

MacIntyre's insight is useful in the context of the Song of Songs. The editor has chosen the form of the love song (or perhaps more correctly a series of love songs carefully woven together) through which to express views not just on the art of wooing but also, as we have seen at various points already, on how two ordinary lovers can compare their love to those who are apparently 'superior' to them. The 'king' is the male lover, not the real king. Standard ideas of the time are challenged. The female lover argues for example against being judged simply because she works in the field (1.6). Walls and rafters in nature are preferable to those in the temple. In MacIntyre's terminology, the reasoning transcends the traditional mode of thought.

But perhaps most challenging of all is not just what is said but who says it. As I mentioned previously, the majority of the verses in the Song of Songs have been spoken by the female lover and we will have cause to examine this in more detail shortly. No other work in the Hebrew canon has this feature. It implies an egalitarian outlook completely at odds with the prevalent patriarchy. Moreover, what she says implies utter rejection of most of the norms to be expected in ancient Israel. To do so within the framework of an apparently conventional format - the lovesong was a staple of Middle Eastern literature of the period - is what makes the

---

[239] Alasdair MacIntyre: *After Virtue* (1981) Duckworth, London, 222.

Song of Songs one of the finest works to have come down to us from the ancient world. It combines this with some of the most soaring poetic imagery we have in the Bible.

Furthermore, the female lover's ability to give expression to her inner emotions seems, in turn, to give confidence to her lover. As we will see, his reticence is shortly to disappear. He will also launch into passionate descriptions of her body, the detail of which is entirely new.

Before that occurs, there is one more crucial scene. The criticism of normative values, already implied and hinted at, will shortly become more explicit. In verses 2.8-3.5, Solomon has not appeared overtly (or even covertly, as far as we can tell). He is about to reappear in the longest scene in which he is directly referred to. But, as we will see, this is merely a launchpad to further implied criticisms of Solomon and all that he stood for. The skill of the author is to add these criticisms into an apparently conventional love story. But, as I have been stressing, there is nothing conventional about the Song of Songs. I now turn to the rest of chapter 3 and consider how Solomon is woven again into the lovers' story.

SONG OF SONGS 3.6 - 3.11

The Solomon Interlude

The following six verses introduce a complete change of mood. Gone is the dialogue between two lovers, and the female lover's anxiety which followed it. In its place are episodic verses containing three direct references to Solomon - first, sixty soldiers guarding his bed, then his construction of a palanquin and, finally, a description of his crowning on his wedding day. The first of these verses does not mention Solomon and many have sought to identify Solomon with the person being referred to in the verse. That identification is incorrect as I show in the commentary below but, even though the verse does not directly refer to Solomon, it forms an integral part of this Solomonic interlude.

The mysterious woman

ו מִי זֹאת עֹלָה מִן־הַמִּדְבָּר
כְּתִימְרוֹת עָשָׁן
מְקֻטֶּרֶת מֹר וּלְבוֹנָה
מִכֹּל אַבְקַת רוֹכֵל:

Narrator/Chorus?

**3.6 Who is this coming up from the desert
like pillars of smoke
Rendered more fragrant in myrrh and frankincense
than all the powder of the merchant?**

Much is unclear about this verse. First, we do not know who speaks it. It might be a chorus, if the Song of Songs were to be performed. I think though that the preferable view is that this is the poet speaking without intercessory. The sentence itself might be a question (I have rendered it in English as such). On the other hand, it might be a statement of excitement - 'look who's coming up....'. Whichever it is, we are not told directly in the Song of Songs who that person is. The fact that the next verse refers to Solomon has meant many have seen him as the person being referred to - and that he is therefore the answer to the question being posed. That cannot be correct. The form 'Who is' and the adjective 'fragrant' in this verse are both in the feminine, indicating that the person being referred to might be a woman.

Some have suggested that the referent is Solomon's bed in 3.7 (which is feminine in Hebrew). That is also impossible. The verse starts 'who' not 'what' and so the bed must be dismissed as the object being described. It must be a person and that person being referred to must be a woman.

So who is the woman? The obvious, immediate answer of course is that it could be the female lover. We know, however, that, as Solomon is about to be mentioned in the next verse, the reference could also be linked to his life. Some have identified this figure as the Queen of Sheba who would have come up from the desert with her retinue when she visited King Solomon. I find that persuasive. We have considered earlier in chapter 3 of this book her role in bringing spices. Spices were not mentioned in Solomon's building of the temple, though they played a crucial role in the tabernacle. We noted two further points in chapter 3 which are relevant here. First, the books of Kings and Chronicles mention that the Queen of Sheba brings spices; they do not name them specifically. Second, the two main spices commanded to be used in the tabernacle were myrrh and frankincense. Here they are the two spices identified with the mysterious woman coming up from the desert. Previously in the Song of Songs, the female lover had described her own lover as a 'bundle of myrrh' (1.13) but this is the first time the word 'frankincense' has been used. Frankincense is only used three times in the whole of the Song of Songs but, as we will see, it plays a crucial role because of its similar sound in Hebrew to another key word, Lebanon, which has yet to make its appearance. I will refer to this again later in this section in more detail.

There are a number of further questions arising from this verse. First, the identification with the Queen of Sheba is not explicit, yet the reader is obviously invited to make the link given the theme of a woman bearing spices and its location in the Song of Songs immediately prior to an express reference to King Solomon. Second, an either/or decision is not necessary. It is entirely possible to read this reference as being both to the Queen of Sheba *and* to the female lover. In such a reading, the female lover, perfumed in her spices, is portrayed as imitating the Queen of Sheba. Supporting the view that there is an identification here with the female lover is the fact that the phrase 'who is this….' (in Hebrew '*mi zot*') appears on two other occasions in the Song of Songs (6.10 and 8.5). On both such occasions, the person being referred to appears to be the female lover. Indeed, in 8.5, the first five words in the Hebrew are identical (rendered in English 'who is this coming up from the desert?').

Another telling link is that the female lover has stated: 'black am I and beautiful …. do not look upon me because I am dawn-darkened, that the sun has tanned me' (1.5-

6). She is a young woman who works in the fields but does not see herself as inferior just because her work involves an involuntary suntan. Her comment implies that others do look down on her. To whom would such a woman wish to compare herself, if not the Queen of Sheba? The exact location of Sheba is uncertain, but it is certainly a long way south of Jerusalem. Modern scholarship considers that is most likely to have been situated in modern day Yemen,[240] some two thousand kilometres south of Jerusalem. In a later era, legends about the Queen of Sheba proliferated. One can assume therefore that, at the time that the Song of Songs was written, the Queen of Sheba would also have been renowned as the prime example of royalty from the south. She would of course have been darker-skinned. The Queen of Sheba would therefore have presented a perfect example for the young woman of a positive black role model which she could channel for her own dark skin, a skin colour which she saw projected in a negative light in her society.

Of course, we cannot be certain of an identification of the lover with the Queen of Sheba, but it is entirely in line with a work where the distinctions between royalty and others are blurred or even cast away. If the male lover is her 'king', why cannot she be his 'queen'?

She is rendered 'more fragrant ..... than all the powder of the merchant'.[241] This may be a further reference to Solomon who, shortly after meeting the Queen of Sheba, engages in trade. Again, on this basis, the comment would appear to hint that the female lover's fragrance can compare favourably to Solomon, as she is more fragrant than the temple in which Solomon omitted to place any of the spices prescribed for the tabernacle in the book of Exodus.

The fearful king

ז הִנֵּה מִטָּתוֹ שֶׁלִּשְׁלֹמֹה
שִׁשִּׁים גִּבֹּרִים סָבִיב לָהּ
מִגִּבֹּרֵי יִשְׂרָאֵל:
ח כֻּלָּם אֲחֻזֵי חֶרֶב
מְלֻמְּדֵי מִלְחָמָה
אִישׁ חַרְבּוֹ עַל־יְרֵכוֹ
מִפַּחַד בַּלֵּילוֹת:

---

[240] Cogan, 310-11

[241] The more common translation of this passage 'perfumed in myrrh and frankincense from all the powder of the merchant' misses the comparison 'than'. The Hebrew allows for both 'than' and 'from' as translations.

Narrator/Chorus?

3.7 Look: Solomon's bed,
    sixty heroes surround it
        from the heroes of Israel.
3.8 All carrying a sword,
    trained in warfare,
Each man has a sword by his thigh,
    because of fear at night time.

Again, the person who says these verses (together with verses 3.9 - 3.11) is unclear. As with verse 3.6, it could be a narrator or, in performance, it could have been assigned to a chorus. Any number of further questions then face the reader of these two verses. What is meant by Solomon's 'bed' in this context? Why does it need sixty heroes surrounding it? Why do they need (presumably) to protect him and why should heroes fear the night? Or is it possibly Solomon who fears the night?

I considered some of these issues briefly when I addressed verses 3.6 - 3.11 in chapter 1 earlier. At that stage, I dealt with all those verses together. To divide them up helps further understanding (though the enigmatic quality of many parts of these verses will remain). Few others have chosen to analyse these verses separately. Verses 3.7-8 and 3.9-10 both refer to Solomon but may be talking about two different episodes. It is useful, at least to start with, to analyse them separately and only thereafter to reconsider them together.

First, let us consider the bed. There have been a number of 'resting places' referred to earlier in the Song of Songs which I have variously translated as 'couch' (for two different Hebrew words - '*eres*' and '*mishkav*') or 'divan' (for '*mesiv*'). The Hebrew word here is '*mitah*' which has become the standard, modern Hebrew word for 'bed'. Yet a translation implying some sort of permanent, fixed resting place within a house may be misplaced - the heroes and the fear of the night could imply security within a palace but why make the reference to 'night' if this is meant to be a reference to a bed indoors? It is more likely (but not certain) that this is a reference to the outdoors. We have no reference in any other Biblical text to Solomon's 'bed' so ultimately we are left with conjecture and context, from which an outdoor setting seems preferable.

The number 'sixty' is not random. We know from a wider context than the Song of Songs that the number sixty was a basic unit number in Babylon[242] (from which the

---

[242]For example, we owe sixty minutes in an hour to the Babylonians.

number twelve for the twelve tribes of Israel makes sense as one fifth of a unit). It therefore indicates a typical large number. We can understand it better, though, from the context of the number within the Song of Songs.

In 6.8, sixty queens are contrasted to the one woman whom the male lover loves. The number sixty in 6.8 therefore contrasts the futility of over-abundance of queens to the perfection the male lover expresses in having but one lover. The contrast in 6.8 is clearly to Solomon even if the proverbial number of a thousand wives is not used. It is a clear attack on Solomon's polygamous instincts which are contrasted to the male lover's very singular intentions. The number sixty, therefore, takes on a negative connotation and ought to be read, in relation to Solomon, as such. One can even sense that, in performance, it would be delivered in a mocking tone.

There are two words which this night time scene uses which were first introduced by the female lover in her own night time scene (3.1-4). The text in 3.7 has the same word ('*saviv*') for 'surround' which was used in 3.2 to describe the woman 'roaming' the city, reminding us of Solomon's need for security and contrasting it with her desire to abandon the constrictions of the town.

The word in 3.8 for 'carrying' a sword is '*achuz*' in Hebrew. This is the word which the female lover used in 3.4 when she said that she 'caught hold' of her lover and would not let him go. Again, the use of the word for Solomon's protection contrasts to its passionate use by the female lover and is probably an intended comparison.

The phrase 'each man has a sword by his thigh' appears to be a direct quote from Exodus 32.27 (these are the only two instances in the Bible where the phrase appears). The intertextual context is very different and the quote is puzzling. In the Exodus passage, Moses commands the Levites that 'each man has a sword by his thigh' and they should kill those who have committed the sin of the golden calf. There seem two possibilities: first, that the author is seeking to make a contrast between the zealotry of the Levites and the timidity of King Solomon or second, that the phrase was a common one in ancient Israel and that no comparison and/or contrast was intended. That remains a possibility but the fact that the phrase appears only twice implies a link.

The 'fear at night time' again, at first, seems an odd phrase for a king. Of course any one who is outside needs to protect him or herself against robbers and others who intend harm. A king could afford such protection. Yet, we are never told about the protection of a modern day politician or king unless the issue of security is relevant to the discussion. So, in this instance, where nothing happens which indicates that King Solomon came to any harm, why does the text need to say something so mundane?   It clearly has an ulterior motive.   There appear to be at least two reasons why the phrase has been inserted.

First, the word translated as 'night time' is '*leilot*'.   We have seen its use before in 3.1 where the female lover was on her couch at night time and could summon up the strength to rise up and seek her lover.   The second is that, in the book of Proverbs, we are told: 'When you lie down, do not fear, so that when you lie down your sleep will be sweet.   Do not worry about sudden fear and the plight of the wicked if it comes'.[243]   Of course, the author of the book of Proverbs claimed Solomonic authorship of his work by use of Solomon's name in the superscription to the book of Proverbs (which was discussed in chapter 1 above).   In the Song of Songs, the night time fear is all too obvious.   The intertextual link also seems to provide an answer to the question whether the reference to 'night time' fear is that of the sixty heroes or of Solomon (the text is capable of both meanings).   The implication in the Song of Songs text is that Solomon needs bodyguards because of his own fear.   The ironic contrast of the Solomon portrayed in the Song of Songs to the Solomon portrayed in the book of Proverbs only heightens the impression that this, otherwise unnecessary, comment has, as its purpose, the mocking of Solomon.   Added to that, of course, is that the immediately preceding scene contains a single woman prepared to venture away from her home, alone at night in disregard of all convention.   Her bravery in search of her lover contrasts starkly with a king frozen in fear on his bed surrounded by his security guards.

Rabbinic understanding of the 'bed'

The Rabbis were often finely attuned to the psychological make-up of many of the characters in the Bible.   As I explained in chapter 5, they tended to avoid such analysis in relation to the Song of Songs because they sought to fit it in to their more general theological worldview.   For example, they do not focus on the character of the two lovers.   However, one midrash relating to the scene with Solomon's bed seems to me to go to the heart of the real Solomon being described in this passage.

'Resh Lakish said 'At the beginning, Solomon reigned over the high [i.e. heavenly/spiritual] places as it is said "And Solomon sat on the throne of God" (I Chronicles 29.23) and in the end he reigned over the lower places as it is said that he ruled over each side of the river from Tifsach to Gaza' (I Kings 5.4) …..

---

[243] Proverbs 3.24-25. I have deliberately used the translation 'fear' in this passage only when the Hebrew uses the term '*pachad*' which is the same term used in the Song of Songs 3.8 to which comparison is being made.

Rav and Samuel said '...In the end he only reigned over Israel as it is said: "I, Qohelet, was king over Israel" (Ecclesiastes 1.12). And later he only reigned over Jerusalem as it is said: "The words of Qohelet, the son of David, in Jerusalem" (Ecclesiastes 1.1) and then he only reigned over his bed as it is said: "Look Solomon's bed, sixty heroes surround it" (Song of Songs 8.7) and then he only ruled over his stick as it is said: "This was my portion in all my toil" (Ecclesiastes 2.10).'[244]

The Solomon whom the Rabbis portray in this passage is a diminished (and indeed diminishing) figure. The Rabbis knew that he ultimately lost almost all his kingdom and they linked that material loss to a spiritual loss though they do not give the reason why. Of the four quotations which Rav and Samuel bring to the discussion, this is the only one from the Song of Songs. The other three are all from the book of Ecclesiastes where the description of the limitations on the powers which humans have over their own lives is set out starkly. The fact that these Rabbis chose to intermingle this passage from the Song of Songs with others only from Ecclesiastes is revealing. Within such a context, this scene concerning Solomon's bed portrays a parody of a king. He reigned only over his 'bed' but still had the retinue appropriate for a king (sixty heroes surround it). We can certainly conclude that the negative impression which this scene makes has clearly not been lost on the Rabbis.

The temple of love

ט אַפִּרְיוֹן עָשָׂה לוֹ הַמֶּלֶךְ שְׁלֹמֹה
מֵעֲצֵי הַלְּבָנוֹן:
י עַמּוּדָיו עָשָׂה כֶסֶף
רְפִידָתוֹ זָהָב
מֶרְכָּבוֹ אַרְגָּמָן
תּוֹכוֹ רָצוּף אַהֲבָה

מִבְּנוֹת יְרוּשָׁלָֽם:

Narrator/chorus?

3.9 King Solomon made himself a palanquin
     from the trees of Lebanon.
3.10 Its pillars he made from silver,
     its back from gold,
its seat was purple,

---

[244] BT Sanhedrin 20b

115

in its midst it was inlaid with love.
[from the daughters of Jerusalem *moved to the next verse*].

These two verses give us some of the most important language enabling us to link the Song of Songs with the life of Solomon. The separation of verses 3.9-10 from 3.7-8 allows us to look at them independently of the previous two verses first, and then to see what, if any, connection there is between them.

When I first referred to verses 3.6-11 in chapter 1, I posed a number of questions about the 'palanquin' (in Hebrew '*apiryon*'). This is the standard translation of the word which appears nowhere else in the Bible and therefore is extremely difficult to comprehend fully. *Chambers* Dictionary (11th Edition) defines 'palanquin' as 'a light litter for one passenger, a box borne on poles on men's shoulders'. Our translation is based on the Septuagint's translation of the word into Greek as '*phoreion*' which conveys the idea of 'carrying'. That however begs more questions than it answers in this context. Why would a moving structure refer to 'pillars', the Hebrew word for 'pillars' implying something even more permanent than the English translation ('*amud*' deriving from the Hebrew root meaning 'stand')? There are perfectly good Hebrew words for 'poles' which could have been used but were not chosen.[245] This seems to be a more permanent structure than would be allowed for by the standard definition of the word 'palanquin'. On the other hand, the 'bed' which we discussed in verses 3.7 and 3.8 is clearly discussed in an ambulatory context as referred to above. The separation of the two passages allows us to consider each on its own terms.

On that basis, verse 3.9 and the first half of 3.10 are completely clear. Solomon did indeed build himself a structure from the trees of Lebanon. In fact he built both the temple and his palace from Lebanese cedar wood. Pillars feature prominently in both buildings. In neither building were the pillars made of silver nor the back from gold but, given the amount of gold and silver which poured into both the temple and the palace, the parallel intended by the author of the Song of Songs is clear.

Why does verse 3.9 use the word 'Lebanon' and not describe the wood used - namely cedar wood? This is the first time that the Song of Songs uses the word 'Lebanon' and its use is deliberate and poetic. In verse 3.6, we saw a reference to frankincense, also that word's first appearance in the Song of Songs. The Hebrew word for frankincense is '*levonah*'. The Hebrew word for Lebanon is '*levanon*'. Clearly the

---

[245] Such as the word '*bud*' which appears frequently in the building of non-pillars in the tabernacle - e.g. Exodus 37.15.

words sound very similar and the poet is making a deliberate word play. The word frankincense appears three times in total; on each occasion, it is paired closely with a reference to Lebanon - either by the word Lebanon being used in close proximity or because of the way in which the word 'frankincense' is being used, as we shall later see.

Is there anything else, apart from word play, which links Lebanon and frankincense? 'Trees of Lebanon' provides an obvious link to the palace and temple. Frankincense, however, was absent from the temple even though it was one of the staple parts of what had been required to be used as one of the spices in the tabernacle.[246] The possibility must be left open that there is an intended criticism of Solomon for failing to carry out the precise requirements for the spices as set out in the book of Exodus. At this stage, such a possibility must remain tentative to be re-examined once we see the other references to frankincense and the spices which will shortly bring forth their fragrance to full effect in chapter 4 of the Song of Songs.

In the commentary to 1.11, I noted that the only two references to gold and silver together were in verses 1.11 and 3.10. The contexts of these two passages apparently could not be more different. In 1.11, the male lover is describing the jewellery on his lover's neck and cheeks. Here, the gold and silver describe the wealth belonging to Solomon. The implication of the link is clear. Gold and silver are not just appropriate for the wealthy. We know that the female lover is sun-darkened and therefore looked down on by many (1.5-6); the gold and silver link asks us to look on her, and our understanding of who deserves our respect, very differently.

What is meant by the palanquin's 'back' being made from gold? The Hebrew word used ('*refidato*') is rare. What does it mean and why has it been used here? The English translation masks the fact that the root of the word has already been used in the Song of Songs. In 2.5, the female lover asks the male lover to 'uphold me with apples because I am lovesick'. The words 'back' in 3.10 and 'uphold' in 2.5 both derive from the same Hebrew root ('*r-f-d*') meaning 'support'. There was no 'support' for either the palace or the temple except for the pillars described in great detail in the book of Kings. So what is being described in 3.10? It seems very likely that the reference is to King Solomon's throne which we are told was made of ivory overlaid with refined gold.[247] The use of such a rare Hebrew word twice should alert us to the fact that something unusual is intended in the text. Both words occur in close connection to the word for 'love'. In 2.5, the reference is to the female lover's

---

[246] See chapter 3.
[247] I Kings 10:18 - see also chapter 3 above.

lovesickness. Here, it is to the middle of the palanquin/structure being inlaid with love from the daughters of Jerusalem. Again, the link between the apparently ordinary love of an unpretentious woman for a man is being compared to love in the context of the throne of King Solomon.

The next phrase 'its seat was purple' appears purely descriptive but creates its own challenges. To what might this be referring? The word translated as 'seat' ('*merkavo*') appears three times in the Song of Songs (1.9, 3.10, 6.12). On both other occasions, it clearly means the seat of a chariot. The word's more general meaning is anything on which to sit so it could come to mean the throne, or something to be placed on a throne such as a cushion.[248]

What are we to make of the 'purple'? There is no reference to the colour purple in the Solomon story except for a passing reference in the book of Chronicles.[249] In the tabernacle, however, purple is mentioned frequently as one of the colours for the various objects it required. Mostly it is paired with the colour '*techelet*' (light blue). However, it is first introduced in the tabernacle by being linked to gold and silver, as it is here.[250] Purple is mentioned once again in the Song of Songs (7.6) in describing the locks on the female lover's hair. At that point, there is also a royal link as we will see - but the 'king' will no longer be Solomon but an epithet for her lover.

The final section of 3.10 ('its midst was inlaid with love from the daughters of Jerusalem') is such a strange ending to this description of Solomon's structure that most commentators have suggested that the text is corrupt and that it needs to be amended. The word 'love' (in Hebrew '*ahavah*'), in particular, seems out of place in such a context - a 'pointless metaphor' in one commentator's words. Through changes of vowelling and addition of an extra consonant, suggestions are that the midst of the structure was inlaid with ebony or stone. The text may have needed to be twisted into shape but at least now a meaning has been worked out - or so the theory goes.

There are good reasons to reject this. First, the Song of Songs was not written to be conventional. It may have used standard formats (ancient love poems) but its message is rarely anything other than radical. Within an apparently conventional description of Solomon's throne comes a comment about love. As Robert Alter notes, the sequence here sets out a familiar Biblical pattern of three similar terms

---

[248] Fox 1985, 121.
[249] II Chronicles 2.13.
[250] Exodus 25.4,

(silver, gold and purple) and then a switch (love). As he says: 'the effect of surprise at the end is exquisite'.[251] Second, the word love (*ahavah*) appears in both 3.10 and 2.5 as does the word 'uphold' in 2.5 ('*rapduni*') and 'back' in 3:10 ('*refidato*') which, as we saw, have the same Hebrew root. The fact that these two words appear close to each other twice is not a coincidence. Those who have sought to change the text have failed to spot this beautiful link.

A further attempt to amend the text comes as a result of the phrase 'from the daughters of Jerusalem'. If we now accept that the reference to love is correct, how does 'love from the daughters of Jerusalem' fit in? The point is more pressing because verse 11 begins with the words 'go out and rejoice, daughters of Zion'. If we move the phrase 'from the daughters of Jerusalem' into verse 11 and remove the Hebrew letter *mem* at the beginning (meaning 'from'), we get a perfect parallelism: 'daughters of Jerusalem go out, and rejoice, daughters of Zion'. Whilst 'love' and 'daughters of Jerusalem' appear together in the oaths we have already considered (2.7 and 3.5), it is difficult to see exactly how they are intended to link together in this passage (in the oath they are required to swear not to arouse love until it is ready, which seems a very different context). In such circumstances, the emendation is appropriate and the last two Hebrew words of 3.10 ('from the daughters of Jerusalem') form the beginning of the next line of the poem without the letter '*mem*'.

The king's coronation

בְּנוֹת יְרוּשָׁלָ͏ִם: יא צְאֶנָה ׀
וּרְאֶינָה בְּנוֹת צִיּוֹן
בַּמֶּלֶךְ שְׁלֹמֹה
בָּעֲטָרָה שֶׁעִטְּרָה־לּוֹ אִמּוֹ
בְּיוֹם חֲתֻנָּתוֹ
וּבְיוֹם שִׂמְחַת לִבּוֹ:

Narrator/Chorus?
Daughters of Jerusalem, 3.11 Go out,
      and rejoice, daughters of Zion,
about King Solomon, about the crown,
      with which his mother crowned him,
On the day of his wedding,
      on the day of his heart's joy.

---

[251] Alter 2015, 22.

Many commentators have been puzzled by this reference to King Solomon being crowned by his mother on the day of his wedding. It appears nowhere else in the Bible. Indeed, it has led in the Jewish tradition to a welter of Midrash intending to explain the gap. Of course, this is poetry and not meant to be taken literally. Whilst a literal explanation of this passage is therefore impossible on the basis of external Biblical evidence, that does not preclude us understanding a considerable amount about the poet's non-literal intention from that same extraneous Biblical material.

First, if taken literally, the reference to Solomon's mother is, of course, to Bathsheba. There is no other Biblical reference to Bathsheba crowning Solomon on the day of his wedding. However, this is not the only puzzling reference in this passage. It also refers to 'the day of his wedding' implying 'one' wedding day. This seems strange in the extreme, given that Solomon proverbially had a thousand wives and so could have participated in a thousand wedding ceremonies. Does this therefore mean that Solomon was crowned a thousand times in a thousand weddings by a mother whose arms got more exercise than she bargained for? Most of those wives are described in I Kings 11 as part of the description of Solomon's fall. They are not named except for their geographical origins. If the reference is intended to be to Solomon's first marriage to the daughter of Pharaoh (I Kings 3.1-2), it would be surprising if his mother 'crowned' him then. First, he was already king at this stage. Second, the marriage was clearly a political alliance, given the terminology used.

The probable answer to this conundrum is that this is a reference not to Solomon's wedding but to his coronation, given the reference to a 'crown'. On that occasion, he was not directly crowned by his mother - he was anointed by Zadok the priest. From that act of anointing, he was recognised as king by the people in preference to his competitor, Adonijah. Yet, as I outlined in chapter 2 above, Bathsheba's role in ensuring her son's accession to the throne was absolutely crucial. Her interaction with both her husband, David, and with Adonijah could serve as a paradigm of how a powerless person can manipulate others to achieve their own ends. It is entirely conceivable that an author/editor, such as the person who wrote/edited the Song of Songs, who was so aware of the importance of those apparently without power, would have recognised Bathsheba's actions as a master-stroke, providing the crucial intervention allowing her son to reign. In that sense, Bathsheba crowned Solomon.

Conclusion

These six verses are entirely different from any of the previous verses in the Song of Songs. Where previously there had been dialogue between the two lovers, anxiety from the female lover and a brief interjection from another voice, these six verses seem to be a more sustained consideration of an entirely new area. They also serve a further purpose. They raise new issues which the lovers can consider as they re-institute their dialogue.

In summation, the verses seem to indicate the following. Verse 6 hints at the Queen of Sheba - all the more so because of the references to Solomon in the next verses. Verses 7-11 directly refer to Solomon. Any positive construction of these verses with regard to the character of Solomon is mistaken. In verses 7-8, he is seen in a processional bed where his bodyguards are emphasised for no good reason except to mock him. Verses 9-10 change the scene to Solomon's 'palanquin', a word which appears only here. Commentators are unsure as to its exact meaning. At first, we might think that Solomon's bed and his palanquin are intended to parallel each other. That, as we realise, is mistaken. Given its context, the palanquin must come to refer either to Solomon's palace or to his temple or to both. It describes its construction in poetic fashion but contains a twist in the tail by seeing love in its very midst. That then links us to Solomon being crowned by his mother on his wedding day in verse 11 (the female figures in verses 6 and 11 showing the beginning and end of this unit). The irony should not be lost on us that a man who had a thousand wives surely never truly experienced real love. Solomon's temple appears to have been appropriated by the narrator. As we will see, the lovers will increasingly adopt the terminology of the temple.

But this Solomonic interlude also marks another turning point. Until now, as I have already mentioned, the dialogue between the lovers has been heavily slanted in favour of the female lover. At the very most, the male lover has uttered eleven verses[252] whereas she has spoken twenty-four verses at the very least.[253] In a best case scenario, she has spoken more than twice as much as he. In a (more likely) worst case scenario, she has spoken four times as much. From now on, their speech is much more equal. He has found his voice.

---

[252] 1.8-11, 1.15, 2.2, 2.10-13 (which should more appropriately be assigned to the woman as they contain her description of what he has said), 2.14.

[253] 1.2-7, 1.12-14, 1.16-17, 2.1, 2.3-6, 2.8-9, [2.10-13 probably], 2.16-17, 3.1-4. All verses prior to 3.6, not referred to in either of these two footnotes, are either unclear as to the speaker or belong to the narrator or chorus.

It is not just that her eyes are doves: there is much more to her than that. Just how much more, we are about to find out.

In great detail.

SONG OF SONGS 4.1 - 5.1

Great Detail

The '*wasf*'

What we are about to encounter is the first of three detailed descriptions by the lover of the other's body. First he describes her (4.1-7). Then she describes him (5.10-16) and finally he describes her again (7.2-10).[254] These elaborate descriptions of the body were frequent in ancient middle Eastern cultures and were later given the name '*wasf*' in Arabic. It is a standard word in Arabic for 'describe', 'depict' 'portray' or 'picture'.[255] In Arab culture, it implied an idealised version of the 'perfect' other.

The *wasf* description became seen over time as entirely unrealistic. No person ever has the untarnished physical features which these poems suggest. Shakespeare's 130th sonnet is an excellent example of a rejection of the ideal without a rejection of the lover:[256]

> My mistress' eyes are nothing like the sun;
> Coral is far more red than her lips' red;
> If snow be white, why then her breasts are dun;
> If hairs be wires, black wires grow on her head.
> I have seen roses damask'd, red and white,
> But no such roses see I in her cheeks;
> And in some perfumes is there more delight
> Than in the breath that from my mistress reeks.
> I love to hear her speak, yet well I know
> That music hath a far more pleasing sound;
> I grant I never saw a goddess go;
> My mistress, when she walks, treads on the ground:
> > And yet, by heaven, I think my love as rare
> > As any she belied with false compare.

---

[254] Arguably there is a fourth as well, given that much of the material in the first description is repeated with crucial differences at 6.5-7 (which will be discussed in the commentary at that stage).

[255] A Dictionary of Modern Arabic: Hans Wehr, page 1072, SLS, New York 1976.

[256] I am extremely grateful to the (anonymous) author of the Wikipedia entry on '*wasf*' who initially brought this link to my attention (accessed 12.11.2017).

Matched against Shakespeare's grounded representation of the lover, the description of the lovers in the Song of Songs will appear very different and idealised in the extreme. So, for example, in verse 4.7, he describes her as totally beautiful without blemish. It would therefore be easy to scorn the beauty of these *wasf*s in the Song of Songs as merely unrealistic. As we will see, the Song of Songs may retain the idealised representation of the beloved that Shakespeare so memorably rejects, but its purpose is much more than the unrealistic, idealised description which was the subject of Shakespeare's scorn in sonnet 130. Each *wasf* serves other purposes besides physical description. Yes, we can enjoy the sensuousness of the descriptions but, if this is all we do, we lose the other messages in these poetic masterpieces. Therefore, as we go through the erotic descriptions of the bodily parts, we need to keep our eyes open to what lurks beyond the flesh.

א הִנָּךְ יָפָה רַעְיָתִי
הִנָּךְ יָפָה
עֵינַיִךְ יוֹנִים
מִבַּעַד לְצַמָּתֵךְ
שַׂעְרֵךְ כְּעֵדֶר הָעִזִּים
שֶׁגָּלְשׁוּ מֵהַר גִּלְעָד:
ב שִׁנַּיִךְ כְּעֵדֶר הַקְּצוּבוֹת
שֶׁעָלוּ מִן־הָרַחְצָה
שֶׁכֻּלָּם מַתְאִימוֹת
וְשַׁכֻּלָה אֵין בָּהֶם:
ג כְּחוּט הַשָּׁנִי שִׂפְתוֹתַיִךְ
וּמִדְבָּרֵךְ נָאוֶה
כְּפֶלַח הָרִמּוֹן רַקָּתֵךְ
מִבַּעַד לְצַמָּתֵךְ:
ד כְּמִגְדַּל דָּוִיד צַוָּארֵךְ
בָּנוּי לְתַלְפִּיּוֹת
אֶלֶף הַמָּגֵן תָּלוּי עָלָיו
כֹּל שִׁלְטֵי הַגִּבֹּרִים:
ה שְׁנֵי שָׁדַיִךְ כִּשְׁנֵי עֳפָרִים
תְּאוֹמֵי צְבִיָּה הָרוֹעִים בַּשּׁוֹשַׁנִּים:
ו עַד שֶׁיָּפוּחַ הַיּוֹם
וְנָסוּ הַצְּלָלִים
אֵלֶךְ לִי אֶל־הַר הַמּוֹר
וְאֶל־גִּבְעַת הַלְּבוֹנָה:
ז כֻּלָּךְ יָפָה רַעְיָתִי
וּמוּם אֵין בָּךְ:

He speaks to her

4.1 Look, how beautiful you are my beloved,
look how beautiful you are.
Your eyes are doves
through your veil.
Your hair is like a flock of goats
which has cascaded from Mount Gilead.
4.2 Your teeth are like a flock just shorn,
which has come up from being washed.
All are twinned
and none are barren.
4.3 Like a crimson thread are your lips
and your speech is lovely.
Like a pomegranate slice is your palate
through your veil.
4.4 Like David's tower is your neck,
built in turrets,
A thousand shields hung on it,
all the bucklers of the heroes.
4.5 Your two breasts are like two deer,
twin gazelles who are pasturing amongst the lilies.
4.6 Before the day breathes
and the shadows have fled,
I will get myself to the mountain of myrrh,
to the hill of frankincense.
4.7 You are wholly beautiful, my beloved
and you have no blemish.

The male lover now sets out his love for his beloved. This lasts for some fourteen verses, somewhat surprisingly given his previous, relative reticence. It is indeed considerably longer than any of the previous speeches of his female lover. These fourteen verses go over disparate themes. I have therefore divided them up for the purpose of analysis. There is though a constant thread linking them, notwithstanding the apparently disparate themes. In particular, the vocabulary introduced by the six-verse Solomon interlude will begin to add to and, in so doing, embellish the powerful passion we have already seen from the woman.

4.1

His speech starts in a way with which we are very familiar. He declares how beautiful she is and that her eyes are doves. He has said so previously. The first part of verse 4.1 repeats verbatim 1.15. However, this is not redundant repetition, for two reasons.

First, the image of her eyes is a deliberate, ongoing one to which he will refer again in verse 6.5, in a striking image, set in a way which deliberately reminds us of this verse. I will come back to it when we consider 6.5.

Second, he immediately adds the phrase 'beyond your veil'. The veil has a dual purpose here. It obviously plays a role by adding a sense of mystery to her beauty; yet the dove image linked to the veil is also no coincidence. In 2.14, he had described her as being 'in the crags of the rock, in the crevice of the cliff, let me see glimpses of you'. Now the image of seeing and concealment links to her dove-like eyes, glimpsed behind her veil. It all adds to the sense of enticement.

What then follows is the first full, detailed description of her body. As we have seen, this becomes a running theme in the next few chapters. In each of the descriptions, however, there is a method to the manner in which the body is referred. In this version, he describes her body 'top down' (eyes, flowing hair, teeth, lips, palate, neck and breasts). We therefore now need to examine the language in more detail.

He chooses the image of a flock of goats for her hair. We have seen the use of the term 'flock' (in Hebrew '*eder*') earlier in 1.7 when she enquired, in what might have been a teasing way, why she should be like someone 'roaming amongst the flock of your friends'. He latches on to this word now (using it also to describe her teeth in 4.2) as part of the pastoral imagery. The word translated as 'cascaded'[257] only appears in this passage and its twin passage at 6.5. It has almost certainly been used because of the alliteration of the Hebrew word ('*galshu*') with Mount Gilead.

Geographical locations

Mount Gilead is the seventh geographical location we have seen in the Song of Songs (following Jerusalem, Qedar, Ein Gedi, Sharon, Israel and Lebanon). Different references clearly have different purposes. Sometimes, as in the case of Qedar and Lebanon, the references are not to a geographical place but are inserted

---

[257] The Arabic cognate word means 'sit' or 'sit up' but the meaning here appears clear.

because those places indicate something to the author (darkness for Qedar, the temple and/or palace for the trees of Lebanon). On other occasions, the reference is ambiguous (we earlier considered whether the reference to the vineyards of Ein Gedi in 1:14 was to the place itself or a metaphor for, and parallel to, the preceding reference to her breasts). In this verse, the reference seems a direct identification with the actual Mount Gilead east of the Jordan river. Further geographical references will follow and, on each occasion, we will have to consider whether they are intended to be understood literally or metaphorically or - a third possibility - whether the author had a deliberate ambiguity in mind.

4.2 - 4.3

Much of the beauty of the poetry comes from the way in which the Hebrew uses similar sounding words. Intricate wordplay abounds. The word for tooth in Hebrew is '*shen*'. This is its first use in the Song of Songs and it will appear a total of five times. It is a homonym for 'ivory' (perhaps unsurprisingly, given its shape and texture). We will see the word again on his body in the form of ivory (5.14) and we will note there the role it plays. There is however a more immediate wordplay using the word for teeth. The word for 'your teeth' (in Hebrew '*shinayich*') in verse 2 clearly links with the word for 'crimson' (in Hebrew '*shani*') in verse 3 to describe the female lover's lips.

The text also makes allusions by the way it uses certain words. In verse 2, the sheep (i.e. teeth) are described as being 'twinned'. Shortly thereafter we see the reference to 'crimson'. The words 'twinned' and 'crimson' are both relatively sparsely used in the Bible. Their close proximity reminds the reader of their use in a completely different context - the aftermath of the story of Judah and Tamar in Genesis 38:

'And at the time she gave birth, look, there were twins in her womb. And when she gave birth, one of them stretched out a hand which the midwife took and bound crimson on it saying "This one came out first".'[258]

The link between the two passages is striking in terms of wording; yet there is no obvious thematic link between the use of the twins and the crimson in each of the two texts. However, if we look back at the Judah and Tamar story we see remarkable thematic similarities to the Song of Songs. The passage in Genesis also involves flocks of sheep and shearing (38.13), a veil (38.14 and 38.20), and goats (38.17 and 38.23).

---

[258] Genesis 38.27-28.

Of course, rural stories of a similar period will, inevitably, involve similar themes; but the linguistic as well as the thematic similarity is striking. If deliberate, (and of course one can never be sure) then the message is clear. Tamar, the underdog, was able to assert herself notwithstanding the odds stacked against her in the patriarchal society in which she lived. She managed to make Judah, a powerful man, recognise the error of his ways. Here the two lovers recognise the power of their own love for each other, spurning those more powerful than themselves.

Almost impossible to convey in any English translation is the sound of verses 2 and 3a. The letter shin appears at the beginning of five words ((a) '*shinayich*' - 'your teeth', (b) '*she'alu*' - 'which has just come up', (c) '*shekulam*' - 'all of which', (d) '*ve-shakulah*' - 'and barren' and (e) '*ha-shani*' - 'crimson'). The words '*shekulam*' and '*shakulah*' create an alliterative effect particularly striking to the listener.

I have translated one word in verse 3 as 'speech'. The original is '*midbaraich*' and only appears in this context here, so its meaning is doubtful. Others render it 'tongue' (Alter), 'mouth' (Fox, Exum and Pope), 'voice' (Bloch). Clearly, within the context, the reference must be to her mouth, but the root of the word means 'speech'. Its form is remarkable because it links to the word for 'desert' in Hebrew ('*midbar*') which appears throughout the Bible and has appeared at 3.6 in relation to the mysterious woman coming up from the desert (whom we identified probably with the Queen of Sheba as well as the female lover). The reason why I have chosen to suggest a non-body part as the translation is because of a parallel within the Song of Songs itself. Here the male lover says that 'your speech is lovely'. In verse 2.14 he had said that 'your voice is sweet and a glimpse of you is lovely'. The implication of the reference to the mouth here is that it is her speech, not just the shape of the mouth from which it emanates, which is so lovely. He is interested in her beyond the surface; he wants her for more than her body.

The second half of verse 3 compares her palate to a pomegranate slice. This is the first time that the word 'pomegranate' has been used and it will appear six times in the Song of Songs. Pomegranates were a staple part of the Biblical world and are mentioned frequently. Their shape was used as an adornment both in the Tabernacle (e.g. for Aaron's tunic)[259] and in the temple, as we noted in chapter 3 above, where pomegranates served, together with lilies, as figures of decoration at the top of the pillars which Solomon constructed.[260] At the end of verse 5 he compares her breasts

---

[259] Exodus 28.34.
[260] I Kings 7.18-22.

to deer grazing amongst lilies. The fact that these two natural symbols, (pomegranates and lilies), artificially constructed on the temple, have been reappropriated by the lovers for descriptions of parts of their bodies may well be significant.

He says her 'speech' is lovely 'through her veil', repeating the words which were introduced at the beginning of the male lover's speech. The veil was seen then as an object increasing the lover's enticement by reason of its mystery. If the identification of the word '*midbaraich*' with 'speech' is correct, then the veil creates an additional effect. A voice is not altered when speaking from behind a veil but the air of mystery produced by that veil enhances its erotic appeal and, thereby, the erotic appeal of the whole.

The description at 4.1b-3 is repeated later in the Song of Songs (at 6.5-7). The repetition is curtailed and a few words are also altered. We will examine the implications of this revised version in the commentary at that stage.

4.4 - 4.5

Her neck is compared to David's tower, adding to our knowledge of the female lover's link to Jerusalem. We have already learnt that the 'daughters' in the chorus (2.7 and 3.5) are from Jerusalem and that she has wandered in a town which has not been explicitly identified (3.2-4) but which, with all the extra references, we are now entitled to link with Jerusalem.

The final word of the first half of verse 4 is '*talpiot*' which I have translated as 'turrets'. It appears nowhere else in the Bible and so the only context we have in which to understand this word is here. It is a conjectural meaning. The Blochs translate it as 'in splendor' which they suggest in their note means 'built to perfection'. Alter suggests 'gloriously'. Segal suggests 'row upon row'. Whether the word is describing the neck, as per Alter and the Blochs, or whether as 'turrets' it forms a parallel to the neck (as per the standard late-twentieth century translation which I have appropriated) remains an unresolved conundrum.

The next line (the second half of verse 4) describing the shields and bucklers of the heroes is clearer. There is much more in this line than at first meets the eye. The Hebrew word for 'hung' ('*talui*') links linguistically to the mysterious word just discussed which I have translated as 'turrets' ('*talpiot*'), since they both commence with the same two Hebrew letters.

The text tells us that a thousand shields can be hung on her neck.[261] Clearly there is a sense of hyperbole in this number in that it indicates the length (and thereby magnificence) of her neck. But it also plays another role. In this verse, the number is used to praise the beloved. Later (8.11-12), the number 'one thousand' will be used in clear fashion to scorn Solomon and everything he stands for. Here the heroes can hang their instruments of war on her elegant neck. We have already seen, however, the reference to heroes in 3.7 prepared for war, whose role is to guard a frightened, night time King Solomon.

Her breasts are described in terms we have already encountered. They are two deer or twin gazelles. At this point, he appropriates her words from 2.9 in which she had asked him to be 'a gazelle or a deer amongst the hinds.' He adds, however, to her image the words 'who are pasturing amongst the lilies'. She has also used this phrase before (2.16). The words of her context are different ('my lover is mine and I am his who pastures amongst the lilies') but the content of unfettered adoration and love is not.

The description of her body now stops momentarily and a new theme is about to be introduced in verse 6. Yet the last two words of 4.5 together with the first line of 4.6 are almost identical to the passage in 2.16 and 2.17. He takes up what she said but transforms it, as we shall now see.

4.6 - 4.7

The male lover's repetition of her phrase at 2.17 moves on entirely differently from its original context. There he was told to turn and imagine himself like various deer on the cleft mountain. He now appropriates the hill country metaphor by talking about going to the mountain of myrrh and the hill of frankincense. This phrase is so rich in meaning that its various layers need to be unpacked.

First, he refers to getting himself to a mountain and then to a hill. In so doing, he is repeating her description of him in 2.8 'striding on the mountains, leaping on the hills'. Whilst the lovers may appear thereby to be self-referential, the magic of the Song of Songs is that this is never fully the case. Something always gets added.

In this case, what appear to be added are not real mountains/hills but spice hills of myrrh and frankincense. Again this seems to be an appropriation of the phrase in

---

[261] The shields are metaphorically hung on the neck and not on the turrets because 'hung on it' (*talui alav*') refers to a masculine word which is appropriate for 'neck' (*tsavar*' in Hebrew) and not for '*talpiot*' which is probably a word in the feminine plural form.

3.6 where a female person (the lover?, the Queen of Sheba?, both?) comes up from the desert '...fragrant in myrrh and frankincense'. But we already saw the import of the Hebrew word for frankincense '*levonah*' being extremely similar in sound to Lebanon '*levanon*', such that a play on words was always implied if the two words were used in close proximity. In the next few verses, the word '*levanon*' appears four times (verse 8 [twice], 11 and 15). On that basis, the hill of frankincense could also be a reference to 'the hill of Lebanon'. Does this make sense? By itself, it is a little strange, since the word for 'hill' (in Hebrew '*giv'ah*') probably implies something much lower than the mighty range of mountains in Lebanon. As such, a reference to the geographical location of Lebanon must be rejected but a link with the name is clearly implied.

What then of the reference to the 'mountain of myrrh'? It is clearly a spice hill but is it something else as well beyond the obvious erotic comparisons to the *mons veneris*? It probably is. 'Mountain of myrrh' in Hebrew is '*har ha-mor*'. This sounds remarkably similar to '*har ha-moriah*' ('Mount Moriah') on which Abraham was commanded to sacrifice Isaac, his 'only son'.[262] It became the location of the temple in Jerusalem. The rewording of '*levonah*' ('frankincense') to '*levanon*' would now render this phrase, 'I will get myself to Mount Moriah to the Hill of Lebanon'. In the context of the Solomonic period which is being described (and probably the period thereafter when this passage was written) this secondary meaning makes perfect sense. The temple on Mount Moriah in Jerusalem was full of Lebanon wood as described in the book of Kings. An allusion here is probably being made to this fact. The Rabbis' linking of every verse to their own narrative of redemption may here reflect the original intention of the author. One Rabbinic explanation of 'I will get to the mountain of myrrh' is 'this is the temple where they used to burn myrrh as incense'.[263]

There is, however, an apparent difficulty with a full comparison of this phrase to the temple and Jerusalem. If the references here are complete, why does the male lover want to go <u>to</u> Moriah and Lebanon. Surely, so much of what we have seen beforehand has been about escaping the city of Jerusalem and its mores. The full answer to this puzzle will become clear in a few verses' time when we realise that the male lover does indeed want to escape from the city. At this stage, though, we can see that he identifies the myrrh and frankincense on his lover (3.6) with Jerusalem but that he chooses his lover over Jerusalem.

---

[262] Genesis 22.
[263] *Tanchuma yashan vayera* 4, quoted in Kasher, 194-5.

He sums up his description of her whole as being beautiful and without blemish. I have referred earlier to the way in which the description is 'idealised' and therefore subject to the sort of criticism which Shakespeare so expertly aimed at such exaggeration. I will address his objection at the end of this section. Yet, the word 'blemish' itself is worth considering in this context. It has interesting antecedents. In the books of Leviticus and Numbers, it was used to describe those people who were or were not able to approach the sanctuary, dependent on blemish or lack thereof. In a non-cultic setting, there is only one use of the word to describe somebody as without blemish. The comparison is noteworthy. The person so described is Absalom: 'And there was no man in Israel whose beauty was so praiseworthy as Absalom; from the palm of his foot to the top of his head, he had no blemish'.[264] There may have been no blemish in his beauty but his real blemish lay in his ambition. He rebelled against his father David, his flowing hair got caught in a tree and he was unceremoniously taken down and butchered by David's men.[265] In the Song of Songs, the male lover knows that his beloved's physical beauty, unlike Absalom's, is matched by her words and her actions. The contrast is quite wonderful.

The phrase 'beautiful, my beloved' in verse 7 repeats the same phrase in verse 1. This is a literary 'inclusio' and thereby indicates the demarcation of a new section which is about to commence. The male lover's description of her body has now come to an end but it is only the launchpad for a torrent of verbal passion he is about to unleash about how taken by her he is.

ח אִתִּי מִלְּבָנוֹן כַּלָּה

אִתִּי מִלְּבָנוֹן תָּבוֹאִי

תָּשׁוּרִי ׀ מֵרֹאשׁ אֲמָנָה

מֵרֹאשׁ שְׂנִיר וְחֶרְמוֹן

מִמְּעֹנוֹת אֲרָיוֹת

מֵהַרְרֵי נְמֵרִים:

ט לִבַּבְתִּנִי אֲחֹתִי כַלָּה

לִבַּבְתִּנִי באחד (בְּאַחַת) מֵעֵינַיִךְ

בְּאַחַד עֲנָק מִצַּוְּרֹנָיִךְ:

י מַה־יָּפוּ דֹדַיִךְ אֲחֹתִי כַלָּה

מַה־טֹּבוּ דֹדַיִךְ מִיָּיִן

וְרֵיחַ שְׁמָנַיִךְ מִכָּל־בְּשָׂמִים:

יא נֹפֶת תִּטֹּפְנָה שִׂפְתוֹתַיִךְ כַּלָּה

---

[264] II Samuel 14.25.
[265] II Samuel 18.9,15.

דְּבַשׁ וְחָלָב֙ תַּ֣חַת לְשׁוֹנֵ֔ךְ
וְרֵ֥יחַ שַׂלְמֹתַ֖יִךְ כְּרֵ֥יחַ לְבָנֽוֹן׃

He speaks to her:

4.8 With me from Lebanon bride,
   with me from Lebanon come,
Come down from the peak of Amanah,
   from the peak of Snir and Hermon,
From lions' lairs
   and leopards' mountains.
4.9 You have stolen my heart my sister bride,
   you have stolen my heart with one of your eyes,
      with one bead in your necklace.
4.10 How beautiful are your caresses, my sister bride,
   how much better are your caresses than wine
      and the fragrance of your oil than all spices.
4.11 Flowing honey drops are your lips, bride,
   honey and milk are under your tongue
      and the fragrance of your dress is like the fragrance of Lebanon.

4.8

He asks her to come with him from Lebanon.[266]   Given the play on the word '*levanon*' ('Lebanon') before in 4.6 with reference to '*levonah*' ('frankincense') and given that the '*atzei ha-levanon*' ('the woods of Lebanon'), referred to in 3.9, are in the temple and palace, one would immediately assume that this is the meaning here - in other words, the intention is to show a desire to escape the clutches of the city of Jerusalem. It almost certainly is; but added to it is a geographic reference to a series of mountains in the Lebanon region. Surely then is it not this region which the lover is inviting his beloved to flee? The geographic references need to be examined. 'Amanah' is a mountain in Lebanon whose name is a homonym for 'treaty'. As for the two other mountains mentioned in 4.8, 'Snir' was the name used by the Amorites for 'Hermon'.[267] In Ezekiel, the prophet is commanded to proclaim a dirge on Tyre. Amongst the various items he mentions, he states: 'They built your planks out of cypresses from Snir, they took cedar from Lebanon to make a mast for

---

[266] One Masoretic tradition re-vowels the Hebrew word '*iti*' ('with me') to '*eti*' ('come') which seems unnecessary in this verse.
[267] Deuteronomy 3.9.

you'.[268] The only other Biblical reference to Snir also mentions it in the context of Hermon.[269]

How are we then to understand this passage? It is a clear reference to the geographic region of Lebanon and other mountains in its vicinity. The primary meaning that the reader senses, on a literal reading of the verse, is the need to escape that area. Yet in so doing, the author has chosen to use areas and mountains associated, so far as we can tell, with the cedar and cypress. So it seems likely that there is also a secondary reference implied to cedar and cypresses: the woods used in the building of Solomon's temple and palace. Added to this, the lions mentioned, as somewhere to escape from, have long been a symbol of regal authority and, specifically, twelve lions were engraved onto the steps leading up to Solomon's throne.[270]

So we have a sentence which, read out of context, seems to refer purely to the mountainous region of Lebanon. However, when read within the context of the extensive word play in the Song of Songs on Lebanon and frankincense, Lebanon is associated with the temple and the palace. What are we to make of this? Any answer must be tentative, of course, as we have no knowledge of exactly how and when the Song of Songs was composed. We have evidence to show that references to these mountains were used in the Lebanon area. Indeed, we have Assyrian inscriptions where 'Amanah' and 'Lebanon' are both referred to as '*Ammananu*'.[271] It stands to reason therefore that this part of the Song of Songs may have had its origins far north of Jerusalem in the Lebanon region. I would therefore suggest that this is an original poem about Lebanon which has been woven into a larger narrative about love and King Solomon. I refer in more detail to the image of 'Lebanon' in the Song of Songs in chapter 6 below.

4.9

There is one important word in 4.8 to which I have not yet referred - he describes her there as his 'bride' (in Hebrew '*kallah*'). He has not done so before and this is the word's first appearance in this developing narrative poem. Over the next few verses, he will use it extensively, including in an entirely new poem. But he will also use it with another word. The first time that this combination of words is used is here in 4.9. He describes her as 'my sister, bride' ('*achoti, kallah*'). This sense of intimacy appears rather touching. He then adds to this the phrase 'you have stolen

---

[268] Ezekiel 27.5.

[269] I Chronicles 5.23.

[270] I Kings 10.20.

[271] Fishbane, 115.

my heart'. This is my attempt to translate the one word equivalent in Hebrew - '*libavtini*'. As Alter points out, the King James version uses the term 'ravished'. The word comes from the root meaning 'heart' and literally means 'you have hearted me'. Clearly, the word is used to link in, as a wordplay, with '*levanon*' and '*levonah*' to both of which it sounds remarkably similar. But in the context of love and a sister, the root linked with the word 'heart' has an altogether darker, more sinister aspect as well. It relates to the story of Amnon and Tamar as told in II Samuel 13.[272]

Tamar is the half sister of Amnon. Amnon decides that, because he is infatuated with Tamar, he must love her. He desires to have sex with her. So he devises a plan with one of his aids to pretend to be sick[273] in order to get her to bring him cakes. When she enters with the cakes, he rapes her. He then realises (somewhat belatedly one might argue) that he hates her more than he ever loved her. The crucial word, for our purposes, is the cakes. The full impact of the Hebrew is rarely, if ever, captured in the English translation. Thus the JPS translates II Samuel 13.8 as follows: 'Tamar went to the house of her brother Amnon, who was in bed. She took dough and kneaded it into cakes in front of him and cooked the cakes'. The Hebrew word for 'cakes', in both references, is '*l'vivot*' from the root 'heart' presumably meaning something like 'heart-shaped'.

So we have a situation in the Amnon and Tamar story where a sister is raped by her brother when the role of heart-shaped cakes is crucial to the narrative. When this intertextual link is transferred to the Song of Songs, it certainly makes one shudder that he describes his 'bride' as both his 'sister' and as having captured his 'heart'. Whether the link was a deliberate one by the author is impossible to tell at this distance of time but, whether or not it was, the comparison also invites a clear contrast. There is nothing non-consensual about what occurs between the two lovers in the Song of Songs. The love is voluntary, and total, in sharp contrast to the rape in the Amnon and Tamar story. The word 'ravish', used by the King James version in its translation of this verse in the Song of Songs, with its implication of abduction and rape, is as far away as could be from the intent of the word here.

The image that he has used about her having captured his heart is one which he develops. He says that this has been brought about through one of her eyes and a bead of her necklace. Both images are familiar from his earlier, much briefer,

---

[272] The reference here to Tamar is to a completely different Biblical figure from the Tamar mentioned in the commentary to 4.2-3 above who appears only in Genesis 38.

[273] The Hebrew word for 'sick' (II Samuel 13.6) is the same word as used for love sick in the Song of Songs at 2.5 and 5.8

description of her in chapter 1 of the Song of Songs. There (1.15), he described her eyes as doves. This could be what the reference here is intended to mean or, as some have interpreted, it could mean that she has captured his heart through a glimpse of her eyes though the word 'glimpse', or something similar, is absent from the Hebrew. The reference to 'bead' and 'necklace' refer us back thematically to his imagery in 1.10 where he had described the beauty of her neck in beads (though using a different Hebrew word for 'bead').

4.10 - 4.11

Odour, and the erotic effect it can have on the lover, are referred to in these two verses which complete this poem. The next poem (4.12-5.1) will also take up the use of fragrances to spice up love and we will consider them again in more detail there. At this stage, it is worth noting that the ends of both verses 10 and 11 refer to her 'fragrance', whereas the beginnings of both verses 10 and 11 refer to other of her qualities ('caresses' in verse 10 and 'honey and milk' in verse 11). On that basis, it is worth taking these two verses together, with this obvious parallelism, and seeing how the two parallels interact.

The non-spice parallel in verses 4.10 and 4.11.

In verse 10 he uses his new name for his lover; his 'sister-bride' has wonderful caresses, which are even better than wine. He is clearly returning her compliment; at the very beginning of the Song of Songs, she had said that his love was better than wine (1.2 and 1.4). Here though, he adds (in the parallel in verse 11), in addition to his reference to caresses, an explanation of why her caresses and lovemaking are so wonderful. The Hebrew phrase uses stunning alliteration - '*nofet titofnah*' reflected in Alter's beautiful translation 'Nectar your lips drip'.[274] The phrase which follows ('honey and milk under your lips') is redolent of the land flowing with milk and honey (Exodus 3.8 and elsewhere). The parallel relates touch (caresses/lovemaking) to touch and taste (lips and tongue with honeycomb, milk and honey). Delightfully, Exum compares it to the final two lines of Kubla Khan by Coleridge: 'For he on honey-dew hath fed/and drunk the milk of Paradise'.[275]

---

[274] Alter (2015), 26.
[275] Exum, 174.

The spice parallel in verses 4.10 and 4.11.

The touch/taste parallel in the first half of each verse changes in the second half to smell. Again the words he uses in verse 10 ('the fragrance of your oil') are an appropriation of the term she had used in 1.3. She had said that his fragrance was 'good'. He repeats the term 'good' but says that her smell is 'better than all the spices'. We would therefore expect a similar fragrance parallel at the end of verse 11. We do indeed get it: 'the fragrance of your dress is like the fragrance of Lebanon'. This is a stunning and, at first, puzzling phrase. The parallel means that 'spices' and 'Lebanon' are being used as a parallelism. Why is there a reference to Lebanon in the context of spices? Moreover, the poem has so far been highly critical of Lebanon. The 'wood of Lebanon' was the choice of wood for Solomon's 'palanquin' referred to in 3.9. The only other direct references so far to Lebanon have been in 4.8 where the male lover had asked her to come away from Lebanon. Now she is identified with the smell of Lebanon which seems, at first sight, to make no sense.

There is a clear answer to this conundrum. We have our constant wordplay on 'levanon' ('Lebanon') and 'levonah' ('frankincense'). Frankincense would apparently have made more sense as the fragrance of her dress. Yet this is clearly not a mistake. The Song of Songs is a work which does not reject the norms which it sees. It merely wishes to transform them. So the 'Lebanon' represented by the temple is only rejected in the sense that it is transformed on her body into the love between the two lovers. Where one would have expected 'levonah' ('frankincense'), the editor deliberately wrote 'levanon' ('Lebanon'). This unexpected use of words will continue in the next poem when a transformation of temple imagery will be forged by the use of the word 'levonah' ('frankincense').

We have been introduced to the idea that the imagery which the male lover is using now serves a dual purpose; first, in apparently conventional literary fashion, to declare his love for his beloved. However, it also serves to compare his lover favourably with the society in which they both live. He does so in his next poem. Again, he introduces us to a new term. We encounter a garden for the first time; his lover is compared to a locked garden. We will never be able to force the garden door totally open to understand fully what was intended but perhaps we will gain some insights into what he intends in this new setting.

יב גַּן | נָעוּל אֲחֹתִי כַלָּה
גַּל נָעוּל מַעְיָן חָתוּם:
יג שְׁלָחַיִךְ פַּרְדֵּס רִמּוֹנִים

עֵם פְּרִי מְגָדִים
כְּפָרִים עִם־נְרָדִים:
יד גֵרְךְ ׀ וְכַרְכֹּם קָנֶה וְקִנָּמוֹן
עֵם כָּל־עֲצֵי לְבוֹנָה
מֹר וַאֲהָלוֹת
עֵם כָּל־רָאשֵׁי בְשָׂמִים:

He speaks to her

4.12 A locked garden, my sister bride,
    a locked spring, a sealed fountain,
4.13 Your branches are a pomegranate orchard
    with the most excellent fruits
        Henna with nard.
4.14 Nard and saffron, cane and cinnamon
    with all the trees of frankincense
Myrrh and aloes
    with all the finest spices.

4.12

The lack of a present tense in Hebrew means that this sentence could be rendered in a number of ways. Naturally, one wants to translate it as 'A locked garden is my sister bride, a locked spring [and] a spring fountain'. The problem with such a translation is that, in this context, he has only just spoken to her and in the next verse he will continue talking to her - so why should he refer to her here in the third person? It would seem therefore that 'my sister bride' is a vocative: he is speaking to her and telling her that she is a mystery rather than in some sense speaking about her and saying that she is unapproachable. Some manuscripts rendered the word 'spring' ('*gal*' in Hebrew) as 'garden' ('*gan*' in Hebrew) assuming a scribal error, but the image of a locked spring and a sealed fountain seem to go together perfectly so there is no need to change the received text.

4.13

The first word in verse 13 (in Hebrew '*sh'lachayich*') appears very rarely in the Bible - so its meaning is difficult. It derives from the base root word meaning to 'send' and, in the context of a plant, has the meaning of 'shooting forth' when used as a verb. I have taken one of the various translations available which I think nearest matches this meaning (others include 'watercourses'). As it is the subject of the pomegranate orchard with fruits and various spices attached, it is a shame that we cannot be sure to what it refers. Lack of certainty, however, allows the mind to read in all sorts of erotic possibilities which may or may not be correct. Without greater knowledge, a true meaning eludes us.

The word translated 'orchard' is often translated as 'pleasure garden'. It is one of the strongest indications that the Song of Songs (or at the very least this part of the Song of Songs) is a late work because the Hebrew word used ('*pardes*') only appears in late Biblical works (such as Ecclesiastes and Nehemiah). The word itself has a remarkable history. It is a loanword from Persian; from there it transferred to Greek, where it became '*paradeisos*', and hence 'paradise' in western thought and languages. Its history in Jewish thought is as important. Via a midrash in the Talmud,[276] it became an acronym for the basis of the various exegetical methods by which the Bible was interpreted by the Rabbis.

We have already seen a reference to a pomegranate (her palate was compared to a pomegranate slice in 4.3). We need to bear this comparison in mind but also that the word here appears in the plural. Later the word will be used twice (6.11 and 7.13) when the male lover wants to know whether the pomegranate has blossomed, adding to the potentially erotic possible meanings of this verse.

There are a total of nine spices mentioned in the Song of Songs. All of them appear in this passage; henna (in Hebrew '*k'far*'), spikenard ('*nard*'), saffron ('*karkom*'), cane ('*qaneh*'), cinnamon ('*qinnamon*'), frankincense ('*levonah*'), myrrh ('*mor*'), aloes ('*ahalot*') and finest spices ('*rashei besamim*'). To understand the significance of these spices in the Song of Songs, one must look at how and where these spices are referred to elsewhere in the Bible. Spikenard and saffron only appear in the Song of Songs. Aloes appear as part of the enticements of the strange woman in Proverbs 7.17 whom we encountered in contrast to the female lover in 3.1-4. Henna is used in the building of Noah's ark.[277] Five of the spices are, as we have seen, required for use in the tabernacle (cane, cinnamon, frankincense, myrrh and finest spices).[278] Yet, none of them were used by Solomon in the building of his temple.

It seems to me that a comparison is being drawn, and a contrast made, between the lovers and Solomon. This is heightened by the description of the frankincense in

---

[276] Hagigah 14b (and other places)
[277] Genesis 6.14.
[278] Exodus 30.22-37.

verse 14 here as being 'the trees of frankincense' or, in Hebrew, '*atzei levonah*' with its deliberate imitation of the sound of '*atzei levanon*' ('trees of Lebanon') out of which, we are told in 3.9, Solomon built his 'palanquin' (i.e. his palace and temple). The message seems to be that the lovers use the spices mentioned in the building of the tabernacle but a wise and wealthy king such as Solomon chose not to do so.

טו מַעְיַן גַּנִּים
בְּאֵר מַיִם חַיִּים
וְנֹזְלִים מִן־לְבָנוֹן׃
טז עוּרִי צָפוֹן וּבוֹאִי תֵימָן
הָפִיחִי גַנִּי יִזְּלוּ בְשָׂמָיו
יָבֹא דוֹדִי לְגַנּוֹ וְיֹאכַל פְּרִי מְגָדָיו׃
א בָּאתִי לְגַנִּי אֲחֹתִי כַלָּה
אָרִיתִי מוֹרִי עִם־בְּשָׂמִי
אָכַלְתִּי יַעְרִי עִם־דִּבְשִׁי
שָׁתִיתִי יֵינִי עִם־חֲלָבִי
אִכְלוּ רֵעִים
שְׁתוּ וְשִׁכְרוּ דּוֹדִים׃

He speaks to her:

4.15 A fountain of gardens,
       a well of living waters,
             and flowing from Lebanon.
4.16 Awake oh North and come oh South,
       blow into my garden, may its spices flow.

She speaks to him:

May my lover come into his garden
       and eat the most excellent fruits.

He speaks to her:

5.1 I have come into my garden, my sister bride,
      I have gathered my myrrh with my spice;
I have eaten my honeycomb with my honey,
      I have drunk my wine with my milk.

Chorus

Eat friends,
> **drink and be drunk with love.**

4.15 - 4.16

Having described all the spices on his lover's body, he now returns to the image of the garden with which he has compared her. The double meaning of the garden as his lover's body is added to by the reference to Lebanon. Again the movement of the living waters is flowing from Lebanon (as in 4.8).

Much of the focus on gardens in the latter part of the Song of Songs has led some to compare it to the story of the garden of Eden.[279] Indeed, one Jewish text has it that the garden of Eden sang verse 4.16 of the Song of Songs.[280] This is perhaps unsurprising - the image in verses 15 and 16, of the wind blowing and living waters, readily links to the garden of Eden. In that seminal story, God blows the breath of life into Adam's nostrils and a river flows to water the garden.[281] The other obvious image which links with verse 16 is the beginning of the book of Ecclesiastes where the wind 'goes to the south, turns to the north, the wind goes and turns and turns and in its turnings, the wind returns'.[282] In the Song of Songs, though, the transformation of these garden images into metaphor for the body is wholly new. Any comparisons therefore between the Song of Songs and any other Biblical text can only be entertained with this obvious, but crucial, difference in mind.

As if to heighten the sexual frisson, in the second part of verse 16, we hear again, for the first time since the Solomonic interlude, directly from the female lover.[283] She mentions her beloved coming into his garden and eating the most excellent fruits. We have seen how in chapter 4 of the Song of Songs the male lover has appropriated her earlier language where she had spoken so much more than he. Now, she returns the favour and adopts his choice of language. He has introduced the garden metaphor, which she now latches on to, and he has referred to the most excellent fruits (4.13) which she now repeats.

---

[279] e.g. Paradoxes of Paradise, Francis Landy.

[280] Perek Shirah - referenced Landy, (1983), 183, (2011), 172.

[281] Genesis 2.7,10.

[282] Ecclesiastes 1.6.

[283] It is possible that verse 15 and the first part of verse 16 are words spoken by the female lover as they are not gendered.

5.1

As has been recognised universally, the traditional chapter ending makes no sense as 5.1 is clearly the ending of this poem. The verse itself contains two different sections.

First, the male lover confirms and summarises his actions. As such, this verse clearly demarcates the ending of a section. He also uses the terminology 'my sister, bride' for the last time. We noted at its first appearance at 4.9 the ironic use of the term in the context of the Amnon-Tamar story and its transformation in the Song of Songs into something quite wonderful and utterly different. The 'sister-bride' terminology also transforms his female lover. In verse 8.1, she will refer to him as her brother by saying that life would be so much easier if he had been her brother because public embraces between them would go unremarked.

The poetry used by the male lover in this section is somewhat lost in translation. All the 'I' and 'my' references in the translation reflect the ending *-i* at the end of nine out of the thirteen Hebrew words. Moreover, by the end of the verse, the connection between garden and lover is made explicit. There are four parts to this summary-cum-conclusion. The second part links myrrh with spice, the third links honeycomb with honey, and the final links wine with milk. In this manner, the link between garden and lover in the first part 'I have come into my garden, my sister bride' is made obvious. The garden and lover are as inextricably linked to each other as the other phrases link myrrh to spice, honeycomb to honey, and wine to milk.

The second section is addressed to more than one person. It could therefore be addressed to the two lovers or to a whole group of people. The text does not make this clear, though within the context it makes sense that it is addressed by a chorus to the two lovers.

Beyond physical description - concluding remarks on 4.1 - 5.1.

On one level, the *wasf* which forms the launchpad for chapter 4 of the Song of Songs fails the challenge posed by Shakespeare. The male lover describes his lover with the express comment that she is entirely without blemish (4.7); indeed his detailed portrayal of her backs up that image of physical perfection. We need not sneer at such utopian impossibility. The first *wasf* in the Song of Songs has two very clear purposes which take us beyond the limits of corporeality.

First, we learn that the male lover has a voice. As has been made clear in the commentary previously, he is extremely reticent in the first three chapters. We now find that he is able to respond to her. He does so by appropriating her language.

But he is in fact not only responding to her. He is also responding to the Solomon interlude. His language, as I have shown, is full of the terminology which we first encountered in Solomon's threefold direct appearances in 3.6-11. In this fashion, he appropriates the poetic language referring to the temple contained in that passage, and reinterprets it within the context of his love for the girl. Solomon is therefore central to the passage we have just considered without being mentioned once.

Of course, let us never forget that we are dealing here with a pure fiction. The male and female lovers are not real. They are figments of the imagination of the author/editor of the Song of Songs. We see in 4.1-5.1 perhaps as clearly as anywhere else in the Song of Songs what genius that person had for weaving apparently separate descriptions of different love scenes into one whole by the use of wordplay.

An abrupt change of scene

This section ends with the lovers apparently blissfully happy and drunk with love. One would therefore assume that the next poem would carry on where we have just left off. Such an assumption would be wholly incorrect. The next scene finds the female lover in all sorts of distress. It also serves a literary function which, as we shall see, takes time to reveal itself.

SONG OF SONGS 5.2 - 5.8

Distress and Departure

The next episode is totally different from the scene we have just encountered. It clearly mirrors the episode in 3.1-5 in which the female lover was on her bed at night and sought her lover. It raises any number of questions as a result. Why is there such an abrupt change in mood by the time this brief episode is over? What is the reason for having these two scenes and why are there these differences between them? As we analyse the individual verses, we need to bear such questions in mind and work out the degree to which we can answer them by the end of this episode.

ב אֲנִי יְשֵׁנָה וְלִבִּי עֵר
קוֹל ׀ דּוֹדִי דוֹפֵק
פִּתְחִי־לִי אֲחֹתִי רַעְיָתִי
יוֹנָתִי תַמָּתִי
שֶׁרֹאשִׁי נִמְלָא־טָל
קְוֻצּוֹתַי רְסִיסֵי לָיְלָה:
ג פָּשַׁטְתִּי אֶת־כֻּתָּנְתִּי
אֵיכָכָה אֶלְבָּשֶׁנָּה
רָחַצְתִּי אֶת־רַגְלַי
אֵיכָכָה אֲטַנְּפֵם:
ד דּוֹדִי שָׁלַח יָדוֹ מִן־הַחֹר
וּמֵעַי הָמוּ עָלָיו:
ה קַמְתִּי אֲנִי לִפְתֹּחַ לְדוֹדִי
וְיָדַי נָטְפוּ־מוֹר
וְאֶצְבְּעֹתַי מוֹר עֹבֵר
עַל כַּפּוֹת הַמַּנְעוּל:
ו פָּתַחְתִּי אֲנִי לְדוֹדִי
וְדוֹדִי חָמַק עָבָר
נַפְשִׁי יָצְאָה בְדַבְּרוֹ
בִּקַּשְׁתִּיהוּ וְלֹא מְצָאתִיהוּ
קְרָאתִיו וְלֹא עָנָנִי:
ז מְצָאֻנִי הַשֹּׁמְרִים הַסֹּבְבִים בָּעִיר
הִכּוּנִי פְצָעוּנִי
נָשְׂאוּ אֶת־רְדִידִי מֵעָלַי
שֹׁמְרֵי הַחֹמוֹת:

ח הִשְׁבַּעְתִּי אֶתְכֶם בְּנוֹת יְרוּשָׁלָ͏ִם
אִם־תִּמְצְאוּ אֶת־דּוֹדִי
מַה־תַּגִּידוּ לוֹ
שֶׁחוֹלַת אַהֲבָה אָנִי׃

She speaks

5.2 I am asleep but my heart is awake.
   Listen! My lover knocks:
"Open for me my sister beloved,
   my dove, my perfect one,
Since my head is full of dew,
   my locks with the drops of the night".
5.3 "I have taken off my clothes,
   how will I dress?
I have washed my feet,
   how will I soil them?"
5.4 My lover took away his hand from the keyhole
   and my innards yearned for him.
5.5 I arose to open up for my lover
   and my hands dripped myrrh,
And my fingers, flowing myrrh
   on the handles of the bolt.
5.6 I opened up for my lover
   but my lover turned and passed on.
      I nearly expired when he spoke,
I sought him but did not find him,
   I called him but he did not answer me.
5.7 The guards who roam in the city found me,
   they hit me and manhandled me,
They took my shawl off me,
   the guards of the walls.
5.8 I have made you swear, oh daughters of Jerusalem,
   that if you find him,
what should you tell him?
   That I am lovesick.

5.2

The scene opens with two words in Hebrew '*ani yeshenah*' ('I am asleep') which immediately alert us to the fact that the next verses are likely to parallel those we saw earlier which started (at 3.1) with the words 'on my bed at night'. Yet the next words in Hebrew '*ve-libi er*' ('but my heart is awake') indicate that her comments now will be different. First, she has never used the word 'heart' before. There are two places from which she could have taken it. It was first used to describe the rejoicing of Solomon's heart at the time of his wedding (3.11). It was then used by her lover in 4.9 to describe how she had stolen his heart. The fact that she has now appropriated a word that he had used to proclaim heightened passion[284] indicates a sense not only that he has listened to her but that she is now returning the compliment. Not only do these two lovers love each other but they clearly listen to each other. From a literary point of view, it therefore also becomes increasingly difficult to conceive of these apparently fleeting scenes as entirely independent of each other. If they were created separately, they have been brilliantly woven together.

The next three Hebrew words '*qol dodi dofeq*' ('Listen! My lover knocks') now recalls her own previous comment (2.8-2.9) where she had used the same opening words ('*qol dodi*') to describe her lover coming toward her and then peering in by the window. In this sense, these words seem a continuation of that earlier episode.

In the next line she tells us what he says. She is apparently quoting him. She had done so previously at 2.10-2.13. Again, remarkably, when she now quotes him, we see that she uses language both from that earlier quote and the language that he has used in the long speech/description of her which we have just read. She refers to four pet names he has used ('my sister, beloved, my dove, my perfect one'). In 2.13 he had referred to her as 'my beloved, my beautiful'. Here she repeats his use of pet names but alters them to 'my sister, my beloved' which now reflects his adoption of the word 'sister' in 3.9. Similarly, here she now quotes him as saying 'my dove, my perfect one'. He had called her 'dove' on a number of occasions (1.15, 2.14 and 4.1) but he had never previously called her 'my perfect one' ('*tammati*'). The word '*tam*' means 'completion' or 'perfection' or 'wholeness'. It appears to be her direct reflection of the comment he has just made to her that she has no blemish (4.7).

---

[284] The word for heart in Hebrew '*lev*' is understood as meaning the faculty of the intellect in much Hebrew writing. It seems impossible so to understand it in the two contexts set out above. Here the word is obviously being used in connection with emotion.

Most important, as a literary device which is not as obvious in any English translation, is that she quotes him by using seven words ending '-*i*' (generally, but not always, meaning 'my …'). This mirrors his use of the same device twelve times in his peroration in 5.1. She imitates his style of speech. The lovers are therefore clearly in dialogue with each other and what they say indicates a reliance, not only on their own thought processes, but an ever-increasing reliance on that of their counterpart.[285]

His next words ('my head is full of dew, my locks with the juices of the night') are surely capable of literal or erotic interpretation but again, as we will see, will be used later as a device by which she describes him (see comments below on 5.11).

5.3

The next line is clearly spoken by her. We can infer that this is not a comment she makes to herself (meaning something like 'help, he's come at an inconvenient time') but rather, as Alter and others have suggested, that this is her response to him. Alter reads it,[286] I think persuasively, as a tease which goes very wrong. Even so, the author has again produced word play intended to link her comment with his previous speech. The word translated 'soil' appears only here in the Bible. It has the Hebrew root '*t-n-f*'. The word for 'drip' which the male lover introduced in 4.11 has the root '*n-t-f*'. In other words it uses the same three Hebrew letters in a different order. This is a clear attempt on her part to use his language, made even more obvious in two verses' time where she adopts his language and uses his word 'drip'.

5.4

His reaction to her comment is to withdraw his hand from the keyhole (the three letters 'key' have been inferred by me - perhaps incorrectly! - these verses are full of erotic overtones). Her innards then yearn for him. These comments appear merely to show that he is about to leave. Things in the Song of Songs are rarely as they appear at first glance, though. In fact, the words 'hand' and 'innards' will become in 5.14 parts of her description of praise of him (changed in the new context to mean 'stomach'). In other words, she transforms their original use in a time of distress to an entirely different joyous meaning.

---

[285] Any number of arias from Mozart operas exhibit a very similar phenomenon.
[286] Alter 2015, 30.

She refers to her lover as '*dodi*' which I have translated as 'my lover'. She so describes him in the rest of this episode. Increasingly, this will be her pet name for him for the rest of the Song of Songs. In the passage parallel to this in 3.1-5, she had described him regularly as 'my soulmate' ('*et she'ahavah nafshi*').

5.5

As in the first night time sequence, she gets up (see 3.2). In the previous version, she got up to search round the city. Here, with her lover much nearer, she does so with the purpose of letting him in. She mentions the myrrh on her hands and fingers. She had first introduced the image of myrrh (1.13) in which instance it was on his body and not hers. He had then used the image of myrrh extensively in chapter 4, playing on its similarity to the word for Mount Moriah. He had combined this with the fact that the word for frankincense resembles Lebanon, thereby creating a link with the temple built out of Lebanese cedar wood. I remarked that this may be an implied criticism of the fact that Solomon did not use the prescribed spices in the temple. In a text where the lovers swap images regularly for literary purposes, one might expect her to latch on to this striking imagery. In fact, there is no hint of that link in what she says at this stage. Instead, she refers to something he mentioned on a different occasion. She is clearly influenced by what he has said because he had used the image of 'dripping' to describe the honey on her lips (4.11). Now it is applied to the myrrh on her body. Another participle is also used (in Hebrew '*over*') meaning 'passing'. This is a deliberate choice because the same word will describe how his lover goes away in 5.6 (in Hebrew '*avar*' deriving from the same root). I have used 'passed on' in 5.6 to retain the link.[287]

The root of both 'bolt' and 'locked' is '*n-a-l*'. By using the word 'bolt' she has appropriated his language of a locked garden and spring in 4:12, again adapting his use to her situation.

5.6

She finally opens up the door to him but finds that he turns away and passes on. The Hebrew word for 'turns away' ('*chamaq*') appears only twice in the Bible. The other occasion is also in the Song of Songs at 7.2. As we will see there, the male lover uses it and transforms its meaning into something much more positive about his female lover.

---

[287] In Exodus 30.23, the myrrh required in the tabernacle is described as '*mor dror*', 'free flowing myrrh'. Whilst not using the same adjective, the implication surely is that the type of myrrh to be used in the tabernacle was similar to that being described here.

I have translated the next words 'I nearly expired when he spoke', (literally it means 'my soul departed when he spoke'). This could imply fainting (Alter 'went faint') or loss of any ability to think straight. What seems to remain a mystery is what it was that he said. We are told he spoke - we are not told, however, what it was that he said which caused this effect on her.

It is only at this point that the narrative again clearly begins to resemble the original night scene. 'I sought him but did not find him' repeats the phrase she used in 3.1 and 3.2. She then adds that she 'called him but he did not answer'. Previously in 2.10 he had answered when she had heard her lover (2.8). She has also heard her lover at the beginning of this episode (5.2) where the words '*qol dodi*' appear as they did in 2.8. Presumably the lack of answer has been inserted to make the contrast to the earlier joy of the two lovers even greater.

This would be one of the lowest points of the narrative were it not for the next verse which takes us to a new nadir.

5.7

As in the previous night scene, the guards who roam the city find her. On the previous occasion she asked them whether they had seen her soulmate (3.3); she then passed them by (using the same verb used in the passage just discussed to describe how her lover 'passed' on in 5.6) and found her soulmate. Here that is not allowed to happen as we now find out. At the very least, the guards of the walls beat and assault her. Implied though in the phrase 'they took my shawl off me' might also be that they raped her.

The word for 'wall' here (in Hebrew '*chomah*') has not been used previously and will be adopted by the woman at the end of the Song (8.9-10). It implies the city walls. Previously she used the image of the wall of a building (in Hebrew '*qir*') to describe the walls/beams of the lovers' 'houses' being cedar and the rafters cypresses (1.17). The idyllic use of an architectural term in 1.17 transformed to the (imagined) countryside contrasts sharply with the real wall of the city which forms the location for manhandling, if not rape.

5.8

Any listener to the first four Hebrew words of this verse ('I have made you swear, oh daughters of Jerusalem') would assume that the next words would imitate the exact format already heard twice before (2.7 and 3.5). Indeed at 3.5, it formed the ending of the equivalent night time scene. In fact, this time, we do not get as far as deer and hinds masquerading as God as we did on those two previous occasions. Rather, the adjuration abruptly moves on; she asks that if her lover be found the only thing he should be told is that she is lovesick (echoing her comment directly to him in 2.5).

In the next verse, we see that the daughters of Jerusalem ask her to explain that love. This implies a continuation which is what most commentators see at this stage. As a result of what is set out below, I have chosen to see a break here for what are good structural reasons.

Conclusion - the two night episodes (3.1-5 and 5.2-8)

The two night episodes need to be examined to note the similarities and differences between them.

The similarities seem to be the following:

1. Both episodes start with her alone on her couch at night.

2. They both involve her meeting the male lover.

3. Both end in the city which both episodes view as a negative place.

4. Both scenes end with an adjuration.

The differences between the two scenes can be summarised as follows:

1. The male lover's appearance in the scenes is reversed. In the first episode, she does not have her lover with her at the beginning but she then finds him. In the second episode, he appears at the beginning but then she loses him.

2. In the second, most of the action takes place in her chamber and then moves outside for a short period. In the first, there is only the briefest of references to her couch at night after which she goes out for the rest of the scene.

3. In the first scene, she describes her lover as her 'soulmate' ('*et she-ahavah nafshi*') whereas in the second, he is referred to as exclusively '*dodi*' ('my lover').

4. The two adjuration scenes start the same but veer off into very different places.

5. Above all, in the first episode, because he has yet to say very much, she has scarcely any of his material to use that she can adopt and then adapt to her own use in her poem. The second episode, on the other hand, follows his long description (*wasf*) of her. This allows her to take his language and use it for her own purposes, which she does to full effect in this second episode.

What this analysis has not been able to achieve is a satisfactory answer to the question posed at the beginning of the section concerned with this night scene, namely why there is such an abrupt change of mood - from elation to despair within a few verses. Has he left her for good? Is it all only in her mind? Is it a lovers' tiff? We do not know. These appear to be questions which elude any answer.

There is, however, another important function which the two night time episodes fulfil. One must not just note what these scenes say but also where they fit into the Song of Songs chronologically. The first night time episode occurs after she has described their love (2.8-17). What then follows is the description of Solomon (3.6-11). The second night time episode follows his description of their love and precedes the next scene which, as we will see, is her detailed description of his body. This could be set out as follows:

1. description by her of love (2.8-2.17)

2. first night time episode (3.1-5)

3. description of Solomon (3.6-11)

1. *wasf* description by him of female lover (4.1-5.1)

2. second night time episode (5.2-8)

3. *wasf* description of male lover (5.9-16).

On this basis, there is a structural parallel between the description of Solomon in 3.6-11 and the *wasf* description of the male lover in 5.9-16. They each follow the different night time episodes. This parallel therefore invites not only structural but also literary comparison. What literary comparisons can be made between the description of Solomon in the Solomon interlude in 3.6-11 and the *wasf* description of the male lover in 5.9-16? As we shall shortly see, Solomon is not mentioned expressly in this *wasf*. Yet he pervades it in a number of references.

So we now turn to the *wasf* description by the woman of her male lover. It is the only occasion on which she provides such a full description of her lover's body. Will she compare him or contrast him to Solomon? We are about to find out.

SONG OF SONGS 5.9 - 6.3

Statuesque Royalty

ט מַה־דּוֹדֵךְ מִדּוֹד
הַיָּפָה בַּנָּשִׁים
מַה־דּוֹדֵךְ מִדּוֹד
שֶׁכָּכָה הִשְׁבַּעְתָּנוּ:

The daughters of Jerusalem to her:

**5.9 How is your lover better than another lover,
    most beautiful of women?
How is your lover better than another lover
    for you have made us swear as such?**

It is extremely difficult to render this sentence in English with its original conciseness. The twenty-eight words in this English translation reflects a mere ten in the Hebrew.

In the phrase 'how is your lover better than another lover' (three words in the original repeated), 'better than' could also be rendered 'different from'. Both capture the essence of the particle '*mi-*' in the Hebrew.

The final two words of this verse (rendered in English 'for you have made us swear as such') appear odd in the context of what has immediately gone before. They seem to parallel 5.8 where the female lover has also just made the daughters of Jerusalem swear. But there they had sworn that they would tell her lover, if they encountered him, that she was lovesick. So what is this adjuration all about? When were the daughters of Jerusalem made to swear about the superiority of her lover? This seems to be a different adjuration about which we had not been told previously. How (if at all) this scene links with the previous one thematically is uncertain. As we are about to see, the nature of the question is crucial for the next poem - a *wasf*, describing his body.

The Second *Wasf* - her description of him - and the answer to their question

This verse, therefore, poses a question to the woman. She is not asked merely to describe her lover. Rather, she is asked to do so as a comparison to another - why is he better/different? That context is crucial for what is about to come. She is about to describe his body in the second of the *wasf*s in the Song of Songs; moreover, it is the only one of the *wasf*s in which she describes him. Like his description earlier, there is a method to how she depicts him; her description of his body is from his head down his body, as had been his description of her (4.1-7).

As we go through the description we need to bear in mind that she is answering a comparison question and determine how the nature of the question (tell us why he is better/different) assists us in understanding the *wasf*.

י דּוֹדִי צַח וְאָדוֹם
דָּגוּל מֵרְבָבָה:
יא רֹאשׁוֹ כֶּתֶם פָּז
קְוֻצּוֹתָיו תַּלְתַּלִּים
שְׁחֹרוֹת כָּעוֹרֵב:
יב עֵינָיו כְּיוֹנִים
עַל־אֲפִיקֵי מָיִם
רֹחֲצוֹת בֶּחָלָב
יֹשְׁבוֹת עַל־מִלֵּאת:
יג לְחָיָו כַּעֲרוּגַת הַבֹּשֶׂם
מִגְדְּלוֹת מֶרְקָחִים
שִׂפְתוֹתָיו שׁוֹשַׁנִּים
נֹטְפוֹת מוֹר עֹבֵר:
יד יָדָיו גְּלִילֵי זָהָב
מְמֻלָּאִים בַּתַּרְשִׁישׁ
מֵעָיו עֶשֶׁת שֵׁן
מְעֻלֶּפֶת סַפִּירִים:
טו שׁוֹקָיו עַמּוּדֵי שֵׁשׁ
מְיֻסָּדִים עַל־אַדְנֵי־פָז
מַרְאֵהוּ כַּלְּבָנוֹן
בָּחוּר כָּאֲרָזִים:
טז חִכּוֹ מַמְתַקִּים
וְכֻלּוֹ מַחֲמַדִּים
זֶה דוֹדִי וְזֶה רֵעִי
בְּנוֹת יְרוּשָׁלָ͏ִם:

She speaks:

5.10 My lover is dazzling and red,
**   eminent amongst ten thousand.**
5.11 His head is the finest gold,
**   his locks dangle,**
**   black as a raven.**
5.12 His eyes are like doves
**   at the shore of water,**
washed in milk,
**   sitting in a full pool.**
5.13 His cheeks are like a bed of spice,
**   perfume towers.**
His lips are lilies,
**   dripping flowing myrrh.**
5.14 His hands are rods of gold
**   studded in emerald**
His stomach is a tablet of ivory
**   adorned with sapphires**
5.15 His thighs are marble pillars
**   set on pedestals of fine gold.**
His appearance is like Lebanon,
**   chosen like cedars.**
5.16 His mouth is mellifluous
**   and his all is alluring.**
That is my lover and that is my friend,
**   oh daughters of Jerusalem.**

Many commentators have seen something statuesque[288] in this description by the female lover of her beloved. It is certainly less intimate than his description of her in chapter 4 but that is hardly surprising given that he was speaking to her whereas here she is speaking about him to the daughters of Jerusalem. Others have rejected this, saying that only the head has such statue-like imagery.[289] What is not in dispute is that the use of metals in describing him renders the poem very different from the way he had described her. We need to analyse it in detail to see what conclusions we can draw.

---

[288] Bloch 185, Exum 202.
[289] Fox 1985, 147.

5.10

There is a clear link to King David in this verse. First 'my lover' (in Hebrew '*dodi*') links to 'David' (meaning 'beloved') in Hebrew. Of course, the David link could not be made only if this word were used (given that it is the most common word in the Song of Songs). However, it combines in this verse with other themes which make the link clear. The lover is described as 'red' just as David is described as 'red-like'[290] with beautiful eyes and handsome. Moreover, the word rendered in English as 'ten thousand' (in Hebrew '*revavah*') is crucial in the life of David. It is the word used after his successful battle with the Philistines to describe him: 'And the women who were celebrating answered and they said, "Saul slew by the thousands and David by the ten thousands". And Saul was furious and this matter angered him greatly and he said: "they have given David the ten thousand and me they have given the thousands - shortly they will give him the kingdom". And Saul eyed David warily from that day on.'[291] The link may be subtle but it is also profound and unmistakable. We are put on notice that the comparison to be made is royal.

The word I have rendered as 'eminent' is rare (Alter uses 'standing out') and it is difficult to elicit the exact meaning. It is the same root as appears in 2.4 where I translated it as 'banner'.[292]

5.11

The royal image seems to continue with the description of his head as the finest gold, with its implication of a crown.[293] Yet suddenly the imagery becomes more realistic and enticing and altogether more down to earth. His locks dangle. These locks were referred to in 5.2 when she described him as using this word to refer to his own hair.[294] Moreover, his locks are 'black as a raven'. The compliment she pays to his hair colour here is reminiscent of her comment early on (1.5-6) where she saw her

---

[290] I Samuel 16.12, 17.42

[291] I Samuel 18.7-9

[292] See also commentary on '*nidgalot*' at 6.4 below

[293] The book of Daniel, in one of its Hebrew language visions, has a passage which contains remarkably similar language ('*ketem*' '*ufaz*' '*tarshish*') - Daniel 10.5-6. It suggests that the author of the book of Daniel (which was written after the Song of Songs) was familiar with the Song of Songs or, at the least, the poem from which this passage emanated.

[294] The word I have translated 'dangle' is '*taltalim*' and only appears here. It literally means 'hill-hill'. It follows the word 'locks' ('*qvutzotav*') here. In 5.2, 'locks' appears immediately after the word for 'dew' (in Hebrew '*tal*'). Whilst dew (*tal*) is spelt with a *tet* and *taltaltim* is spelt with a *taf*, there is still an alliteration of sound notwithstanding that modern Hebrew has rendered *tet* and *taf* more similar in pronunciation than they probably sounded at the time.

own black or sun-darkened skin colour as something to be cherished, rather than scorned as accepted norms would have had it. It also contrasts with the red referred to in 5.10. Presumably, therefore, his complexion is red in contrast to his dark hair.[295]

5.12

She describes his eyes as like doves, which is an image he has used of her eyes before (1.15); indeed, it is one of his pet names for her (5.2). She has appropriated it from him as she had not previously availed herself of this comparison. Her geographical location of the doves, though, is completely new - 'at the shore of water'. It is used to describe a gazelle by the water in psalm 42.[296] So the pupils are the doves and the water is the rest of the eye, as the doves 'wash in milk'.

The word '*milleyt*' I have translated as a 'full pool'. It is difficult because it only occurs here in this form. Its root is the idea of fullness and it probably appears in this unusual form to parallel a word with the same root '*memullaim*' in verse 14.

5.13

She then uses imagery from previous poetry. She has not used the image of spice before, which he introduced (4.10,14 and 16), and she now adopts it to describe his cheeks as being like a bed[297] of spices. He has not used spices imagery to describe her cheeks and lips. She now does so whilst again adopting his terminology. They are perfume towers. Previously, he has used the term 'tower' but to describe her neck (4.4). She describes his lips as lilies. He has used 'lilies' in a metaphor for her breasts (4.5). Her lips now drip with flowing myrrh as her hands and fingers had when she opened the door for him in the previous scene (5.5).

5.14-15

The description in the following two verses to describe his hands, stomach and thighs is remarkably full of imagery of fine stones and metal. There seems to be a

---

[295] We are not told whether David's 'red-like' description in I Samuel 16 and 17 is a reference to his hair or his complexion. It is probably to his complexion because, when Esau is similarly described as 'red-like', a direct reference to his hair is made (see Genesis 25.25) which does not exist in either of the David references.

[296] Psalms 42.2.

[297] The word '*arugah*' (bed) is also used in psalm 42 where it means 'yearn' - so that the gazelle yearns for the water shore. Here the word appears shortly after a reference to a water shore. Whether this confluence of words is coincidental or not is impossible to tell.

dichotomy between the stones on the one hand and the mainly metal elements on the other. The two stones mentioned, '*tarshish*' (which I have translated as 'emerald') and '*sapirim*' (sapphires), both appear in the tabernacle described in the desert in the book of Exodus.[298] The metals, on the other hand, seem deliberately to imitate wording described in Solomon's temple and palace. His hands are described as 'rods' of gold - as were the supports to the doors in the temple.[299] The words 'ivory' (in Hebrew '*shen*') and 'fine gold' ('*paz*') used to describe his stomach and thighs are two words very rarely used in the Bible which had both been used to describe Solomon's throne: 'And the king made a great throne of ivory which he inlaid with the finest gold'.[300] Added to this is the fact that his thighs are marble pillars - a word associated with both the tabernacle and the temple.[301]

The body, Solomon and Lebanon

We have thereby been put on notice that appearances are deceptive. This may be a *wasf* but it is a *wasf* with a symbolic meaning. The references to images associated with power and King Solomon are deliberately used in this description of the male lover. There even seems to be a hint of King David as explained in 5.10 above. The female lover seems to be telling us that he may just be her lover but he can be compared favourably to anyone including kings of Israel.

Her reference in 5.15b to his 'appearance is like Lebanon, chosen like cedars' therefore must be understood in two ways. First, cedars in Lebanon were known to be tall and his height could therefore be compared to them. But the Lebanon and the cedars, with which the author of the Song of Songs would probably have been familiar, were those in Jerusalem used by Solomon for the temple and his palace. Given the other explicit references in this *wasf* to items built for Solomon, the comparison seems highly likely. Moreover, this is another example of the cross-fertilisation of vocabulary between the two lovers. This is her first use of the term 'Lebanon' though she has used 'cedar' to describe the lovers' own house (1.17), a word with similar connotations of both the North and Jerusalem. He used the term 'Lebanon' extensively in his own *wasf* (4.8, 4.11 and 4.15). Indeed, he played on its similarity with the sound of the Hebrew word for 'frankincense' ('*levonah*') and heart ('*libavtini*').

---

[298] Exodus 28.20 (*tarshish*), 28.18 (*sapirim*).

[299] I Kings 6.34 (*gelilim*).

[300] I Kings 10.18.

[301] The words went on to have a further royal connection in Esther 1.6. The book of Esther is almost certainly a later book and so could not have influenced the Song of Songs.

In her adopting the term 'Lebanon' with its implication of the temple and palace, we now see the degree to which the lovers intermingle each other's vocabulary. It is a vocabulary which she uses here to invite comparison between her lover and 'Lebanon' (i.e. the temple and palace). In so doing, with the surrounding vocabulary in the *wasf* expressly using language taken from the temple context, we realise that the female lover is comparing her lover to a cedar and, above all, to 'Lebanon'. We are beginning to realise that the reader of the Song of Songs is being invited to share this secret lovers' language. The irony is that it is not their own language originally; 'Lebanon' was an idea introduced by the narrator in 3.9 to describe Solomon's 'palanquin'. It now forms part of the lovers' story.

The word I have translated 'chosen' (in Hebrew '*bachur*') also means 'young man'. It appears to have been carefully selected since both meanings apply. He is both a young lad which renders him tall as the cedars but there is also an element of chosenness about him - certainly in her eyes.

5.16

It is almost impossible to capture in English the beautiful alliteration in the Hebrew words '*chikko mamtaqqim vechullo machamaddim*'. 'His mouth is mellifluous and his all is alluring' is my attempt at it. Literally it translates as 'his mouth is sweet and his whole is desirable'.

The final line of the poem, telling the daughters of Jerusalem that this is my lover and this is my friend, clearly serves the purpose of providing a snapshot answer to the question posed at its beginning.

It is at this stage that we need to ask what the purpose of this *wasf* is. A *wasf* is commonly understood to be a description of the lover's body in poetic form. The issue that we face is that the question to which the answer is 'this is my lover' (5.16) was not 'please describe the body of your lover' but, as we saw from verse 5.9, a question asking something else - 'please tell us why your lover is better than/or different from another lover'. It is crucial to understanding the full meaning of this *wasf* to appreciate that this is the nature of the question to which the *wasf* is the response.

This therefore means that a mere description does not suffice. To describe is not to compare or, indeed, to assert difference in any way. In using the *wasf* form, the description is express and transparent but, hidden behind the layers of description, are references to both David and Solomon. Within the context of a poem which compares and contrasts the lovers favourably with all others, this *wasf* is clearly part of that ongoing theme.

However, its location within the structure of the Song of Songs is also important. I discussed the issue of location after considering the second night scene (5.2-8). As I said, the first night scene (3.1-5) is followed by the longest explicit, direct reference to Solomon and his temple-like 'palanquin' (3.6-11). As we can now appreciate, the second night scene is also followed by a reference to Solomon - this time transformed into references from his history transposed onto the male lover's body. For her, he is becoming Solomon but a superior version to the original. That is how she answers the daughters of Jerusalem's comparison question.

א אָנָה הָלַךְ דּוֹדֵךְ
הַיָּפָה בַּנָּשִׁים
אָנָה פָּנָה דוֹדֵךְ
וּנְבַקְשֶׁנּוּ עִמָּךְ:
ב דּוֹדִי יָרַד לְגַנּוֹ
לַעֲרֻגוֹת הַבֹּשֶׂם
לִרְעוֹת בַּגַּנִּים
וְלִלְקֹט שׁוֹשַׁנִּים:
ג אֲנִי לְדוֹדִי וְדוֹדִי לִי
הָרֹעֶה בַּשׁוֹשַׁנִּים:

The daughters of Jerusalem to her:

6.1 Where has your lover gone,
**   most beautiful of women**
Where has your lover turned,
**   so that we make seek him with you?**

She replies to them:

6.2 My lover has gone down to his garden
**   to the spice beds**
To pasture in the gardens
**   and to gather lilies.**
6.3 I am my lover's and my lover is mine,
**   who pastures in the lilies.**

The daughters of Jerusalem now ask the female lover a 'where' question about her lover. This is noteworthy because it appears to have little to do with, or possibly even ignores, the previous erotically charged description of the lover that they have just heard.

While it may show a desire on the part of the daughters of Jerusalem to hunt for the lover, it links more naturally to the issue of finding him which we considered in the second night scene (5.2-8). The problem however is that, in that episode, it was she who was asking the daughters of Jerusalem to say, if they saw him, that she was lovesick. Previously, she had sought him. Now they are prepared to assist her in seeking him.

Her answer to their question implies that she knows where he is but that they do not. This does not sit easily with what we heard in the night scene. We seem to have moved on. Of course, if we read the Song of Songs literally, this appears as a (probably insoluble) contradiction. There is no need to seek to resolve any such contradiction. To see a clear plot in what is a series of episodes has been the aim of too many commentators over the centuries. We live in an age, post Eliot, Pound and Celan, which has accepted fragmentation as part of poetic discourse. There is an obvious element of fantasy in the Song of Songs and a realistic resolution is not necessary.

Rather, we should examine the poetic beauty in what has been written. These three verses comprise five bi-cola lines (which I have sought to reflect in the translation). 6.1 comprises the question of the daughters of Jerusalem and consists of two lines. Her answer is in 6.2 and also comprises two lines. 6.3 is then her joyous summation at the end.

The subtlety and beauty of the original is difficult to reflect in translation. The first word of each of the first four lines is 'where' (in Hebrew '*ana*' 6.1a), 'where' ('*ana*' 6.1b), 'my lover' ('*dodi*' 6.2a) and 'to pasture' ('*lir'ot*' 6.2b). The poet takes these four words, changes '*ana*' to '*ani*' (meaning 'I') and appropriates them in 6.3 as the basis of the final fifth line. The lilies ('*shoshanim*') at the end of the line reflect its use as the final word in 6.2b.

As before, words used previously are adopted. His cheeks were a 'bed of spice' (5.13). He now goes down to the beds of spice in his garden (also echoing the garden motif which he had brought in in 4.12 and following the language in 4.16).

The episode therefore ends with harmony between the lovers. We have been told that the lover has been identified with Solomon, or, rather, a better version of Solomon than the historical one. In the next episode, 'Solomon' will again describe her.

SONGS OF SONGS 6.4 - 6.12

She is One

6.4 - 6.10

ד יָפָה אַתְּ רַעְיָתִי כְּתִרְצָּה
נָאוָה כִּירוּשָׁלָ͏ֶם
אֲיֻמָּה כַּנִּדְגָּלוֹת:
ה הָסֵבִּי עֵינַ֫יִךְ מִנֶּגְדִּי
שֶׁהֵם הִרְהִיבֻנִי
שַׂעְרֵךְ כְּעֵדֶר הָעִזִּים
שֶׁגָּלְשׁוּ מִן־הַגִּלְעָד:
ו שִׁנַּ֫יִךְ כְּעֵדֶר הָרְחֵלִים
שֶׁעָלוּ מִן־הָרַחְצָה
שֶׁכֻּלָּם מַתְאִימוֹת
וְשַׁכֻּלָה אֵין בָּהֶם:
ז כְּפֶלַח הָרִמּוֹן רַקָּתֵךְ
מִבַּעַד לְצַמָּתֵךְ:
ח שִׁשִּׁים הֵמָּה מְלָכוֹת
וּשְׁמֹנִים פִּילַגְשִׁים
וַעֲלָמוֹת אֵין מִסְפָּר:
ט אַחַת הִיא יוֹנָתִי תַמָּתִי
אַחַת הִיא לְאִמָּהּ
בָּרָה הִיא לְיוֹלַדְתָּהּ
רָאוּהָ בָנוֹת וַיְאַשְּׁרוּהָ
מְלָכוֹת וּפִילַגְשִׁים וַיְהַלְלוּהָ:
י מִי־זֹאת הַנִּשְׁקָפָה כְּמוֹ־שָׁחַר
יָפָה כַלְּבָנָה
בָּרָה כַּחַמָּה
אֲיֻמָּה כַּנִּדְגָּלוֹת:

He speaks to her

**6.4 You are beautiful, my beloved, like Tirtzah,
        lovely like Jerusalem,
                fearsome as stars.
6.5 Turn your eyes away from me**

since they have overwhelmed me.
Your hair is like a flock of goats
    which has cascaded from the Gilead.
6.6 Your teeth are like a flock of ewes
    that have gone up from being washed.
All are twinned
    and none are barren.
6.7 Like a pomegranate slice is your palate
    through your veil.
6.8 Sixty are the queens,
    and eighty the concubines
        and the young maids are without number.
6.9 She is one - my dove, my perfect one;
    she is one to her mother,
        radiant to her who gave birth to her
The daughters saw her and were happy about her,
    queens and concubines praised her.
6.10 Who is this observed looking like the dawn,
    beautiful as the moon,
radiant as the sun,
    fearsome as the stars.

6.4

The comparisons for her beauty now range from places such as Tirtzah (capital of the Northern Kingdom until the time of King Omri,)[302] to Jerusalem and then the phrase ending with the word '*nidgalot*' which I have translated as 'stars'. Various proposals have been made for its translation: 'most eminent' (Fox) 'splendour' (Exum) 'on high' (Alter) and 'stars in their courses' (Blochs). The word appears again at the end of verse 10 where its context implies a planet - hence the translation here as 'stars'. As Alter notes, its root does not imply a star[303] so this (or indeed any) translation remains problematic. Its normal meaning is a banner or flag and has already appeared twice in 2.8 (where it meant 'banner') and 5.10 (where it meant 'eminent' or 'standing out').

---

[302] I Kings 16.23.
[303] Alter 2015, 37.

6.5a

Is this another tease? Or perhaps it is a compliment. He asks her to turn her eyes away - they overwhelm him. The context of this comment is revealing. The lines which follow (6.5b-7) largely repeat 4.1b-3 (as discussed below). The previous version of these lines was itself preceded by the words 'your eyes are doves through your veil' (4.1a). Whilst both introductions contain references to 'eyes', this introduction here is very different - it seems like a tease or compliment or, possibly, both!

6.5b - 7 (Repetition of a fragment of the first *wasf*)

These verses repeat 4.1b-3 but contain a few minor differences. In 1b it was 'mount' Gilead. In 4.2 the flock was 'shorn'; here we find that it is a flock of ewes. Verse 4.3a is wholly omitted ('like a thread of crimson are your lips and your speech is wonderful'). It is not clear that these differences are significant. What may be much more significant is that this fragment exists at all. I discuss its implications at the end of this section.

6.8 - 6.9

The obvious comparison is here being made between the one and perfect lover and the sixty queens, eighty concubines and young maidens without number. Many have made the link with Solomon and argued that this is a reference to his wives. If one takes this literally according to the Biblical account of his relationships with women, then it cannot work. Solomon proverbially had a thousand wives; they are described in I Kings 11.3 as 'seven hundred princesses and three hundred concubines'. Whilst the numbers do not tally, the sentiment clearly does. The link to King Solomon is invited by this reference. Moreover, the number 'sixty' has a significance from within the Song of Songs itself; it is the same as the number of guards who guarded Solomon from fear of the night in 3.7. Let us also not forget the immediate context of this comment about the sixty queens. The female lover has just told the daughters of Jerusalem why her lover is so much better than any other. Within that context, it is clear that the male lover, having been compared by her favourably to all other lovers, responds in kind. Sixty guards and sixty wives may be what Solomon needs but I have my one and only love whom the daughters, queens and concubines praise.

Two phrases in this sentence recall the tension of the two night episodes which now seem to have been resolved.

First, in 5.2, she quotes him as asking her to open up to her and he uses the words 'my dove, my perfect one' (in Hebrew '*yonati, tammati*'). The night scene ended with her losing him. Here he uses exactly the same phraseology in circumstances where they are now together.

Second, he describes her here as 'one to her mother, radiant to her who gave birth to her'. The reference to her mother reminds one of the first night scene in 3.4 where she says that she will not let him go until 'I have brought him to my mother's house, to the chamber of my parent'. The implication of his comment to her referring to her mother is that, whilst she may not have succeeded in physically bringing him to her mother's house, that was hardly the true purpose of the comment in 3.4. In effect she has succeeded in winning him, which was her real motive.

6.10

He now portrays her as looking like the dawn. This recalls her own description of herself (1.5-6) where she had depicted herself as 'black' and then added 'do not see me as dawn-darkened'. The word '*shachar*' meaning 'dawn', as mentioned in the commentary to 1.5-6, is closely linked to the word '*shachor*' (meaning 'black'). This meaning comes to the fore in this context where she is described as being 'beautiful as the moon'. The poetic word for 'moon' used is '*levanah*'. Its primary meaning is 'white' meaning that images of black and white in relation to her description are clearly implied. Hinted at in the sound of the Hebrew word '*levanah*' is, of course, the word '*levanon*' ('Lebanon'). She had described his appearance as 'like Lebanon, chosen like cedars' (5.15). Now in comparing her to the moon with a word sounding so similar, the implication is that he is returning the compliment in this subtle reference to what she had previously said.

The four descriptions of her in this verse relate to dawn, moon, sun and what are probably stars (see discussion above at 6.4). He has described her body from the top down. He has now chosen to end his depiction with similes which all appear in the sky. In one fell swoop, his gaze moves up to the heavens where her beauty is now located for him.

יא אֶל־גִּנַּת אֱגוֹז יָרַדְתִּי
לִרְאוֹת בְּאִבֵּי הַנָּחַל
לִרְאוֹת הֲפָרְחָה הַגֶּפֶן
הֵנֵצוּ הָרִמֹּנִים:
יב לֹא יָדַעְתִּי נַפְשִׁי
שָׂמַתְנִי מַרְכְּבוֹת עַמִּי נָדִיב:

He speaks?

6.11 I went down to the walnut garden
**   to see the buds of the stream.**
To see whether the vine has bloomed,
**   whether the pomegranates have blossomed**
6.12 I did not know myself;
**   she placed me in lavish chariots.**

These two verses fit neither with the previous verses nor with what follows and therefore the consensus amongst commentators, that they are a fragment, seems correct. It is also not clear who is speaking. I am tentatively suggesting that it is the male lover, given that he raised the issue of the garden in the first place. On the other hand, given the degree to which the two lovers adopt each other's terminology, an opposite view is certainly plausible.

The word for 'walnut' appears only here in the Bible so its translation is conjectural and based on later Jewish tradition (the word is popularly used in modern Hebrew for a 'nut').

6.12 has proved problematic for all commentators. The Masoretic text punctuates it in a way entirely different from the manner in which I have translated it above as I do not feel able to follow the traditional version. The verse literally reads: 'I did not know myself, she placed me chariots my people noble'. The final two Hebrew words *'ami nadiv'* make little sense. The reverse wording *'nedivei am'* is frequent in the Bible and means 'nobles of the people'. Alter suggests emending the plural 'chariots' to singular and therefore arguing that the reference to 'chariot[s]' is in fact a reference to her body.[304] There is no obviously flawless solution but in the context of two ordinary lovers, who see their love as special and above that of those of royal birth, the suggestion makes eminent sense.

Conclusion

Much of the material in these nine verses is fragmentary in nature. At one stage, as noted, it repeats almost verbatim lines seen previously (6.5b-7) where they formed part of the first *wasf* description of the female lover's body. The final verses refer to material which appears to be much better integrated later on. So, for example, the

---

[304] Alter 2015, 40.

difficult reference in 6.12 to '*nadiv*' ('noble') reappears in 7.2 where its context allows us to understand it far more clearly. Similarly, the words 'whether the vine has bloomed, whether the pomegranates have blossomed' in 6.11 are repeated later in 7.13. The context in the latter case (going to the field and the vineyards) seems to fit the context much better than going to the budding of the stream as referred to here.

But it is, I think, the repetition of the fragment of the first *wasf* at 6.5b-7 which is most revealing. What I am about to suggest must be pure conjecture but there nevertheless seems to have been a recognition on the part of the author/editor, when inserting this passage, that the two *wasf*s which we have already considered (at 4.1-7 and 5.10-16) were not sufficient. We still retain this fragment at 6.5b-7, indicating that a further description of the female body was required. Perhaps this fragment formed a rough draft or a reminder that more was required. We cannot be sure. The reason that this supposition has merit is that we are about to encounter the final *wasf*, containing a new description, where he again depicts her body, largely (but not entirely) free of the sentiments contained in the first *wasf*.

But we have learnt that, in this great work, no material is free of the influence of what has gone before. We have progressed in the Song of Songs and our male lover has more material to adapt to his new-found willingness to articulate how wonderful she is, as we shall now see. And he has even found a new pet name for her which he is about to reveal.

SONGS OF SONGS 7.1 - 7.14

The Shulamite

The third and final *wasf*

א שׁוּבִי שׁוּבִי֙ הַשּׁוּלַמִּ֔ית
שׁוּבִי שׁוּבִי וְנֶחֱזֶה־בָּ֑ךְ
מַה־תֶּחֱזוּ֙ בַּשּׁוּלַמִּ֔ית כִּמְחֹלַ֖ת הַֽמַּחֲנָֽיִם:
ב מַה־יָּפ֧וּ פְעָמַ֛יִךְ בַּנְּעָלִ֖ים
בַּת־נָדִ֑יב
חַמּוּקֵ֣י יְרֵכַ֔יִךְ
כְּמ֣וֹ חֲלָאִ֔ים
מַעֲשֵׂ֖ה יְדֵ֥י אָמָּֽן:
ג שָׁרְרֵךְ֙ אַגַּ֣ן הַסַּ֔הַר
אַל־יֶחְסַ֖ר הַמָּ֑זֶג
בִּטְנֵךְ֙ עֲרֵמַ֣ת חִטִּ֔ים
סוּגָ֖ה בַּשּׁוֹשַׁנִּֽים:
ד שְׁנֵ֥י שָׁדַ֛יִךְ
כִּשְׁנֵ֥י עֳפָרִ֖ים
תָּאֳמֵ֥י צְבִיָּֽה:
ה צַוָּארֵ֖ךְ כְּמִגְדַּ֣ל הַשֵּׁ֑ן
עֵינַ֣יִךְ בְּרֵכ֣וֹת בְּחֶשְׁבּ֗וֹן עַל־שַׁ֙עַר֙ בַּת־רַבִּ֔ים
אַפֵּךְ֙ כְּמִגְדַּ֣ל הַלְּבָנ֔וֹן צוֹפֶ֖ה פְּנֵ֥י דַמָּֽשֶׂק:
ו רֹאשֵׁ֤ךְ עָלַ֙יִךְ֙ כַּכַּרְמֶ֔ל
וְדַלַּ֥ת רֹאשֵׁ֖ךְ כָּאַרְגָּמָ֑ן
מֶ֖לֶךְ אָס֥וּר בָּרְהָטִֽים:
ז מַה־יָּפִית֙ וּמַה־נָּעַ֔מְתְּ
אַהֲבָ֖ה בַּתַּֽעֲנוּגִֽים:

He speaks to her:

7.1 Again, again, the Shulamite,
　　　again, again so that we can see you.
What will we see in the Shulamite, like the dance of the two camps?
7.2 How beautiful are your feet in shoes,
　　　daughter of a noble.
The curves of your thighs

are like jewels,
      the handiwork of a craftsman.
7.3 Your navel is a crescent moon goblet,
      never lacking mixed wine.
Your stomach is a heap of wheat,
      surrounded by lilies.
7.4 Your two breasts
      are like two deer,
         twin gazelles.
7.5 Your neck is like a tower of ivory,
your eyes are pools in Heshbon by the gate of Bat Rabbim.
Your nose is like the Lebanon tower overlooking Damascus.
7.6 Your head on you is like Carmel
      and the locks of your head are like purple,
         a king is bound up in the curls.
7.7 How beautiful and wondrous you are,
      love amongst pleasures.

7.1

The reference to 'the Shulamite' (in Hebrew '*ha-shulamit*') is both striking and, at first sight, perplexing. Striking in that the reference is introduced for the first time in this verse. Perplexing because this verse is the only occasion when the word is used in the Bible. I will shortly analyse its role which I consider crucial to the literary narrative of the Song of Songs. In order to do so, we must start by considering, and weighing up, the various meanings attributed to the word. Those meanings can only provide hints as to what is intended, given the chasm between our time and when the Song was written. Hopefully, though, they will assist us in understanding it and provide a launchpad for an analysis.[305]

First, we have to ask whether the word is a proper name or not. It is feminine in form. The modern Hebrew name '*Shulamit*' clearly derives from here but, as it appears only twice in the Bible, and both times in this verse, it may well not have been a proper name in the conventional sense, given that '*Shulamit*' is preceded by the letter '*he-*' indicating 'the'. If it is not a name, then what could it be? Perhaps it

---

[305] I acknowledge here my indebtedness to Michael V Fox's analysis - see Fox 1985, 157. As will be seen in what follows, I seek to build on it.

is some sort of title? Or the reference could be to a place called 'Shulem' from which the woman being spoken to originates?

Second, we have to ask who is being addressed? Is 'the Shulamite' being identified with the female lover who, after all, has just been addressed by her lover at the end of chapter 6? Or is this some sort of dance being enacted by someone else who is being spoken to?

These are of course questions which have been addressed by many commentators over the centuries and no consensus has emerged. It is worth considering some of the theories because, in so doing, we should be able to form clearer views of how this reference is intended to play out within the context of the Song of Songs.

The meaning of 'the Shulamite'

The first suggestion is that the reference to the 'Shulamite' should be to the 'Shunamite' involving the changing of just one letter in the Hebrew original, as in the English. This argument is based on the proposition that, since the word 'Shulamite' occurs nowhere else other than here in the Bible, it must be incorrect and therefore needs to be replaced by a similar sounding word, appearing more frequently. There is no place called 'Shulem' in the Bible but the place name 'Shunem' appears three times.[306] It was a town in the territory belonging to the tribe of Issachar. The first two references in the Bible are passing. The third reference, in II Kings 4.8, is more substantial; it is the place where Elisha performs miracles for a Shunamite woman. Yet there is no clear connection with the Song of Songs or the life of Solomon.

Much more obviously linked is that David's servant, Avishag, is only ever described as 'Avishag the Shunamite'. She appeared in one scene when David was old in order to warm him but did not have sexual relations with him.[307] In the second scene, as we saw in chapter 2 above, Adonijah, the defeated pretender to the crown, requested Avishag the Shunamite as his wife from the newly anointed King Solomon. He did so via Bathsheba. As we saw in chapter 3 above, this was almost certainly an attempt by Bathsheba to goad her son into killing a potential threat to his kingdom, an attempt which proved to be entirely successful.[308] However, it is difficult to see how these references are being used in the Song of Songs. Neither Shunem nor Avishag the Shunamite seem to have any other role in the Song of Songs. Given also that the

---

[306] Joshua 19.18, I Samuel 28.4, II Kings 4.8.

[307] I Kings 1.1-4.

[308] I Kings 2.16-25.

amendment would involve changing the text by one letter, one ought to reject such a proposal for the purpose of what now appears to be reading in an implausible meaning.

Another suggestion is that the war goddess 'Shulmanitu' has been confused and combined with the more common name 'Shunamite' to create the word 'Shulamite'.[309] Whilst the word 'Shulamite' certainly has an air of mystery about it, it seems far-fetched, in the extreme, to explain it as an incorrectly written name for a war goddess who otherwise plays no role in the Song of Songs. Again this suggestion ought to be rejected.

There are at least two other, much more plausible, explanations for the reference to 'the Shulamite'. The first focuses on the meaning of the word. Its root is *sh-l-m* which obviously means 'peace' as in '*shalom*'; however, the root also signifies 'completion' 'wholeness' and 'perfection'. Michael Fox's suggestion is therefore that the word is to be translated 'O perfect one'. This translation has the advantage over the other two discussed above in that it involves neither an emendation of the text nor any implication that its author has in some way incorrectly set out the name of a war goddess. Moreover, it fits perfectly into the text. The implication of 'perfection' or 'completeness' is exactly how the male lover has described his beloved previously, even if he has not used this particular term before to express the sentiment. '*Ha-shulamite*' could therefore, on this basis, be translated as 'perfect one' or 'complete one'.

The second possible meaning argues that the word '*ha-shulamit*' derives from the name Solomon and is, as it were, its female form. Solomon in Hebrew is '*Shlomoh*'. The alternative female form '*Shlomit*' appears elsewhere twice in the Bible.[310] On both occasions, the reference is fleeting and seems to bear no relation to Solomon. On this occasion, however, in a song which is expressly stated to be about Solomon, a reference to its female form, however fleeting, cannot be so easily dismissed. Given the number of direct and indirect references to Solomon in the text, this female form must therefore be significant.

It seems to me that the choice made by many commentators as to whether the meaning here is 'oh perfect one' or a female version of Solomon is a false dichotomy. The two meanings work perfectly together side by side and consequently there is no need to decide between them. To make a choice between

---

[309] William F Albright: 'Archaic Survivals in the Text of Canticles'. In *'Hebrew and Semitic Studies presented to G.R.Driver'*. Oxford: Clarendon 1 - 7, quoted Fox (1985) 157.
[310] Leviticus 24.11, I Chronicles 3.19.

the two implies that the author could not work with more than one meaning; given the sophistication of the entire work, that is a proposition which ought to be rejected. The name Solomon means 'perfection' and, as with all Hebrew names, the Bible is perfectly willing to play with the original derivation of a name when it suits its purpose. As we will see later in the Song of Songs, the text does exactly that - to devastatingly withering effect on the image of Solomon.[311]

Moreover, we have not discussed another possible meaning of the word; namely, that it is in addition a reference to Jerusalem, literally 'the city of peace' or 'the city of perfection'. Jerusalem occurs frequently in the Song of Songs - directly through the reference to the daughters of Jerusalem. But it is also probably the city in which the female lover roams in the two night scenes. To accept this possible meaning should not involve a rejection of the other meanings. Indeed, they all play on the root *sh-l-m*.

An interesting feature of 'the daughters of Jerusalem' and 'Solomon' as explained by Segal is that they both appear seven times in the Song of Songs.[312] Use of a word seven times seems to be a frequent Biblical technique to indicate perfection but of course such a number indicates little unless the number of appearances parallels the context. That is clearly the case here. The Solomon being described here as '*ha-shulamit*' is perfection indeed - in contrast to the historical one.

The conclusion one ought to reach regarding the enigmatic reference to 'the Shulamite' is therefore that only one English rendering fails to capture the nuance and ambiguity of the original. In not being a person's name (by using the Hebrew letter '*he*' ['the']), the reference is to 'the perfect one'. But the obvious link with Solomon also, paradoxically, does lend the word a quasi proper name status. It is as if this is not her real name but has been given to her, as a term of affection.

The reference to 'the Shulamite' is therefore packed with layers of meaning which need to be revealed. We are about to embark on considering the third *wasf*. 'The Shulamite' also has a clear structural purpose which can only be clearly appreciated once the *wasf* is complete. This will be considered at that stage.

---

[311] See commentary below on 8.10-11.
[312] Segal, 152.

Who is being addressed?

So far we have focused exclusively on one word in 7.1. We now need to examine it in the context of the rest of the verse to see whether we can come to a conclusion as to who 'the Shulamite' is. That is difficult. The context is dancing again and again like the 'dance of the two camps'. The exact meaning of this phrase eludes us. 'Two camps' ('*machanayim*' in Hebrew) is the word used by Jacob to describe the camp where he encountered God.[313] Alter takes the word and proposes 'two rows'[314] - presumably some form of communal dance.

On the basis of this verse alone, it is highly likely that the male lover is addressing the female lover. He has just said that she is one/unique (6.9) and, if Alter is correct that this is some sort of communal dance, then he appears to be showing off his lover. He wants everyone to gaze lovingly at her as she dances. The imagery of a communal dance also seems to fit the context. In 6.8 he had compared her to sixty queens, eighty concubines and maidens without number. Here he is asking his companions to admire her uniqueness within the context of a communal dance.

We do not know (and indeed are never told) her real name but I would suggest that the best way to understand 'the Shulamite' reference is that this is his pet name for her. We should never lose the linguistic derivation of the word 'Solomon' in attributing this meaning. He is therefore openly referring to her as a female version of Solomon. By saying that she is a female 'Solomon' (which could mean Solomon's lover in this loose poetic terminology) he also implies that she is whole, complete and perfect, given the root meaning of the word '*sh-l-m*'.

Let us not forget the context for this new pet name. In her previous *wasf* description of him, she deliberately incorporated temple and royal imagery, associated with King Solomon, into her depiction of his body (5.10-16). In both cases, of course, the implication is not that each lover is like Solomon. Rather the context each time implies that those lovers are better than the original version.

It is at this point, when seeing how wonderfully his lover dances, that he decides to describe her again. We noted that 7.1 refers to her being seen by many others. So when he addresses her now, he does so within the circumstances of what looks like a social occasion - rather than an intimate encounter under a tree or in the hills.

---

[313] Genesis 32.2.
[314] Alter 2015, 41, following Bloch, 199.

That, then, is the immediate context in which this the third, and final, *wasf* commences. It is also different from the other two *wasf*s in that it describes her body from the ground up, whereas the previous two *wasf*s had started with the head and worked their way down. Perhaps it is because we have been presented here with the image of a dance that the male lover first describes his female 'Solomon' by considering her feet.

7.2

Some (but unfortunately not all) of the mystery in the Song of Songs can be overcome by revealing the Solomon comparison which the lovers make so often. Perhaps he has not seen her in shoes until he sees her dancing - leading to this comment about her beauty in shoes. The reference to her being a 'daughter of a noble' of course may not be true of his real lover but that is scarcely the point. To him, she is just as noble as Solomon's wife (the first of whom, we know was the daughter of Pharaoh[315]) and so, the reference makes perfect sense in context. It also assists us in understanding the 'noble' reference in 6.12 which, nevertheless, still presents formidable difficulties.

He then proceeds to describe the 'curves' of her thighs. The word he uses ('*chamuqei*') is one referred to previously. It only appears twice in the Bible - both in the Song of Songs - and the other appearance is at 5.6 where she used it to describe the 'turn' her lover made to leave her and the concern which that engendered. That is now forgotten as he adopts her word and uses it, in a wholly positive light, to describe her curvaceousness. The notion that her curvaceous thighs remind him of jewels and then of 'the handiwork of a craftsman' may also have the resonance of the handiwork of the temple. 'Handiwork' consists of two Hebrew words - '*ma'aseh*' ('work') and '*yedei*' ('hands of'). There are a number of Hebrew words for 'work'; the word chosen is the one used for both Bezalel[316] in the tabernacle and Hiram[317] in the temple, for their creative talent. That is the context here; her body is also the handiwork of a craftsman. It is only a hint, but the male lover may be picking up her far more overt reference to temple/royal vocabulary in her description of him (5.6-10).

---

[315] I Kings 3.1.
[316] e.g. Exodus 39.8.
[317] e.g. I Kings 7.17.

7.3

The words in the first part of this verse describing her navel have never previously appeared in the Song of Songs and thereby introduce new imagery. The reference, though, to the 'crescent moon' (in Hebrew '*hasahar*') reminds one of the previous use of such imagery in 6.10 where he described her as 'beautiful as the moon' and used a different word ('*levanah*') for moon. Whether 'sometimes a navel is just a navel' as Alter has it,[318] or whether other parts of the body are intended remains, of course, ambiguous and for the reader to interpret.

The lilies surrounding the heap of wheat which comprise her stomach are also interesting. The tops of the pillars in the temple were lily handiwork[319] - thereby consisting of the word for 'work' ('*ma'aseh*' as before) in 7.2 and the word for 'lilies' (in Hebrew '*shoshanim*') in 7.3. The author of the Song of Songs may have wanted to alert us to the temple link by carving, as it were, these temple images onto the female lover's body. We cannot be sure: to misquote Alter (misquoting Freud), 'sometimes a lily is just a lily'! Yet the fact that the image in both cases consists of lilies does beg the question whether, in the context of a poem so full of Solomonic imagery, a deliberate analogy was being made.

7.4

The first *wasf* in making its way down the female body described the breasts in exactly the same form at 4.5. The two *wasf*s meet, as it were, at this point. Apart from minor vowel changes to one word, with no impact on meaning, 7.4 parallels 4.5 in every other respect. From now on, a number of the parts of her body have been previously described. We therefore have comparison points to compare them and to see how each *wasf* differs.

7.5

He proceeds to compare her neck to an ivory tower. Previously her neck had been compared to 'the tower of David built on turrets' (4.4a). The image stops here abruptly; commentators have suggested that a further description of the ivory tower is missing. The 'ivory' imagery is an adoption by him of her description in 6.14 of his stomach as a tablet of ivory. That had clear royal references as discussed in the

---

[318] Alter 2015, 42.
[319] I Kings 7.22.

commentary at that point. We do not know whether what is missing may have been a clearer, royal link.

When we look at the description of the eyes, we see how the imagery has developed in the three *wasf*s. The eyes are described in all three. In 4.1 he describes her eyes as doves, an image he had also used previously (1.15). In the second *wasf* she also describes his eyes as doves but then introduces a water metaphor - they are doves at the edge of water (5.12). On this occasion the dove has disappeared but the water imagery is pursued. Now her eyes are pools in Heshbon. In so doing the author is playing with the double meaning of the word 'eye'. In Hebrew the word '*ayin*' ('eye') is identical to the word for 'fountain' or 'spring'. So 'your eyes' implies something entirely natural about the eyes when being referred to in the context of a pool. Heshbon was located in Moab and, whilst known for its vineyards (see Isaiah 16.8 where the vineyards are withered), no reference to its pools has otherwise been left to us in Biblical literature. Either this is an image made up by the poet or, as seems more likely, it was a reference familiar to readers at that time.[320]

Having been told that her eyes are in Heshbon, we are now informed that they are located at the gate of Bat Rabbim. The name is unfamiliar, except for this reference - so how should we understand it? Most commentators have sought to identify it with another name for Heshbon. It means 'daughter of many' or 'daughter of great ones'. So what is it doing here? Inevitably any answer is not merely geographical in a poem layered with so many meanings. Bat Rabbim also serves a literary purpose within the context of the Song of Songs as a comparison to the description of her in 7.2 as '*bat nadiv*' ('the daughter of a noble'). As such, the extra name for Heshbon doubles as another compliment to her. Her spring-like eyes make her an important person.

He now describes her nose. This constitutes a break in the upward description of her body. Why does the nose follow the eyes? Perhaps the eyes are more enticing, or perhaps he sees the face as one whole and describes it together (though no such reasoning has been needed before where a strict order has been followed).[321] This is

---

[320] For another wordplay on eyes/spring, see Genesis 38.14 where Tamar waits for Judah at '*petach aynaim*'. This means both 'the entrance to the two springs' which is its physical location and 'opening of the eyes' which is exactly what Tamar proceeds to do to Judah to show him the error of his ways.

[321] A somewhat unlikely proposal to resolve the conundrum is that, in 1.16, she had told him 'behold you are beautiful, even handsome'. The word in Hebrew for the English 'even' is '*af*' whose other meaning is 'nose'. Thereby she also describes him as having a handsome nose. This would be of little relevance were it not for the fact that, immediately prior to this, he had described her eyes as doves (1.15). In other words, the order of eyes and nose mirrors the previous hidden reference. Such radical suggestions of course are rarely promoted above the purgatory of footnotes!

the first use of the word '*af*' ('nose') in the Song of Songs. It reappears later in this poem (7.9).[322]

Her nose is like the Lebanon tower overlooking Damascus. Given the use of Lebanon as a metaphor for Solomon and/or his temple and palace, it would be tempting to read such a use in this context. However, that does not appear to be the case here. We do not know whether a well-known Lebanon tower did indeed overlook Damascus to its east or whether this is a metaphorical reference to the way the mountain appears, tower-like, when viewed from the east. The purpose of the references to the northern part of the Biblical area has an entirely different purpose which we see in the next verse.

7.6

The comparison of her body to the northern Biblical area continues. Her head is now likened to the Carmel mountain. As Michael Fox has pointed out,[323] the comparison is more than it seems. If the word for the Carmel mountain ('*carmel*') had appeared in the form '*carmil*', it would have meant 'scarlet'. The words obviously sound very similar. This is clearly deliberate word play for a number of reasons. First, we have a colour motif - we see that he goes on to describe the locks of her head as 'like purple'. But there are a number of other literary motifs being played out. It links back to another mountain, Lebanon, in the previous verse. Let us not forget, however, that the image of scarlet or red has been an ongoing motif in the descriptions. He had described her lips as 'crimson' (in Hebrew '*shani*') in 4.3. Perhaps even more, though, it is intended as a reminder of 5.10 where she describes her lover as 'red'.

The locks of her hair are like purple. We know that purple was a sign of wealth. Its use here is not coincidental. We saw the word 'purple' used in 3.10 where it was part of the description of the 'palanquin' which Solomon built for himself. There 'its seat was purple, its midst inlaid with love'. The colour purple clearly is associated in the male lover's mind with royalty because he immediately adds, 'a king is bound up in the curls'. Here, he freely admits his own enchantment by the delights of her curls[324] and, in so doing, compares himself to a king. That king, given the previous purple reference, must be King Solomon where purple was identified with love.

---

[322] At 7.9, the word in context stands for 'breath' - see comment in this regard at commentary to 7.9.

[323] Fox 1985, 160.

[324] The Hebrew word translated as 'curls' appears otherwise in the Bible as water-troughs (e.g. Genesis 30.38). The idea of curls seems to make sense in the context here.

By the end of this *wasf* description, we have therefore come to the following position. He started (7.1) by identifying her through the use of a word portraying her ('*ha-shulamit*'), amongst other things, as a female version of Solomon. Now he self-identifies as King Solomon; not, however, the polygamous version described in the Bible and clearly associated at that time with the historical King Solomon. This version of King Solomon is the non-historical, monogamous version created by the lovers in this poem.

An intriguing suggestion for this verse comes from a recent Israeli commentary which suggests an even greater link between 'purple' and 'king'. By a simple act of moving the break between lines, 7.6 could read: 'your head on you is like Carmel / and the locks of your head are like the purple of a king / bound up in the curls'. In so doing, it is the female lover who is, after all, being described, who takes on the regal aspect.[325] As an alternative explanation, Gurevitch suggests that 'a king bound up in the curls' is a king bound up in his palace who cannot realise true, free love.[326]

7.7

As if to stress the links between 'king' and 'love' in the male lover's mind, the *wasf* description ends with an ecstatic sentence praising the delights of love above anything else. The Blochs make the point that comparison is a staple part of the worldview of the Song of Songs.[327] And of course the lovers are always better than anyone else in the Song of Songs. The word 'love' (in Hebrew '*ahavah*') itself is used differently at the beginning of the Song from the way it is used at the end. At the beginning, it appears frequently.[328] After the first love scene, its use is limited only to adjurations (3.10, 5.8 and 8.4) and to the most heightened of emotional states, as here, and in the Song of Songs' most famous references to love in 8.6 and 8.7. Love has become a state of mind and precious.

The structural purpose of 'the Shulamite' reference

The Shulamite reference introduces the final of the three *wasf*s. He has then described her body in the next five verses. If we examine the previous two *wasf*s,

---

[325] Gurevitch, 86.

[326] Gurevitch, 99. Gurevitch bases this argument on a link between the 'curls' (Hebrew '*rehitim*') in 7.6 and the 'rafters' (Hebrew '*rechiteinu*') in 1.17. Despite apparently different roots, this argument has force. Brown Driver Briggs ('BDB') considers that the words in fact derive from the same root - see BDB, 923. The Masoretic marginalia at 1.17 also understand the word as identical, seeing the word which is written ('*ketiv*') '*rechiteinu*' with a *chet* as being required to be read ('*qeri*') as '*rehitenu*' with a *he*.

[327] Bloch, 204.

[328] It appears ten times before 3.10.

we have already seen that they were identified by the author by means of an inclusio; in other words, immediately before and after the *wasf* were words which were repeated. In this manner, they indicated the beginning and end of the poem.

So for example, the first *wasf* (4.1b-6) is preceded by the words: 'Look, how you are beautiful, my beloved, how you are beautiful' (4.1a). It is followed by the words: 'You are wholly beautiful, my beloved, and you have no blemish'. The second *wasf* (5.11-16a) is preceded by the words: 'My lover is dazzling and red, eminent amongst ten thousand' (5.10). It is followed by the words: 'That is my lover and that is my friend, daughters of Jerusalem' (5.16b).

A similar pattern of inclusio also exists in the third wasf. The first two words of the description - '*mah yafu*' ('how beautiful' 7.2) - are repeated in slightly different grammatical form immediately after the *wasf* - '*mah yafit*' ('how beautiful' 7.7). The image of absolute perfection '*ha-shulamit*' ('the perfect one') in the pet name he uses for her immediately precedes the first reference to her beauty in 7.2. The phrase where the delights of love are praised above anything else (7.7b) immediately follows the final reference to her beauty. In this way 'perfection' and absolute 'love' are linked as part of the inclusio.

חּ זֹאת קוֹמָתֵךְ דָּמְתָה לְתָמָר

וְשָׁדַיִךְ לְאַשְׁכֹּלוֹת:

ט אָמַרְתִּי אֶעֱלֶה בְתָמָר

אֹחֲזָה בְּסַנְסִנָּיו

וְיִהְיוּ־נָא שָׁדַיִךְ כְּאֶשְׁכְּלוֹת הַגֶּפֶן

וְרֵיחַ אַפֵּךְ כַּתַּפּוּחִים:

י וְחִכֵּךְ כְּיֵין הַטּוֹב

הוֹלֵךְ לְדוֹדִי לְמֵישָׁרִים

דּוֹבֵב שִׂפְתֵי יְשֵׁנִים:

He speaks to her:

**7.8 This, your stature can be compared to a palm tree
and your breasts to bunches.**

He speaks to himself:

**7.9 I say, "I will climb on the palm tree,
I will take hold of its stalks"**

180

He carries on speaking to her:

And may your breasts be like bunches of grapes
      And the smell of your nose like apples.
7.10 And your mouth like good wine
      going smoothly to my lover,
            gliding on the lips of sleepers

7.8

Commentators identify this as a new poem but such delineations, whilst true, are also often misleading. It has an obvious link with what has just gone before. The male lover is building on his description of her body. Where her description of him had been of a cedar (5.15), he now proceeds to describe her as a palm tree. Both trees were familiar from the temple in Jerusalem (or the 'house of the Lord' - see Psalm 92.13-14).

Her breasts are compared to bunches by him. Here he is adopting her wording from the earlier part of the Song of Songs; she had said that 'He will lie between my breasts. A bunch of henna is my lover to me in the vineyards of Ein Gedi' (1.13b-14). The bunch moves from being near the breasts to being identified with the breasts, an allusion which he will expand shortly.

7.9a

There is a wonderful irony in the use of the term '*amarti*' (meaning 'I said' but possibly having a 'present' meaning here). This most common of Hebrew words is used only twice in the Song of Songs (the other occasion being at 2.10). On both occasions, the 'speech' is internal.[329] This of course is in a poem where the lovers regularly speak to and about each other.

He 'says' he will climb on the palm tree and take hold of its '*sansinnav*', a difficult word where I have adopted the common view (or perhaps 'educated guess' may be a more appropriate term) that its meaning is either 'stalks' or 'branches'.

---

[329] The context here clearly indicates that he addresses this line to himself and only reverts to his lover with the other lines in this poem.

Her breasts had been compared to bunches in 7.8. They are now bunches of grapes, mirroring in even fuller fashion the parallel to 1.13-14 we identified in 7.8 above.

7.9b - 10

The final part of verse 9 ('the scent of your nose is like apples') seems more linked to the beginning of verse 10 than the rest of verse 9. This is because so much of the vocabulary is parallel to the opening section of the Song of Songs (1.2-4); the words '*re'ach*' ('smell'), '*yayin*' ('wine'), '*tov*' ('good'), '*dodi*' ('my beloved') and '*mesharim*' ('smoothly'/'straight away') all appear in both. As we will see, the language of the opening sections of the Song of Songs comes strongly to influence its final verses.

Commentators understand the reference to the nose to be taken to mean 'breath'. Her breath is therefore likened to an apple. He had been described as an 'apple in the trees of the forest' (2.3). Thereafter the apple was associated with love and love sickness (2.5).

The final part of the verse (translated 'gliding on the lips of sleepers') is difficult because of the final word 'sleepers'. It makes little sense and a number of suggestions have been made. A minor change of vowelling would render it 'old' ('gliding on the lips of the old') and it appears as such in 7.14 ('new as well as old'). Clearly wine has a soporific effect but it is unclear how or why, in this context, wine flows onto sleepers' lips. Michael Fox suggests deleting one letter and rendering the phrase 'crimson lips'.[330] Exum suggests 'lips and teeth' again with only a minor emendation of the text.[331] None of these proposals is watertight and the phrase remains problematic.

In addition to the difficulty regarding the meaning of the last word, the final phrase presents a further obstacle to understanding. It is unclear who has said it. For many commentators the last words in this verse are spoken by the woman though there is no clear delineation of where she would start speaking.

יא אֲנִי לְדוֹדִי
וְעָלַי תְּשׁוּקָתוֹ:

---

[330] Fox 1985, 163.
[331] Exum, 239.

She speaks to him

7.11 I am my lover's
and his desire is for me.

This sentence has brought a rare unanimity among modern commentators as to its importance. This has nothing to do with the fact that, at first sight, the phrase appears to be a reworked repetition of 2.16 and 6.3. In both those instances (with slight variation of order), my lover was for me and I was for him amongst the lilies. Here the lilies have vanished and been replaced by the word 'desire'. Within the context of the increased use in chapter 7 of abstract ideas ('perfect one', 'love'), the use of 'desire' can be seen as an additional example of this trend. But what has fascinated commentators is also the word's linguistic basis.

Desire

The Hebrew word for 'desire' used here is '*teshuqah*'. As all modern commentators make clear, the word appears only three times in the Bible. The other two occurrences are both early in the book of Genesis. First, it occurs within the context of God's curses to Adam, Eve and the snake in the garden of Eden. The woman's curse is as follows: 'To the woman, [God] said, "I will greatly increase your pain and suffering in pregnancy, in pain will you give birth; to your husband will be your desire and he will rule over you"'.[332] The other reference in the book of Genesis is not to the relationship between a man and a woman but to that between one particular man (Cain) and sin: 'And God said to Cain why are you angry, why has your face fallen? If you do right, then you can bear it; if you do not do right, sin lies in wait at the door - its desire is for you but you will rule over it'.[333]

The contrast between the use of the word '*teshuqah*' in the two Genesis passages, on the one hand, and in the Song of Songs, on the other, is remarkable. In both instances in Genesis, the term 'rule' is used in connection with 'desire' - both times by a man: first of a husband who rules over his wife who 'desires' him and then by Cain who rules over sin which 'desires' Cain. The man can 'rule' over both his wife and sin. In the Song of Songs, by contrast, the man desires the woman just as much as vice versa. Moreover, it is she who is permitted to say so. The word 'rule' never appears in the Song of Songs. The lack of hierarchy and the lack of domination are at the very heart of the ideology of the Song of Songs. The contrast in terminology

---

[332] Genesis 3.16.

[333] Genesis 4.6-7. Parts of Genesis 4.7 are notoriously difficult and my translation reflects this. However, the relevant part using the word 'desire' ('*teshuqah*') is clear.

and context between the Song of Songs and Genesis highlights the radicalism of the Song of Songs.

Yet there is much more to be added to the importance of the way the word '*teshuqah*' is used within the context of the Song of Songs. If one's only focus is on the linguistic triliteral root, then there is little more to say. The root of the word 'teshuqah' is '*sh-v-q*' and of course it appears nowhere else in the Song of Songs. But the poet and listeners were not in the least interested in triliteral roots, beloved by so much of nineteenth-century German academia. As we are more than aware from some of the mistranslations of the Bible into Greek in the Septuagint, later translators often mistakenly linked words which we now know from other semitic languages were in fact linguistically unrelated. In this regard, a fascinating Rabbinic 'mistranslation' yields a surprisingly rich result.

Consider the following Rabbinic conundrum which appears in *Shir hashirim Rabbah*.[334] They wondered whether the rare word '*teshuqah*' 'desire' in this verse derived from the same root as '*neshiqah*' meaning 'kiss' as in 'let him kiss me with the kisses of his mouth' from the beginning of the Song of Songs (1.2) or did it perhaps derive from the word '*nesheq*' meaning 'weapon'. The Rabbis were completely wrong on their grammar - the word in fact derives from neither. But by making their point, the Rabbis encapsulated the two contexts of the word with precision. In the book of Genesis, 'desire' is a means of rule, as is a weapon. In the Song of Songs, 'desire' is a means of love, as is a kiss. The same word can have entirely different connotations in different contexts.

For the Rabbis then, the word 'desire' in the Song of Songs was intimately linked to the word 'kiss'. To see this as merely a grammatical error is to do a disservice to the Rabbis' feel for the text and to miss the poetry of the Song. The poet has just introduced terminology (see commentary on 7.9b-10 above) alluding directly to the beginning of the Song of Songs. The word 'desire' here points back through its verbal links to that beautiful opening. On both occasions the speaker is the woman. Moreover, she continues the passionate desire to kiss him in 8.2 (discussed below) where further wordplay ensues on what the Rabbis thought may be the same root.

Needless to say, the Rabbis did not write the Song of Songs and therefore their insight, whilst interesting, does not answer the question as to how the author would have intended this striking reference. The author would have sought wordplay without reference to (or most probably any knowledge of) the exact grammatical

---

[334] Quoted in Kasher, 15.

forms so beloved of nineteenth-century Biblical professors.   Accordingly, the Rabbinic feel for the text in this instance is highly likely to match authorial intent. Intertextual references, based on triliteral roots, have an enormous role to play in Biblical analysis but we also need to look beyond them and search for, and examine, the wordplay which is at the heart of the way that the poet crafts the relationship between the two lovers.

יב לְכָה דוֹדִי
נֵצֵא הַשָּׂדֶ֔ה
נָלִ֖ינָה בַּכְּפָרִֽים:
יג נַשְׁכִּ֙ימָה֙ לַכְּרָמִ֔ים
נִרְאֶ֞ה אִם־פָּֽרְחָ֤ה הַגֶּ֙פֶן֙
פִּתַּ֣ח הַסְּמָדַ֔ר
הֵנֵ֖צוּ הָרִמּוֹנִ֑ים
שָׁ֛ם אֶתֵּ֥ן אֶת־דֹּדַ֖י לָֽךְ:

She speaks to him

7.12 Come my lover,
>   **let us go out into the field,**
>>   **let us rest amongst the henna,**

7.13 let us go early to the vineyards,
>   **we will see if the vine has blossomed,**

if the bud has opened,
>   **if the pomegranates have bloomed,**
>>   **there I will give my caresses to you.**

From a grammatical point of view, the speaker in the rest of chapter 7 is not clear. There are no gender endings to assist (both references 'to you' in 7.13 and 'for you' in 7.14 are ambiguous because of their position at the end of the sentence which changes the vowelling in Biblical Hebrew, obscuring otherwise clear gender differences).   The best clue is that the pet word '*dodi*' ('my lover') is used.   This of course is the word which she has used consistently previously and so it is highly likely that she is speaking.   In any case, this speaker is picking up the reference to '*dodi*' in the previous verse.   These two verses also mirror two previous sections of the poem and must be examined in that context.

7.12 - 7.13a-b

The words 'rest', 'henna' and 'vineyards' in 7.12 have all been referred to in 1.14. Yet here the word 'henna' (in Hebrew '*kofer*') has a further meaning which it did not have in 1.14 when it appeared in the singular form. In this verse by contrast, 'henna' is in the plural ('*k'farim*'). This is also the way in which the plural of the word 'village' (singular '*k'far*') is formed. The word could therefore also mean 'villages'. So which of the two meanings should one choose? Both meanings make perfect sense of the sentence and the context of the poem. There is a constant longing to leave the town and to escape to the countryside. The alternative translation 'let us go out into the field, let us spend the night in the villages, let us go early to the vineyards' therefore also reflects both the Hebrew and the general intent of the author. We should not force ourselves to choose between the two meanings; rather, we should enjoy the author's, no doubt deliberate, ambiguity.

Given the link to verse 1.14, one wonders whether the written link between 'field' (in Hebrew '*sadeh*') in 7.12 and 'breasts' (in Hebrew '*shadai*') in 1.13 is also deliberate.[335] '*Sadeh*' and '*shadai*' do not sound particularly similar but in written form there is more of an obvious link. This raises the question of the degree to which written, as opposed to oral, similarities were intended for an audience largely likely to be listening to, as opposed to reading, the poem.

7.13c-e

We are now introduced to three images of fecundity. Two of the phrases appeared in the fragment at 6.11 (relating to the vine and the pomegranate) and two appeared again in much more fragmentary form at 2.13 where 'the vines are giving off blossom scent'. One way to read these three images is that they summarise the previous images of blossoming in the Song of Songs. They form a sharp contrast, however, to the only other references to vineyard and fecundity imagery to follow (in 8.11-12) which are entirely negative about wealth and Solomon (as we shall see in the commentary at that point).

As if to prove that these three images form a climax to this particular poem of the Song of Songs, the final words of the verse make clear what their purpose is - to say that she will make love to him there. The word 'there' (in Hebrew '*sham*'), appearing at the beginning of the phrase, clearly is intended to indicate that the word is to be stressed. One would have expected it at the end of the phrase. But there is

---

[335] See Fox 1985, 170. Moreover, the word 'breasts' appears again in 8.1.

also another reason why it does not appear as the final word. Whilst themes run throughout the Song of Songs, the poet has also clearly delineated for us separate poems - in particular, where this poem ends and where it starts. It ends here and it starts at 7.12. That is because there is a clear inclusio - the first two words of the poem in Hebrew are '*lecha dodi*' ('come, my lover' 7.12a) and the final words are the similar sounding '*dodai lach*' ('my caresses to you' 7.13e).

יד הַדּוּדָאִים נָתְנוּ־רֵיחַ
וְעַל־פְּתָחֵינוּ כָּל־מְגָדִים
חֲדָשִׁים גַּם־יְשָׁנִים דּוֹדִי
צָפַנְתִּי לָךְ:

She speaks to him:

7.14 The mandrakes have given off their scent,
choice fruits are at our door,
new as well as old, my love,
I have hidden away for you.

The clear delineation of the end of the previous poem is immediately put into question by the reference to mandrakes as the first word in the next verse. The Hebrew word is '*dudaim*' and inevitably is a play on the word '*dodi*' ('my love') which is the most frequently appearing word in the Song of Songs. The mandrake was considered to be an aphrodisiac, as is probably hinted here and as we can certainly see from the following intertextual reference.

Like the word '*teshuqah*' ('desire') in 7.11, its only other use in the Bible is in the book of Genesis: 'And Reuben went at the time of the wheat harvest and found mandrakes in the field. He brought them to Leah his mother. Rachel said to Leah, "give me some of the mandrakes of your son". She said to her, "was it not enough that you took my husband and now you take my son's mandrakes". And Rachel said, "he will therefore lie with you this evening in return for your son's mandrakes". And Jacob came from the field in the evening; Leah came out to meet him and she said "come to me because I have hired you through my son's mandrakes". And he slept with her that night'.[336]

The contrast between the two contexts of the mandrakes is every bit as stark as that relating to the word 'desire' referred to in 7.11. In Genesis, the mandrakes provide

---

[336] Genesis 30.14-16.

the backdrop and the context of a competition between Rachel and Leah, the two wives of Jacob, for fecundity and their husband's presence. In the Song of Songs, the mandrakes provide the enticement for the one and only love between the two lovers - the choice fruit,[337] available on their (*al fresco*) doorstep, new as well as old, hidden away only for the lover. The word, like the world, has been transformed for the lovers.

Conclusion

With the end of the third *wasf* at 7.7, the Song of Songs breaks off long, clear delineated set pieces for shorter poems often more fragmentary in nature, in some cases clearly delineated, in others not. That process will continue in the final chapter of the Song of Songs which in fourteen verses probably contains eight poems. Let us, though, consider what conclusions we can draw from chapter 7 and how they will follow through into chapter 8.

Shakespeare's critique in sonnet 130 of over-idealised descriptions of the perfect lover preceded the first of the three *wasf*s. It is very useful to measure how those *wasf*s fare against the challenge of the bard. On Shakespeare's own terms, they all fail the test. They are all totally unrealistic and indulge in hyperbole. Yet we instinctively know that these poems are not examples of weak literature. Their beauty lies not just in the descriptions they offer but in their careful cross-referencing of terminology and subtle adaptation of words to fit new contexts. By the end of the idealised descriptions, the poet is prepared to use abstract (and therefore idealised) concepts.

Added to this is that all the *wasf*s follow the Solomon interlude (3.6-11) and combine the vocabulary used to describe Solomon with their own terms of reference. In the second *wasf*, she uses temple imagery to describe him and, just before the final *wasf*, his pet name for her is the female form of Solomon.   The lovers have now appropriated the Solomon story. But for them that story is not, unlike the original, one of domination but rather one of mutuality.   Words such as 'desire' and 'mandrakes' appearing in the book of Genesis, with their implications of control, are transformed into the narrative of the lovers' consensual relationship.

The fragments which we are about to consider in chapter 8 build on this theme. They contain some of the most powerful comments on the nature of love; and in them the lovers are, finally, completely open about what they think of the real King Solomon.

---

[337] Also referred to previously - see 4.13 and 4.16.

SONG OF SONGS 8.1 - 8.14

The Thousand is Yours

א מִי יִתֶּנְךָ֮ כְּאָ֣ח לִי֒
יוֹנֵ֖ק שְׁדֵ֣י אִמִּ֑י
אֶֽמְצָאֲךָ֤ בַחוּץ֙ אֶשָּׁ֣קְךָ֔
גַּ֖ם לֹא־יָב֥וּזוּ לִֽי׃
ב אֶנְהָֽגֲךָ֗ אֲבִֽיאֲךָ֛
אֶל־בֵּ֥ית אִמִּ֖י תְּלַמְּדֵ֑נִי
אַשְׁקְךָ֙ מִיַּ֣יִן הָרֶ֔קַח
מֵעֲסִ֖יס רִמֹּנִֽי׃

She speaks to him:

8.1 Would that you were like a brother to me,
      sucking from my mother's breasts;
I would find you outside and I would kiss you,
      they would also not scorn me.
8.2 I would lead you, I would bring you
      to my mother's house, she who taught me.
I would make you drink from the spice wine,
      from the juice of my pomegranate.

She has never before described her lover as her 'brother' (in Hebrew '*ach*'). Whilst she has referred to her own brothers before (1.6), she did not actually describe them as her 'brothers'; rather she called them the 'sons of my mother' and portrayed them in a negative light. Her 'brother' terminology is clearly influenced by his description of her as 'my sister my bride' (4.9). We have therefore already become aware of its use as a term of endearment. Now we appreciate that she also appears to use it for practical purposes. We have seen how many problems she has had in an open relationship with her lover from the second of the two night scenes (5.2-7) where she was manhandled by the watchmen of the wall when searching in the town for her lover. She has realised that brothers are the only men, besides husbands, with whom one can have a publicly tactile relationship in this society.

189

Yet the way in which that relationship is now described is much more than fraternal. If she found him outside, she would (and would be permitted to) kiss him. The single Hebrew word for 'I would kiss you' is '*eshaqcha*' the root of which, as we saw earlier, the Rabbis thought was linked to '*teshuqah*' ('desire') in 7.11. The lack of any actual grammatical link does not prevent the poet using the alliteration in poetic fashion. 'Kissing' and 'desire' are deliberately fashioned to match each other. The immediate comment 'they would also not scorn me' can only be fully understood after we have read 8.7. At that point, the same phrase is used to indicate the scorn heaped on someone who gives all his wealth for love. Only at that later stage is the contrast between true and false love laid bare for all to see.

The Blochs point out[338] that the woman bringing her lover to her mother's house contrasts with the order of things in Genesis 24.67 where Isaac brings Rebecca to his mother's house. This may therefore be another example of the reversal in this poem of what would otherwise be expected in the book of Genesis, shown so vividly in the Song of Songs by the word 'desire' in 7.11 and the use of the term 'mandrakes' in 7.14.

The phrase 'she who taught me' has puzzled many commentators. Grammatically it could also mean 'you who taught me' referring to the male lover but that seems less likely in the context. The passage here may parallel 3.4 in which the female lover says 'until I have brought him to my mother's house, to the chamber of the one who bore me'. One of the ancient versions has even suggested replacing the text here with that in 3.4. Whilst it makes sense as it stands, one does wonder whether a secondary or implied meaning of 'the one who bore me' in 3.4 (in Hebrew '*horati*') for an ancient listener or reader would be 'the one who instructs me' (from the root *y-r-h*). If so, then a parallel is intended to the passage we are now considering in 8.2. At the very least, a wordplay appears possible.

Further clear wordplay is unfortunately lost in translation. She goes on to say 'I would make you drink....' The Hebrew is '*ashqecha*', obviously being used as a play on words with '*eshaqecha*'[339] ('I would kiss you') in 8.1 and '*teshuqah*' ('desire') in 7.11. Kisses and wine were linked at the beginning of the Song (1.2). Now kisses, the drinking of wine and desire all get intermingled in the passion of the lovers. The drinking here involves wine and pomegranate. These were the two fruits referred to in 7.13 (wine there being in the form of the vine) and they were the place

---

338 Bloch, 210.
339 This is not the only biblical example of a play on words by the use of the words 'kissing' and 'drinking' in close proximity. See also Genesis 29.10-11 for another example.

where she would give her love to him. This is now fulfilled in her mother's house where she hopes to guide him.

ג שְׂמֹאלוֹ תַּחַת רֹאשִׁי

וִימִינוֹ תְּחַבְּקֵנִי:

ד הִשְׁבַּעְתִּי אֶתְכֶם בְּנוֹת יְרוּשָׁלָ͏ִם

מַה־תָּעִירוּ ׀ וּמַה־תְּעֹרְרוּ

אֶת־הָאַהֲבָה עַד שֶׁתֶּחְפָּץ:

She speaks to the daughters of Jerusalem:

8.3 His left hand is under my head,
   and his right hand embraces me.
8.4 I have made you swear, oh daughters of Jerusalem,
   that you should not rouse or arouse
      love until it is ready

Verse 8.3 appeared in identical form at 2.6. Verse 8.4 is paralleled at 2.7 and 3.5. However it is a truncated form of those two identical previous verses. No longer is the adjuration accompanied by gazelles or hinds of the field.

To understand these differences fully, we need to see what they are and how they relate to their own different contexts. The first passage at 2.6-7 followed a scene ending with a declaration of lovesickness (2.5) and preceded the male lover striding over the hills and mountains to encounter his beloved. Indeed, Alter invites us to make the comparison here with the passage in 2.7 because there he had brought her to the bed chamber (2.4) whereas here the position is reversed and it is she who leads him.[340]

But it is the second passage at 3.5 where the parallels are more obvious. The word similarities appear to be clearly deliberate and therefore must serve some intended purpose. 3.5 followed the first night scene where she brought him 'to the house of her mother, to the chamber of the one who bore me' (3.4). Our passage also follows a similar wish to bring him to the 'house of my mother'. 3.5 preceded the words 'who is this coming up from the desert' (3.6) as does this passage (8.5). We are thereby being invited to compare what follows (8.5ff) with the previous passage (3.6ff). As we will recall, the Solomon interlude at 3.6-11 involved what we understood to be a concealed reference to the Queen of Sheba and an explicit

---

[340] Alter 2015, 48.

reference to King Solomon which has been central to the text ever since. Our difficulty is that, unfortunately, the next verse here (8.5) is rather rough and ready and seems more like a first draft than the finished product. We will nevertheless do what we can with it and with what follows it.

The rest of the Song of Songs follows the fragmentary nature of 8.5. Five fragments[341] follow, varied in nature and quality, but often with interlinking themes. Much of the material, whilst brief, is nevertheless sublime and offers fascinating comparisons with other parts of the Song of Songs and the Bible.

ה מִי זֹאת עֹלָה מִן־הַמִּדְבָּר
מִתְרַפֶּקֶת עַל־דּוֹדָהּ
תַּחַת הַתַּפּוּחַ עוֹרַרְתִּיךָ
שָׁמָּה חִבְּלַתְךָ אִמֶּךָ
שָׁמָּה חִבְּלָה יְלָדַתְךָ׃

Narrator/Chorus?:

**8.5 Who is this coming up from the desert,
      leaning on her beloved?**

She speaks to him:

**Under the apple tree I aroused you,
      there your mother was in travail for you,
         she was in travail and gave birth to you.**

This verse appears to be two separate ideas and I will treat them as such.

8.5a

The meaning of the phrase 'leaning on her beloved' is difficult (especially given that the word for 'leaning' appears nowhere else in the Bible) and one presumes something is now missing because this line is obviously distinct from what follows it.

Clearly this makes analysis difficult though not impossible. In the parallel passage in 3.6 which opens with the same words, the words 'leaning on her beloved' are

---

[341] 8.5, 8.6-7, 8.8-10, 8.11-12, 8.13-14.

instead 'like pillars of smoke' from all the incense which the Queen of Sheba/the female lover is wearing. There can, of course, never be smoke without a fire. In verse 8.6, we are about to see a passionate reference to fire providing a further possible link to the passage in 3.6 - one cannot be sure whether the link was intended and it must remain tentative given the fragmentary nature of the line.

8.5b

Again this line appears without much context to assist us. It may have been inserted here because it uses the word 'arouse' as did the adjuration in the previous verse - and the references to his mother parallel the reference to her own mother in 8.2. The location for this sentence is under the apple tree, a place which has been associated previously by the female lover with her lover, who is like an apple tree in the forest in comparison to all the other young men (2.3).

The single Hebrew word used for 'in travail' only appears once elsewhere with this meaning in the Bible.[342] It does, however, use the same three letters for its root as the word in 2.15 describing the 'ruining' of the vineyards by the foxes. How, or if, there is a connection between the two sentences is difficult to say at this distance of time. The word '*yeladatecha*' I have translated as 'she who gave birth to you' though the form does not exactly fit this translation and commentators have argued over its actual meaning. Unfortunately, no better solution seems to have been proposed.

ו שִׂימֵנִי כַחוֹתָם עַל־לִבֶּךָ
כַּחוֹתָם עַל־זְרוֹעֶךָ
כִּי־עַזָּה כַמָּוֶת אַהֲבָה
קָשָׁה כִשְׁאוֹל קִנְאָה
רְשָׁפֶיהָ רִשְׁפֵּי אֵשׁ שַׁלְהֶבֶתְיָה:
ז מַיִם רַבִּים לֹא יוּכְלוּ לְכַבּוֹת אֶת־הָאַהֲבָה
וּנְהָרוֹת לֹא יִשְׁטְפוּהָ
אִם־יִתֵּן אִישׁ אֶת־כָּל־הוֹן בֵּיתוֹ בָּאַהֲבָה
בּוֹז יָבוּזוּ לוֹ:

She speaks to him:

8.6 Set me as a seal on your heart,
as a seal on your arm

---

[342] Psalms 7.15.

Because strong as death is love,
**   tough as Sheol is jealousy;**
Its sparks: sparks of, fire, an almighty flame.
8.7 Many waters cannot extinguish love
**   and rivers cannot drown it.**
Were a man to give all the wealth of his house for love,
**   they would surely scorn him.**

This section sets out probably the most famous words in the Song of Songs. In a few carefully constructed words, we have one of the strongest statements in ancient (or indeed modern) literature about the power of love. Whilst it is contained within one of her declarations to him, it feels totally different. It may, like so many other verses, contain natural imagery - but that only strengthens the contrast. Previous imagery has related the natural world to parts of the body. Whilst that also occurs in these verses to some extent, the fire, waters and rivers are metaphors relating not to part of the body but to what that body craves - love.

If, as we have been told three times previously, love should not be roused or aroused until it is ready, these words seem to have an altogether different quality. They seem to be a summation of what love is and therefore provide a fitting conclusion to the poem. Let us not, in this context, forget the literary drift of the Song of Songs. It opened with speech, mainly from the female lover, using images relating to the body and images from nature to describe the love between the man and the woman. That gave way, following the Solomon interlude, to *wasf* descriptions of the body - again, material in the extreme. The third, and final, *wasf*, however, summarised that description at its beginning and end with images of 'perfection' and 'love' and, in 7.11, we were introduced to the ideal of 'desire'. In other words, the Song of Songs has already set up the notion that generalised, idealised lessons can be learnt from the specific experiences and narratives of the two lovers.

In order better to understand what the purpose is of the poem contained in these two verses, we need to look closely at how it has been fashioned. It was not created in a vacuum. The two verses, making up the poem, in fact consist of five lines. The first line (8.6a) and last line (8.7b) contain material with links to other parts of the Song of Songs whereas the three middle lines introduce imagery which is entirely new to the Song of Songs. We will analyse where that comes from and how it has been constructed.

8.6a

The 'seal' and 'heart' in 8.6a have already appeared. In 4.12, we were introduced to a 'sealed spring' as one of the descriptions of 'my sister bride': 'A locked garden, my sister bride, a locked spring, a sealed fountain'. The 'heart' was first introduced in the Solomon interlude describing the day of his wedding as 'the day of his heart's joy' (3.11). The male lover adopts this term and then also uses it in connection with 'my sister bride' but in verbal form in 4.9: 'you have stolen my heart, my sister bride, you have stolen my heart with one of your eyes, with one bead in your necklace'. So we immediately realise that there is a link with the 'sister bride' image and the 'seal' and the 'heart'. They were his images, which she now uses.

While we may see the imagery of the seal on the heart and on the arm and read it as metaphorical, the reality is that the primary image for the ancient reader or listener was physical. The direct reference to be understood was probably jewellery hung round the neck resting on the heart and a wristband of some sort for the seal on the arm.

The idea that a physical object could, at the same time, represent something symbolic is, of course, well known in all societies. The notion of physical binding creating metaphorical meaning is seen at its most well-known in Judaism in the passage from Deuteronomy 5.4-9, which has become known to Jews as the first paragraph of the Shema: 'And these things which I command you today shall be on your heart. And you shall teach them to your children and you shall speak about them when you sit in your house, when you are walking on the road, when you lie down and when you rise up. And you shall bind them as a sign on your hand and they shall be for frontlets between your eyes.' (Deuteronomy 5.6-8).

While this passage is one of the most well-known in the Bible, where the act of wearing an item represents something beyond the physical, it is not the only such example. There are many others. It is one of those which concerns us now.

The link to the book of Proverbs

Chapter 6 of the book of Proverbs contains guidance from a father to a son as to how to behave. As we discussed in chapter 1 above, the book of Proverbs was attributed to King Solomon though it was almost certainly written well after his reign. If, as seems likely, chapter 6 of the book of Proverbs was also written after[343] the book of Deuteronomy, then it is clear that there is an obvious influence from the Shema on the following verses: 'Guard, my son, the commandment of your father and do not abandon the instruction of your mother. Bind them on your heart always, garland them on your neck. When you are walking about it will guide you, when you lie down it will protect you and when you wake it will converse with you.'[344]

The reason why we have moved from the Song of Songs to the book of Deuteronomy and then to Chapter 6 of the book of Proverbs is that there is a profound link between this passage in the Song of Songs and terminology in chapter 6 of Proverbs. The seal around the heart, in particular, appears in both; the book of Proverbs explains that that which is valued is to be garlanded round the neck so as to be close to the heart. The Song of Songs transforms this message to its own profound statement about the nature of love.

In fact, the link is even stronger.[345] Further on, in chapter 6 of Proverbs, a large proportion of the terminology which we see in these two verses in the Song of Songs also appears: 'Let one not scorn the thief when he steals to fill his body when he is hungry. When he is found, he pays seven-fold, he gives all the wealth of his house. Adultery makes no sense - he who does it corrupts his body. He will receive wounds and insult and his iniquity will not be wiped out. For jealousy angers a man and he will not be consoled on the day of revenge. He will not accept any ransom, will not turn even if you increase the bribe.'[346]

There are many shared words between this passage in Proverbs and verses 8.6-7 in the Song of Songs. 'Let one not scorn..[the thief]' (Proverbs 6.30) parallels 'they would scorn' in the Song of Songs 8.7 (and indeed 8.1). The words 'all the wealth of his house' (Proverbs 6.31 and Song of Songs 8.7) and 'jealousy' (Proverbs 6.34 and Song of Songs 8.6) appear in both passages.

As we have seen so often previously, when we appreciated that the Song of Songs has intertextual links with other Biblical passages, the connection serves also to

---

[343] Dating of both the book of Proverbs and the book of Deuteronomy is not entirely clear. A majority of scholars believe, though, that chapters 1 to 9 of the book of Proverbs were written at a later period than most of the rest of the book. Accordingly, it is probable that chapter 6 of the book of Proverbs was written later than, and therefore was influenced by, the book of Deuteronomy. For further discussion of this influence see Fox (2000), 230.

[344] Proverbs 6.20-22.

[345] Zakovitch brings this out powerfully - see Zakovitch 133-5. He analyses 8.6a as a separate poem to 8.6b-7 but for the reasons set out in these paragraphs, the whole of 8.6-7 seems intricately linked to the Proverbs connection and should be read together.

[346] Proverbs 6.30-35.

highlight the contrast. The words may be similar but the message has been transformed. No longer are we dealing with adulterous men and cuckolded jealous husbands, unwilling to forgive in any circumstances, as in the book of Proverbs. Instead the strength of the passion of jealousy has been channelled into the relationship itself and not the repercussions of its breakdown.

8.6b

The power of the second line in this poem (8.6b) is heightened by its obvious parallelism. 'Strong' parallels 'tough', 'as death' parallels 'as Sheol' (the Biblical netherworld identified with death)[347] and 'love' parallels 'jealousy'.[348] Love and jealousy therefore appear to be different aspects of the same emotion for the poet.

8.6c

We mentioned, earlier in the analysis of 8.6-7, that it is a self-contained poem consisting of five lines. 8.6c is the third line and so comprises the centrepiece of this particular poem in the Song of Songs. As such, given that this poem itself is about the nature of love, its location indicates its importance as much as its physical centrality. It is less well known than the previous line. For reasons which will become clear, it was probably viewed with greater importance in earlier times than the previous line. This is not only because of its content (which I will consider shortly) but also because of a peculiarity regarding its accentuation which I consider immediately below.

Accentuation on 8.6c

One aspect of this line, which I am not aware has been remarked upon, is its accentuation by the Masoretes. The Masoretes were the rabbis in the tenth century who set out the received Biblical text. With this text, apart from providing vowels, they also provided accent marks. Those had two purposes. They indicated musical notes which allowed the text to be chanted as well as read but also created a sophisticated system of punctuation.

The system is based on markings indicating conjunctive words (which were to be linked to the next word or phrase) and disjunctive words (which were to be separated

---

[347] See e.g. Genesis 44.29.

[348] Much as one would want to translate 'jealousy' (in Hebrew 'qin'ah') as some form of immediate sexual passion given the context, Fox argues persuasively that it cannot have this meaning - see Fox (1985) 169-70. This makes the parallel with Proverbs 6 all the more apposite.

from the next word or phrase). A disjunctive accent on a word would therefore indicate to the reader or speaker that there should be a pause before the next word or phrase. The different types of accents for disjunctive words themselves consist of their own hierarchy, indicating that some pauses are longer than others. A much less sophisticated version of this system exists in western languages. When reading or speaking a sentence, we naturally pause longer at a full stop than at a semi-colon; and longer at a semi-colon than at a comma, or a dash. The Masoretic accentuation system works on exactly the same principles but with many more disjunctive punctuation signs than in western languages.[349] The vast majority of Hebrew sentences consist of phrases containing one, two or three words with conjunctive accents followed by a disjunctive, thereby sub-dividing a long verse into more manageable phrases for reading silently or aloud.

What does this somewhat esoteric diversion have to do with our text? 8.6c contains four words, all of which contain disjunctive accents.[350] I have sought to replicate the effect in my English translation above. It indicates an attempt to break up the words, including an obviously syntactically ludicrous pause after 'of' in 'sparks of, fire'. Whilst this is not unique, it is extremely rare. Moreover, it would naturally occur in a longer verse requiring longer subdivisions and so is extremely rare within the context of poetry in clauses as short as 8.6c .

We therefore appear to have been given an indication from the Masoretes in the tenth century as to the importance of these four words. The accent marking clearly indicates their portent by the requirement to pause (unnaturally) between each word. This could of course mirror earlier practice (the Masoretic text reflected traditions from many centuries before) but unfortunately we cannot be sure.

The sparks create a fire which turns into a fiery flame. From where do those sparks derive? 'Its sparks' could refer back to love or (more immediately) to jealousy. The poet does not make it absolutely clear. There is no real need to do so because both apply. Small sparks of love can become, via jealousy, an almighty flame.

One further question arises from the final word of this line - namely, whether it contains the name of God. Its final two letters comprise one of the names of God

---

[349] See *A Treatise on the Accentuation of The Twenty-One so-called, prose books of the Old Testament*, William Wickes, Kessinger Legacy Reprints, Oxford 1887 and *The Music of the Hebrew Bible*, Victor Tunkel, London 2004. A very comprehensive review of the material in Hebrew is *Ta'amei Hamikra*, Mordechai Breuer, Horev, Jerusalem, 1989.

[350] They are respectively, (1) *zaqef gadol*, (2) *zaqef gadol*, (3) *tipcha* and (4) *silluq* (also known as *sof pasuq*). They follow the *etnachta*, the main subdividing sign within a verse and so indicate a second half of the verse entirely disjointed in terms of accent marking.

but they are used in many situations indicating something large in one way or another. On some occasions, God is being hinted at; on others, that does not appear to be the case.[351] In relation to their appearance in the Song of Songs, some manuscripts divide up the final two letters from the rest of the word indicating a divine flame. There is no real evidence that that is the intention in this poem in which God does not otherwise appear. However, the ambiguity may well be deliberate and I could not resist adopting Exum's[352] beautiful phrase 'an almighty flame' which captures that ambiguity perfectly.

8.7a

The power of this fire is so strong that any amount of water cannot douse it. This image of the strength of an unquenchable fire inevitably draws comparison with the burning bush which was not consumed because of the divine presence (Exodus 3.2). The passages do not, however, have any shared vocabulary.

'Many waters' is a frequent image in the Bible. So, in Psalms 93.4, it appears in contrast to God who is more glorious and majestic than the most fearsome of natural images. Love fulfills the same function in the Song of Songs. Love may be the substitute word in the Song of Songs for the divine in the image in Psalms but it is infused with that same divine spirit and power. It is hardly surprising that so many of the ancient commentators saw the secular images of love and read into them divine messages, because the author of the poem was perfectly prepared to take passages with clear, unambiguous references to God and use them as a launchpad for the message which was to be expressed through the Song of Songs.

8.7b

The final line of the poem talks of the contrast between money and wealth. A man is scorned if he seeks to buy love. The irony is that, in this society, real love is also scorned unless the parties are married, as the poet had made clear in 8.1. There, a single woman showing open love to a man could not do so unless that man was her brother.

The relationship between love and money does not end with this comment. The nature of love has been laid bare by the poet and it gets applied to a particular

---

[351] See e.g. Psalms 118.5 where God is clearly hinted at, given the context.
[352] See Exum, 243.

situation, as we will see, in 8.11-12. The lesson of the Song of Songs (written more than two thousand years before the Beatles) is that money can't buy you love.[353]

ח אָחוֹת לָנוּ֙ קְטַנָּ֔ה
וְשָׁדַ֖יִם אֵ֣ין לָ֑הּ
מַה־נַּעֲשֶׂה֙ לַאֲחֹתֵ֔נוּ
בַּיּ֖וֹם שֶׁיְּדֻבַּר־בָּֽהּ׃
ט אִם־חוֹמָ֣ה הִ֔יא
נִבְנֶ֥ה עָלֶ֖יהָ טִ֣ירַת כָּ֑סֶף
וְאִם־דֶּ֣לֶת הִ֔יא
נָצ֥וּר עָלֶ֖יהָ ל֥וּחַ אָֽרֶז׃
י אֲנִ֣י חוֹמָ֔ה
וְשָׁדַ֖י כַּמִּגְדָּל֑וֹת
אָ֤ז הָיִ֙יתִי֙ בְעֵינָ֔יו
כְּמוֹצְאֵ֖ת שָׁלֽוֹם׃

He speaks with others [?] - to her [?]:

8.8 We have a small sister
who has no breasts.
What shall we do for our sister
on the day spoken for her?
8.9 If she is a wall,
we will build on her a turret of silver,
If she is a door,
we will besiege her with a tablet of cedar.

She speaks - to him [?]:

8.10 I am a wall
and my breasts are like towers
Thus I was in his eyes
like one who finds peace.

What are we to make of these words? They do not apparently fit easily into the pattern of love talk that we saw previously. In the first two verses, he is probably speaking but we cannot be sure. Verse 8.8 uses the word 'we' for the speaker. So he could be speaking with others or it could be some form of '*pluralis majestatis*',

---

[353] Cf *Reading Biblical Poetry*. J.P. Fokkelman. Westminster, John Knox, Louisville (2001), 198.

the royal 'we', as it were. In the final verse, she is certainly speaking but is she speaking to him or not? Most commentaries see these verses as a fragment about chastity where walls, doors and tablets of cedar provide the necessary metaphors.

Whilst such a reading cannot be ruled out, it sits uneasily with what we otherwise know concerning the Song of Songs. If the rest of the Song of Songs is about the joys of love, why should there be a passage about the importance of chastity? Indeed, chastity might explain the metaphors in verses 8:8 and 8:9 but it seems difficult to reconcile to her response in verse 8:10, the first line of which indicates her sexual allure and the second line of which is, on first reading, extremely difficult to understand at all within such a context - or indeed any context.

Michael Fox argues[354] that this is actually playful banter and constructs a scenario whereby her brothers are speaking to her. Zakovitch argues[355] that this, like the final two fragments, is full of mocking humour. As we saw, the brothers were angry with her in 1.6, so Fox argues that this is their *volte-face* with banter about her breasts. She then responds to their banter in this version.

I find it difficult to resist the idea that these verses concern playful banter as opposed to a comment about chastity which seems so out of place in the Song of Songs. I also accept Zakovitch's argument that the words are mocking in tone. I find it more difficult to accept Fox's argument that these are the brothers speaking. If so, this would be their only speaking part in the whole of the Song of Songs. We have so far identified three speakers - the male lover, the female lover and the daughters of Jerusalem - plus a narrator. The introduction of a new speaker, only a few verses from the end of the Song of Songs, seems counter-intuitive.

I think there are only two realistic possibilities and slightly favour the second. The first option is that it is the male lover who is speaking in his own voice about his own sister, and using the royal 'we'. Given that each lover has imagined the other as a version of a royal Solomon, this makes sense of the unusual plural. His lover then responds in contrast about herself and her own breasts in verse 10. The second, in my view more plausible, option is that he is speaking as if he were her brothers. This allows for the lack of any evidence in the rest of the Song of Songs that her brothers' anger with her (revealed in 1.6) has in any way dissipated. In this scenario, whilst he may be engaging in playful banter with her, he is also clearly mocking their anger. Her response is then to banter with him about how little her own brothers

---

[354] Fox (1985), 172.
[355] Zakovitch, 136.

understand about her and her body. I will therefore proceed on the basis (counter to most commentators) that it is he who is probably speaking in 8.8 and 8.9 - either in his own voice or, more likely, in imitation of her brothers and mocking them.

8.8

The reference to the day 'spoken for her' is almost certainly a reference to betrothal or marriage. It derives from the standard root for speaking '*d-b-r*' meaning 'speech'. In the Song of Songs this root has more meanings than in any other book in the Bible. It is a homonym for '*midbar*' ('desert') - which we saw in 3.6 and, recently, in 8.5. It also appears in his first *wasf* as a name for her mouth, or possibly her speech (4.3). Now it becomes a synonym for betrothal. If we examine all these instances, we realise that they all add to her enticement. She came up from the desert, scented with myrrh and frankincense (3.6), and her speech was lovely (4.3). The standard word for speech has been transformed by associations into part of her allure.

8.9

The reference which he makes to a 'wall' which she repeats in 8.10 is difficult to interpret as is the 'door' in the next line. A clue may be found in that the Hebrew word used for 'wall' ('*chomah*') was used by her in 5.7. There she said that the 'keepers of the walls took my shawl off me'. In 5.7, the image of a wall was associated with taking off clothes. Here it is associated with the very opposite - in metaphorical language, of building and of strength.

The door symbolises strength, but also the potential for being opened (no doubt with a sexual connotation to be inferred). One wonders about the references to silver and cedar together - both associated in the Song of Songs with Solomon. Silver first appeared on her neck (1.11) as filigree in her jewellery but the only other previous reference to silver was to the pillars which Solomon made out of silver (3.10). Silver is associated with Solomon, one final time, as we shall see shortly in 8.11 where it (and thereby Solomon) is scorned. The cedar was one of the trees which the lovers lay under in 1.15 which, as analysed in the commentary at that verse, must have been a literary device, given that no cedars grew in Israel. Its link with Lebanon and thereby the trees from which Solomon's temple and palace were built, in both the book of Kings and the Song of Songs (3.9), is obvious and may well have been so to readers of this text. She also described her lover as 'choice as cedars' (5.15) in the second *wasf*, full of Solomon metaphors as discussed earlier.

So what is the role of the references to 'silver' and 'cedar' in these verses? They appear as word parallels (each at the end of a line of verse) and so the author is inviting the comparison between them (as is also being done with the similar word parallels in these two lines between 'wall' and 'door', 'build' and besiege' and 'turret' and 'tablet'[356]). The only obvious link between 'silver' and 'cedar' is the wealth associated with both. I discuss below the relationship between 'silver' and Solomon. The wealth associated with 'cedar' is referred to above given its use in the temple. The meaning may be that these are items which are wondrous on his female lover but to be eschewed if associated with Solomon. As with so much else in the Song of Songs, this must remain a tentative explanation of these two verses which present formidable interpretative difficulties.

8.10

This is her response to his banter. Her breasts are towers. He had described her neck as such (4.4 and 7.5). He had thought the appropriate metaphor for her breasts was deer (4.5 and 7.4). She speaks about 'his eyes' as if her lover were not present. Of course this could mean that she is directly speaking to her brothers but, for the reasons I have suggested above, I do not think this is likely given the context. Rather this banter is directly addressed to her lover in the pretence that he is someone else.

The final two words of this verse have vexed commentators. Emendations have been suggested. I have translated them literally 'as one who finds peace'. Given that the word 'find' is in the feminine, the 'one' being referred to is also feminine and presumably to be identified with the female speaker.

There is much about these two words which remains mysterious but the context can assist. In the Song of Songs, the idea of 'finding' only otherwise appears in the two night scenes (3.1-4 and 5.2-8) and 8.1 ('I would find him outside and I would kiss him'). Every time the word is used previously (it has been used eight times), it is associated with the male lover, and it is always linked to the quest to find him or being found instead by others. 'Finding' therefore appears to be intimately connected with the bond between the two lovers and her quest to locate him.

The word 'peace' ('shalom') was discussed in detail in relation to the reference to the Shulamit at 7.1. There we realised that the single Hebrew word 'the Shulamite'

---

[356] The 'turret' (in Hebrew 'tirat') is linked linguistically to the 'rows' of stones on Aaron's breastpiece (in Hebrew 'tur') - see Exodus 28.17-20. The 'tablet' (in Hebrew 'luach') is the same word in Hebrew (as it is in English) which describes the two 'tablets' of stone which Moses brought down from Mount Sinai - see Exodus 31.18 et al.

had a dual meaning. It meant both 'perfect one' and had a Solomonic meaning, given that Solomon's name derives from the same root *sh-l-m*. The word '*shalom*', deriving from the same root, therefore implies that she has both found perfection and also an idealised Solomon in her lover.

That meaning is rendered even more powerful by the next two verses. Solomon reappears. There are four passages in the Song of Songs in which Solomon is expressly mentioned (he appears, as we know, seven times in total in these four passages). We are about to encounter the final such passage.

יא כֶּרֶם הָיָה לִשְׁלֹמֹה
בְּבַעַל הָמֹון
נָתַן אֶת־הַכֶּרֶם לַנֹּטְרִים
אִישׁ יָבִא בְּפִרְיֹו אֶלֶף כָּסֶף:
יב כַּרְמִי שֶׁלִּי לְפָנָי
הָאֶלֶף לְךָ שְׁלֹמֹה
וּמָאתַיִם לְנֹטְרִים אֶת־פִּרְיֹו:

He speaks:

8.11 Solomon had a vineyard
    in Baal Hamon,
he gave the vineyard to the guards,
    a man obtains a thousand pieces of silver for his fruit.
8.12 My own vineyard is all mine in front of you.
    The thousand is yours, Solomon,
        and two hundred to those who guard his fruit.

These two verses were already considered in chapter 1 of this book as a reference to the scorn heaped upon Solomon at the end of the Song of Songs. Now that we are coming to the end of the commentary, we can see that this fits perfectly with the contrast the lovers constantly set out between their own 'perfect' love and that of others, especially Solomon. The following verses are packed with fascinating references to 'vineyards', 'thousands', 'silver' and 'fruit'. There appear to be many influences on them and we will examine how these influences can assist us in interpreting them.

The name 'Baal Hamon' means 'master of plenty'. In verses which scorn Solomon's wealth, one would therefore assume that the name is entirely fictitious. Yet we have the following reference in the apocryphal book of Judith to Judith's husband,

Manasseh: 'He died in Bethulia, his home town, and was buried with his ancestors in the field that lies between Dothan and Balamon'.[357] Whether Balamon in a Greek translation[358] and the presumptive location 'Baal Hamon' are to be identified as the same place is probably unknowable. Of course, it is entirely possible that such a place did exist but that its name also got used for ulterior purposes. On the other hand, it is also possible that no such place existed and the link between the two names is merely coincidental. We cannot be sure. There is, however, further evidence relating Solomon to vineyards that comes from the book of Ecclesiastes; if, as almost all scholars do, we identify Qohelet in Ecclesiastes with Solomon, then we are told that he planted vineyards.[359]

Any attempt at a discussion as to whether Solomon actually owned a vineyard in a real place is largely beside the point. It is abundantly clear that the purpose of this reference is that Solomon is being identified with plenty. Moreover, if we look back at 8.7, we see the Hebrew word *'hon'* ('wealth'). Sounding similar to *'hamon'* ('plenty'), we have been warned that if a man gives all the wealth of his house for love, he will surely be scorned (8.7). Given the scorn shown to Solomon in 8.11-12, the identification of the scorn in 8.7 with Solomon is unmistakable.

So, whether real or imaginary, we are told at the beginning of 8.11 that Solomon owned a vineyard. There are a number of parables about vineyards in the Bible. The format here *'kerem haya l'X'* (i.e. 'X had a vineyard') occurs in two other places. It appears in Isaiah Chapter 5: 'Let me sing for my beloved, a song of my beloved about his vineyard; my beloved had a vineyard in Keren ben Shemen. He broke the ground, got rid of the stones and planted in it a choice vine and built a tower in its midst and he also hewed a wine press within it. He hoped to produce grapes but got wild grapes.'[360] The parable goes on to realise that there was nothing more that the lover could have done for the vineyard but that ultimately 'the vineyard of the Lord of Hosts is the house of Israel'.[361] The use in the Isaiah passage of the language of 'dodi' 'my beloved' immediately raises links with its use in the Song of Songs where it is the most popular word. But the comparison with the parable in Isaiah itself is limited. It is a story of sin and redemption through God whose purpose appears very different to the message contained in the Song of Songs.

---

[357] Judith 8.3 (Translation in the Jerusalem Bible). The original Greek is Βααλαμων.

[358] The book of Judith, being part of the apocrypha, was only handed down to us in the Greek translation in the Septuagint.

[359] Ecclesiastes 2.4.

[360] Isaiah 5.1-2.

[361] Isaiah 5.7.

Of more interest is the parable of Navot's vineyard.[362] Navot had the misfortune to own a vineyard abutting the palace of King Ahab, the king of Samaria. Sensing an opportunity to expand his property and build himself a vegetable garden, the king offered Navot an upgraded vineyard for a good price in a separate location, in place of the one Navot currently owned. This was, in Mafia terms, an offer which Navot could not refuse. Navot made the mistake of doing so - invoking the Lord and the fact that this vineyard was the inheritance of his fathers. Through the not entirely good offices of Queen Jezebel, the king's wife, evidence was manufactured showing that Navot had cursed God, for which the penalty was death. Navot was stoned and thereby King Ahab obtained the vineyard. He was subsequently punished by God, however, for his predatory actions.

No doubt there is a latter-day moral in this story about the dangers of resisting wealthy developers; but for our purposes, the parallels with the Song of Songs are interesting. In both cases, we have a wealthy king and an incident relating to a vineyard. In both cases, money is offered and rejected and the king involved is ultimately scorned/punished.

But we have already mentioned that a link for this short poem in 8.11-12 in the Song of Songs about Solomon also lies much closer to home. As we stated in chapter 1 above, the words 'Solomon' 'vineyards' and 'guards' also appear in 1.5-6 of the Song of Songs. Moreover the motif '*karmi sheli*' ('my own vineyard' 8.12) repeats the same phrase in 1.6. However, the difference is an important one - in 1.6 *she* says the words whereas here, *he* appropriates them as he has done on so many previous occasions. He contrasts Solomon's vineyard to his own. It is quite clear that the 'vineyard' he speaks of is also a metaphor for his lover. In so doing, he is contrasting not only Solomon's wealth to his own, but also Solomon's love to his own. It is in that context that we need to discuss the word 'thousand'.

A thousand

The word 'a thousand' (in Hebrew '*elef*') appears twice in these two verses. First it occurs in the context of the phrase '*elef kasef*' meaning 'a thousand [pieces of] silver' and then it occurs on its own. We therefore need to analyse the word itself but also consider how it works as a phrase, in conjunction with the word for 'silver', which has been analysed previously (see commentary to 8.9 above).

---

[362] I Kings 21.

The word 'a thousand' (*'elef*) has often been seen as a hint at Solomon's wives and, by several commentators within the context of these verses, as a rejection of them and everything that they stand for. Whilst this is undoubtedly true, it must nevertheless be realised that, at no point, does the Bible directly state that Solomon had a thousand wives, or use the term *'elef'*. I Kings 11.3 states that Solomon had 'women, seven hundred princesses and three hundred concubines'.[363] Of course that means that the well-known adage that Solomon had a thousand wives is not wholly incorrect, but it does mean that one is extrapolating from the text in order to reach the number a thousand. Whilst the Song of Songs clearly is linking, in vituperative fashion, to Solomon's women, it also does so by use of the number *'elef'* which does not appear in the passage just quoted from the book of Kings. Moreover, the Song of Songs specifically attributes the actual number to Solomon; 'the thousand is yours, Solomon'.

It therefore stands to reason that, whilst the *'elef'* reference could be to Solomon's wives, it could also be to any other references in the life of Solomon to the number a 'thousand' where the term *'elef'* is specifically used - unlike in the reference to Solomon's women where we infer it. We need to look at these references because they are arguably more likely to be the target of the poem's scorn. I will put references to the word thousand in inverted commas to indicate that the word being used is exactly the same one as used in the Song of Songs.

The term *'elef'* appears regularly in Solomon's life - inevitably, given its meaning, it is associated with abundance. So Solomon sacrificed a 'thousand' burnt offerings at Gibeon.[364] He owned forty 'thousand' stalls for all his horses and twelve 'thousand' horsemen.[365] But the term also applies to Solomon's wisdom; he spoke three 'thousand' proverbs and he wrote one 'thousand' and five poems.[366] It is also the term associated with the servitude related to the building of his temple and palace. The indenture involved thirty 'thousand' men sent in batches of ten 'thousand' each month. Solomon had seventy 'thousand' porters (the Hebrew word for 'porter' literally translates as 'burden bearer') and eighty 'thousand' mountain quarriers - above and beyond the three 'thousand' three hundred supervising the

---

[363] The word I have translated as 'women' could be translated as 'wives' but within a context where it then subdivides between princesses and concubines, this does not seem to make sense. In any event importantly, the word *'elef'* (a 'thousand') is not used. I Kings 11 has no parallel in the book of Chronicles.
[364] I Kings 3.4.
[365] I Kings 5.6. See also I Kings 10.26 where similar references are made.
[366] I Kings 5.12.

work.[367]   Once all Solomon's building work was completed, Solomon sacrificed twenty-two 'thousand' oxen and a hundred and twenty 'thousand' sheep.[368]

This therefore indicates that the word 'thousand' had a number of significances for the author of the Song of Songs. Whilst we associate it (and so probably did the author of the Song of Songs) with Solomon's penchant for women, the Bible directly associates it with Solomon's wealth, wisdom, oppression of his people and displays of opulence before God. It is all these which the Song of Songs is here directly rejecting by use of the word 'thousand' - they are yours, Solomon.

A thousand [pieces of] silver

The reference to a 'thousand' follows a reference to '*elef kasef*' ('a thousand [pieces of] silver'). Its significance in relation to a vineyard is clear from Isaiah 7.23 where a thousand vines obtain one a thousand [pieces of] silver. So the vine was clearly associated with opulence and a thousand [pieces of] silver implies a large amount of money. The phrase is, however, also used in two other Biblical contexts involving scorn and sexual compromise. We need to examine both of them.

First, in II Samuel 18 Absalom, David's son, who has rebelled against him is hanging in the air suspended between heaven and earth as a result of his head being caught in the branches of a tree whilst riding a mule: 'And one man saw it and he told Joab [David's general] and he said "Behold I have seen Absalom hanging in a terebinth [a small tree]". And Joab said to the man who had spoken to him "So you saw and why did you not bludgeon him to the ground - it would have been for me then to give you ten [pieces of] silver and one belt." And the man said to Joab "Even if I could weigh a thousand [pieces of] silver in my palms, I would not touch the son of the king, because the king commanded you, Avishai and Itai within our hearing to guard the lad Absalom.'[369] In this passage therefore, the phrase 'a thousand [pieces of] silver' is used to scorn abusing or killing Absalom, even if he rebelled, because he was the son of king David. Absalom, as a result of that rebellion, never became king. In the Song of Songs, a thousand [pieces of] silver is ironically used to scorn the son of David who was actually crowned.

Second, in Genesis 20, Abraham goes to Gerar in the Negev region with his wife, Sarah. Fearing that both he and Sarah would be in danger if others knew they were a married couple, he passes her off as his sister (which certainly has resonances in

---

[367] I Kings 5.27-30.
[368] I Kings 8.62.
[369] II Samuel 18.10 - 12.

the Song of Songs - see 8.1). Avimelech, the king of Gerar, takes Sarah but God appears to Avimelech, in a night vision, to warn him off what we might now term an inappropriate relationship. Both God and Avimelech agree that Avimelech had had entirely honourable aspirations, with no intention of snatching someone else's wife. Avimelech then asks Abraham why Abraham had placed him in such a compromising position. Abraham replies that he feared being killed were the truth revealed. Avimelech gives Abraham various gifts and returns Sarah to Abraham, her husband, who has doubled up as her brother. Avimelech then says to Sarah: 'Behold I have given a thousand [pieces of] silver to your brother and it will serve you as a covering of the eyes'.[370] This last phrase appears to be some sort of payment in case others suspect what has gone on - Alter translates it as 'a shield against censorious eyes'.[371] So the words seem to indicate some sort of pre-payment for any damage which Sarah might suffer to her reputation as a result of the incident.

The contexts of these two passages are different from each other and each, in turn, from the passage in the Song of Songs. But from both those other passages, we can see the following: the phrase 'a thousand [pieces of] silver' indicates a large amount of money but is associated with payment being made in highly dubious circumstances where a) the murder of the son of the king could have been carried out but was not, or b) an act could have occurred (sexual impropriety) but did not. It stands to reason, therefore, that the phrase 'a thousand [pieces of] silver' itself has a connotation of scorn from both these other contexts in which it appears in the Bible.

It is the 'thousand pieces of silver' which the male lover in the Song of Songs is scorning. He associates it with Solomon. At no point in the book of Kings is the phrase 'a thousand pieces of silver' used in conjunction with Solomon. However, in the book of Chronicles, the words do appear together but in reverse order. We have already referred to it briefly in chapter 4 above. We see a detailed instruction from David to his son Solomon about the building of the temple which does not appear in the book of Kings. The book of Chronicles talks about what David had prepared for Solomon to put in the temple: 'Look, in my poverty, I have prepared for the house of God gold one hundred thousand talents, *silver a thousand* thousand talents, and so much copper and iron that it cannot be weighed as there is so much of it...'[372]

---

[370] Genesis 20.16.

[371] *Genesis Translation and Commentary:* Robert Alter, Norton, New York, 1996, 96

[372] I Chronicles 22.14. See also I Chronicles 29.1-10.

So the phrase 'thousand [pieces of] silver' which appears in other stories in the Bible as a byword for highly dubious payments is also used, in slightly different form, to describe the enormous wealth which Solomon inherited from his father.

We can therefore sum up our conclusions relating to the words 'silver' and 'thousand'. The word 'silver', on its own, in the Song of Songs indicates the woman's body (1.11 and 8.9) as well as wealth and Solomon (3.10 and 8.11). The word a 'thousand' is commonly associated with Solomon's thousand wives but linguistically it is used constantly in the book of Kings to describe various key acts in Solomon's life. The combined phrase 'a thousand [pieces of] silver' has extremely negative connotations in two unlinked stories, and is associated with the great wealth which Solomon inherited from David in the book of Chronicles. It is all this which the lover in the Song of Songs is both scorning and rejecting. Zakovitch puts it well: 'The poet who mocks Solomon wants no part of the royal vineyard, not for wealth, nor for an increase in wives. He is happy with his own vineyard; his one and only woman'.[373]

Two hundred for the guards of the fruit

This phrase is difficult to interpret. In the parallel passage in 1.6 where it is the young woman who is speaking, her mother's sons placed her as guard of the vineyards and then she adds that she had not guarded her own vineyard. We have already identified the 'vineyard' with wealth and the woman herself. On that basis, there are two possible explanations for this difficult phrase. It could be a comment about the rate of payment for those who work Solomon's vineyards (it could be intended to show a low rate of return but that must be a very tentative suggestion) or it could be a possible comment that Solomon has to pay for his women, whereas the male lover certainly does not. Fox suggests[374] that the lover enjoys his own vineyard (i.e. his lover) but Solomon has to share his with the guards. This makes sense of the gender of the guards here (they are masculine) but has to ignore the intertextual link to 1.6 where she is the guard.

יג הַיּוֹשֶׁבֶת בַּגַּנִּים
חֲבֵרִים מַקְשִׁיבִים לְקוֹלֵךְ הַשְׁמִיעִנִי:
יד בְּרַח ׀ דּוֹדִי
וּדְמֵה־לְךָ לִצְבִי
אוֹ לְעֹפֶר הָאַיָּלִים
עַל הָרֵי בְשָׂמִים:

---

[373] Zakovitch, 140.
[374] Fox (1985), 175

He speaks to her:

8.13 O one who dwells in gardens,
friends listen to your voice, let me hear it.

She speaks to him:

8.14 Get away, my love,
and make yourself like a gazelle
or a deer of the hinds
on the mountains of spice.

These two verses, fragmentary in nature, appear to bring us back to the earlier dialogue. In 8.13, he seems to be speaking to her but the text is difficult. The Blochs suggest that he is telling her that, just as their friends listen to her voice, he should now be permitted to hear it.[375] This requires a change in the Masoretic accentuation on the word '*chaverim*' ('friends') to render a disjunctive accent conjunctive. It seems, though, that nothing else will help make sense of this phrase and it appears to be a sensible suggestion.

We have seen how she has previously been compared to a garden (4.12); the metaphor returns now. His reference is now in the plural. One should realise how the word 'garden' (in Hebrew '*gan*') has been used in the Song of Songs. It only appears halfway through the Song of Songs and it is introduced by him (4.12) just after he has found his voice in the first wasf. He then uses the plural '*ganim*' (4.15). She uses 'his' (as it were) garden word to describe to her friends where he is (6.2) and immediately uses the plural a well. So she has learnt from him how to dwell in gardens.

Her reply is deeply enigmatic. It repeats the words of 2.17 with two differences - in the first and last words. Previously, she had commenced the phrase by telling him to 'turn'; now she tells him to 'escape' or 'get away'. Turning has the potential for return - so does 'get away' or 'escape' but return seems more distant in terms both of time and likelihood because the verb indicates a form of fleeing. We will never find out whether he returns. The final word in 2.17 described the mountain as the 'cleft' mountains. Here the mountains are mountains of 'spices'. The word 'spices'

---

[375] Bloch, 220.

(in Hebrew '*besamim*') which occurs eight times[376] in the Song of Songs, and plays such a crucial role, only appears for the first time in 4.10. Like the word 'garden' referred to above, it is, as it were, 'his' word in that she had spoken the vast majority of the lines up to Solomon's first full appearance in 3.6 and had not used the word. He has appropriated so much of her terminology but, now, at the very end, she uses her own previous phrase but adapts it to what she has learnt from him, by changing the crucial last word which we hear to 'spices'.

All commentators remark on the way the poem seems to end inconclusively. We do not know what happens to our lovers. Indeed, we do not know how they first met. Exum says 'without beginning and without end, the poem like the love it celebrates strives to be everlasting'.[377] Yet in one sense the poem really does end - with the sense of smell. In a poem so full of the senses, all we are left with at the very end is the sense that seems to stay longest in our memory: smell.

---

[376] 4.10, 4.14, 4.16, 5.1, 5.13, 6.2(x2) and here in 8.14.
[377] Exum, 245.

Part Three

שִׁיר הַשִּׁירִים

אֲשֶׁר לִשְׁלֹמֹה

The Song of Songs

which is about Solomon

SIX

Solomon and the Song of Songs

A scent often lingers long after its bearer has departed the scene. The male lover disappears into the 'hill of spices' without responding to his beloved, or indeed to our own desire to learn more about him. His incense leaves only a tantalising hint of the figure once present. But perhaps that smoke also provides a suitable metaphor for the fog which has bedevilled much of the effort to interpret the Song of Songs over the millennia.

In part one, we considered the 'Solomon' to whom the editor of the Song of Songs was responding. In part two, we looked at the Song of Songs bearing in mind the analysis undertaken in part one. Now is an appropriate time to bring the two parts together in order to see what themes and motifs run through the Song of Songs without specific focus on individual texts.

So the purpose of part three will be to seek to lift some (but regrettably not all) of the fog. Its three chapters will consider three separate but interrelated areas. This chapter will consider the role that Solomon and the temple have to play in the Song of Songs which, in turn, invites a reappraisal of the poem's structure. Chapter 7 goes on to examine why this leads naturally to a conclusion that the Song of Songs is a radical book. Finally, chapter 8 considers what we can say about the real hero of the Song of Songs, its editor.

In order to analyse the role which Solomon and the temple properly have to play in a full understanding of the Song of Songs, we need to address a common modern fallacy - that the Song of Songs is nothing more than a secular love song.

Simply a secular love song?

Paradoxically, we may owe it to the original Jewish allegorical interpretation that we even know of the Song of Songs' existence. The early Rabbis' own comments leave little doubt that they believed in the allegorical interpretation whereby the text is a love song between God and Israel and nothing else. Yet they were also aware of divergent views and other uses to which their holy book was put. We know from a tradition dating back to the second century CE that Rabbi Akiva criticised those who would sing it in banquet halls or treat it as some ordinary song - such people, he added, had no place in the world to come.[378] It is a hint of the ancient popularity of the Song of Songs, a work which may never have been known to us but for Rabbi Akiva's powers of persuasion (discussed in chapter 5 above) which permitted it to enter into the canon.

This allegorical interpretation is therefore a blessing; without it, the Song of Songs is highly unlikely to have survived. Yet it has also proved a curse - in that it has constantly been subjected to reductionism. The Song of Songs has too often been interpreted as meaning one thing and one thing only. Following swiftly on from the God-Israel reduction in the Jewish tradition was the Church's reduction of the work to a conversation between Christ and the church.

The vast majority of modern readers of the Song of Songs reject these interpretations and, as such, see themselves as free from the interpretive straitjacket of any such form of reduction. In this, most are mistaken. The *weltanschauung* of nineteenth-century scholarly orthodoxy still wields an enormous influence, almost certainly subconscious, on the majority of readers of the Bible in general, and the Song of Songs in particular. No longer a work of allegory, the Song of Songs has been rendered entirely secular and thereby reduced again, this time for different purposes - it has become nothing more than a simple secular love song. It is crucial to a better understanding of the Song of Songs to reject this modern reduction for at least two reasons.

First, our analysis has revealed that there is nothing simple about the Song of Songs. The poetry is remarkably rich and its constant allusions make it one of the most sophisticated and mysterious works to have come down to us from the ancient world. Sometimes, it defies understanding. Whilst it is clearly a love song, it is also much more than that.

Second, the commonly assumed notion that the Song of Songs is 'secular' is, at best, deeply misleading. The word 'secular' is defined in the Chambers English Dictionary as 'relating to the present world, or to things not spiritual; civil, not ecclesiastical; lay, not concerned with religion'.[379] The Song of Songs defies such a definition; at various stages, it is deeply concerned with religion in the course of revealing its love story; themes constantly appear which have a clear or potential link to the spiritual, ecclesiastical mores of the time. That link is often highly critical

---

[378] Tosefta 12:10.
[379] *Chambers Dictionary* 11th Edition 2008.

but this fact does not render it 'secular'; at times, it is deeply theological in the way it connects the two lovers to the power of the temple.

Solomon and the Song of Songs

So why is it that the accepted picture which we have of the Song of Songs is often so different to the one portrayed in this book? I would argue that this is down to the shift of emphasis here. If one asks the question, what does King Solomon have to do with a book in which he is neither of the main protagonists, one is also obliged to re-address many of the issues and interpretations which have become received wisdom. Of course, one must do so with care. When one approaches the Song of Songs, the temptation towards reductionism is great indeed, as its reception history shows only too clearly. The argument in this book could have been that the whole of the Song of Songs is ultimately about Solomon. Such a theory appears untenable, since there is scant or no evidence to back it up in some of the scenes. Yet the reverse argument seems to have been crucial, often unconsciously so, in most modern commentaries - namely that if Solomon is not one of the lovers, the seven passing references to him are largely insignificant, and little or no regard ought to be given to them.

This book has not considered the historical Solomon extraneous to the Bible. Such a figure is elusive. Evidence discovered in 1993 on an inscription in Tel Dan, in modern day northern Israel, refers to the victory of an Aramean king over 'the king of Israel' and 'the king of the House of David'. The inscription has been dated to the ninth century BCE, sometime after the period when David would have lived (probably in the tenth century BCE). Most academics accept this as strong extra-Biblical evidence tending to show the existence of David. No such evidence has so far been comprehensively accepted by the academic community for the existence of Solomon. One theory argues that the historical David and Solomon did exist but that the grandiose descriptions of their achievements simply cannot match the reality of their era when they were little more than local chieftains of an insignificant part of Judah called Jerusalem. They were built up into heroes by one of their ninth-century successors, King Omri, whose scribes created the books of Samuel and Kings. And the rest, as they say, is history - they have played major roles in both Judaism and Christianity ever since.[380]

---

[380] *David and Solomon: In search of the Bible's Sacred Kings and the Roots of the Western Tradition,* Israel Finkelstein and Neil Asher Silberman. Free Press, New York, 2006.

So historical evidence about Solomon extraneous to the Bible is limited in the extreme and, where it does exist, is subject to great dispute. That is not, however, why this book has steered clear of the historical Solomon, whoever that may (or may not) have been. It has avoided it for a much simpler reason; it is simply irrelevant to the portrayal of Solomon in the Song of Songs. There is a wide range of potential dates for the authorship of the Song of Songs but they all put the text several centuries after the time of King Solomon. While not impossible, it is highly unlikely that the editor of the Song of Songs had access to much more material about King Solomon than we have. Of course, the editor had the advantage over us of the contemporary evidence of the Jerusalem of the period in which the Song of Songs was written. That, crucially, included the temple. If, as most scholars accept, the Song of Songs is a relatively late Biblical work, then this would have been the second temple.

Ultimately therefore the editor of the Song of Songs probably only had the same sources to rely on concerning King Solomon as we do - the books of Kings and Chronicles - together, possibly, with any other books about Solomon that have not survived. In other words, the Solomon portrayed in the Song of Songs is a literary figure, reworked from the historical books to depict the same character in a very different situation and therefore in a very different light.

This retuning of our focus on the Song of Songs is necessary to concentrate on the messages which it is actually expressing. Yes, it most definitely is a love song between two lovers; both the Rabbis and the church were wrong initially to ignore, or downplay, this part of the Song of Songs. Yet the subtlety of the message, through the incredibly carefully chosen words, means that it is much more than just an ancient love song.

In his section on 'Solomon in the Song of Songs' Zakovitch makes reference to seven topics in the book of Kings which relate Solomon to the Song of Songs. Five relate to the temple - his wealth in a) gold and silver, b) ivory, c) precious stones, d) spices and e) cedars and cypresses. The other two concern his proverbial ability to compose songs (I Kings 5.12) and his thousand wives (I Kings 11.3).[381] Zakovitch then briefly outlines in a few paragraphs the links to the Song of Songs. Let us do the same - again by topic - but in much greater detail. We will start with the temple and Solomon's palace.

---

[381] Zakovitch 10-11.

The temple and palace in the Song of Songs

We commence where there is the most direct link with Solomon and the events of his life. That leads us to the 'palanquin' referred to in 3.9, a word which appears nowhere else in the Song of Songs or the Bible, leaving its meaning conjectural. Yet the wording surrounding it presents a clear picture of what is being described. The 'palanquin' is made by King Solomon of Lebanon wood - an obvious reference to cedar. It has pillars (as did both the temple and palace), despite the fact that a palanquin (if that is what is intended) is movable. Its seat is purple (a colour associated with royalty). The twist at the end of the verse is that 'in its midst it was inlaid with love' - a real jolt from the royal, to a transformative meaning in line with the assertion of the lovers that their love was special.

As Zakovitch points out, the 'cedars and cypresses' in 1.17 are also 'temple' terminology and thereby linked to Solomon. This should put the alert reader on notice because the context of the reference in 1.17 apparently bears no link to Solomon at all. The female lover is ending a section of *al fresco* 'dialogue' (where she engages in most of the interplay between the lovers) and then says: 'the beams of our houses are cedars, our rafters are cypresses'. The comment points to the contrast between the town-confined temple and the freedom of the lovers in their rural idyll (an idyll which ironically is itself imaginary because the cedar was not native to the Jerusalem area).

Zakovitch refers to the word 'thousand' which is used three times (4.4, 8.11 and 8.12) in the Song of Songs but associates it merely with the 'thousand' wives linked to Solomon. As we noted in the commentary to 8.11 and 8.12, the word 'thousand' is not used in relation to Solomon's women (I Kings 11.3) but it is used regularly in describing Solomon's wealth, his oppression and his 'show' of making sacrifices worthy of his God. It is all this which the lovers scorn, in addition to the polygamy.

In the second *wasf* (5.10-16), she describes his stomach as made of 'ivory' and the 'fine gold' pedestals for the marble pillars which are his thighs. These two, extremely rare Hebrew words, used in close proximity, (5.14-15) are those used to describe the ivory throne of King Solomon made of the finest gold (I Kings 10.18).

The spices mentioned in the Song of Songs appear at various points throughout but all the spices appear together as a cluster at 4.13-14. As analysed at that point in the commentary, the description of the temple is silent on the use of spices, notwithstanding the detailed prescription in the book of Exodus concerning exactly which spices (and in which proportions) ought to be used in the tabernacle. All the spices mentioned in the book of Exodus (and some seem to be very obscure) appear in the Song of Songs; the two which are to be used in the greatest proportions, myrrh and frankincense, occur most frequently in the Song. This may be a jibe at the failure of Solomon to observe the requirements divinely prescribed, a failure stressed in the books of Kings and Chronicles by the arrival of the Queen of Sheba who has to provide the absent spices. We are never told whether those spices ever entered the temple for the purpose of providing the incense for the sacrifices. The lovers sprinkle them liberally on their bodies in contrast to their presumed omission from the temple ritual.

The image of Lebanon and the Song of Songs

The reductionism which has beset so much of the commentary on the Song of Songs is perhaps at its clearest when it comes to extraneous evidence about its imagery. Consider the following from one of the leading late twentieth-century German language commentaries. In translation it comments as follows on 4.6b ('I will get myself to the mountain of myrrh, to the hill of frankincense'):

"It seems unlikely that '*har hamor*' ['mountain of myrrh'] is a play on '*har hamoriah*' ['Mount Moriah'] and '*givat halevonah*' ['hill of frankincense'] a play on '*levanon*' ['Lebanon'], … an ancient Egyptian incantation already has the word pair 'myrrh/frankincense' in an erotic context, where a demon is exorcised with the following words: *Go, please and sleep there/ where your beautiful wives are./ Put myrrh on their hair and fresh frankincense on their members.*"[382]

The implication of this comment appears to be that there is *an* explanation for this difficult line and that academic detective work has solved the mystery of its meaning, by retrieving an ancient source text with its obvious erotic overtones. The flaw in this argument is its failure to acknowledge the complexity of the Song of Songs. Perhaps an analogy can be made to Shakespeare studies. One critical edition of Hamlet opens with the words: 'The basic though not the immediate source of *Hamlet* is a twelfth-century story of Amleth in Saxo Grammaticus's *Historiae Danicae*, which was first put into print in 1514.'[383] No Shakespeare scholar would conclude that Hamlet could be explained by examining those sources, or even the actual history of Denmark. Nor conversely, of course, would such a scholar ignore them. They would form part of the mix. The sources would be used as an aid to

---

[382] Keel, 152, note 14.
[383] *Hamlet Prince of Denmark, The New Cambridge Shakespeare*, 1985, CUP, Cambridge p1.

understanding what went into creating the play we now know as Hamlet, a work of supreme artistry, fashioned by a playwright at the very height of his powers.

Why should we treat the Song of Songs any differently? It is the contention of this book (from which there is little, if any, dissent in other commentaries) that the Song of Songs is also a work of genius, fashioned by a supremely gifted wordsmith. It is of great interest that scholarship over the last two hundred years has informed us that the myrrh/frankincense parallel can also be found in ancient Egyptian love poetry but, unfortunately, this resolves nothing. The editor of the Song of Songs may well have been aware of a parallel Egyptian poem but it is how that source was used which shows us why that editor was such an expert at the craft of writing. As we have seen, myrrh and frankincense were a word pair, not just in Egyptian erotic literature, but also in the tabernacle. They have a context within the Song of Songs; they appear in the first *wasf* which immediately follows the re-introduction of King Solomon into the poem: a re-introduction which, in turn, radically changes the terms, and vocabulary, of the lovers' discourse.

Within such a background, it is entirely conceivable that the editor of the Song of Songs took an old Egyptian love poem and reworked it into both a similar and a very different context, first as the culmination of an erotic tour down the female body (the immediate context of the reference in the Song of Songs) but also as a comparison of these particular spices to the Jerusalem which had just been described in the Solomon interlude. The Song of Songs, like Hamlet, defies an easy solution to its meaning. Both the meanings of this verse, set out above, sit easily with each other. Accepting one should in no way imply rejecting the other.

When it comes to the use in the Song of Songs of the word 'Lebanon', we are even more subject to an implied reductionism. No extraneous evidence is required to make clear that the primary reference for this word is the territory to the north of Israel and it is by this pure geographical reference that many of the commentaries explain away the 'Lebanon' references in the Song of Songs. Again, it is not that I reject such explanations. But as this commentary has sought to show, they can only be partial. That said, twentieth century archeological evidence has revealed fascinating parallels.

The Jewish scholar Michael Fishbane makes the point powerfully in his commentary. His starting point is the fact that the ancient Ugaritic language was rediscovered in 1929 as a result of an archeological find in modern day Syria. It is a language with many similarities to Biblical Hebrew. Fishbane refers to the use of poetic pairs and, in particular, the phrase in 4.8 of the Song of Songs: 'With me from

Lebanon bride, with me from Lebanon come.   Come down from the peak of Amanah'. He then comments: 'This form is of Ugaritic vintage, with exact parallels in the old epic literature. Such similarities point to the strong stylistic influence of this Canaanite literature, with other parallels in the liturgical poetry of Psalms. There was evidently much literary crossover.'[384]

We here have a fascinating glimpse at a potential source for references to Lebanon, and indeed other references, in the Song of Songs. But on each such occasion, we need to exercise extraordinary caution if we wish to ascribe its use to a mere reworking of an old source. In other words, we need to be wary of attributing its function in its new context as having the same intention as that in the Ugaritic original. That is not however to reject such a motivation as the sole purpose of its appropriation but rather to say that this assumption has been far too common in much of the modern reception history. One has to look at the evidence and see where it leads and draw overall conclusions. Beyond other cultures' parallels, such evidence includes other Biblical texts and, crucially, its context within the Song of Songs.

Within that context, let us re-examine the use of the word 'Lebanon' in the Song of Songs. The word appears seven times (3.9, 4.8 [twice], 4.11, 4.15, 5.15 and 7.5). Its first occurrence in 3.9 in the Solomon interlude should alert us to the fact that its use will not merely be that of a geographical reference to the territory to the north of Israel. It immediately follows the first reference to '*levonah*' ('frankincense') in 3.6.[385] 'Lebanon' is associated with wood used in Solomon's 'palanquin' which, given the other new terminology in the Solomon interlude, alerts the reader and/or listener to its links to the temple. Cedars have previously been referred to (1.17) in an apparently rural reference but, when used in connection with cypresses, remind the reader/listener of their use not only in the temple (I Kings 6.15) but also of their connection with Lebanon which makes its first direct appearance in the Solomon interlude.

The next two passages relating to Lebanon in 4.8 contain clear geographical references to the location itself - it is in this context that Fishbane's comment on the Ugaritic link becomes so useful. However, we cannot leave it at that. The word in 4.8 appears soon after the reference to 'frankincense' in 4.6 ('*levonah*') and immediately before the reference to 'you have stolen my heart' ('*libavtini*') in 4.9. In other words, whilst the original meaning of the phrase (given its derivation from Ugaritic literature) relates it to the place, its context with the Song of Songs invites

---

[384] Fishbane, Introduction at xxxiv.
[385] Frankincense appears only three times in the Song of Songs: 3.6, 4.6 and 4.14.

other meanings, linked to the intentions of the editor of the Song of Songs and not to those of the author of the original Ugaritic source. In the commentary at 4.8, those other meanings were discussed and the suggestion was made that the original poem about Lebanon had been woven into a poem about the two lovers and King Solomon.

Foremost amongst those other meanings is the wordplay between '*levanon*' and '*levonah*' which comes to the fore in the rest of chapter 4 of the Song of Songs. Lebanon appears again at 4.11 and 4.15. The female lover's dress is described as having the scent of Lebanon in 4.11 and the fountain of gardens in 4.15 flows from Lebanon. These Lebanon references are interspersed with the only other two references to frankincense. The 'hill of frankincense' in 4.6 has already been discussed. The final reference to frankincense is telling. It appears with all the other spices in 4.14 and at first glance merely seems to be part of a list. Yet it is described as '*im kol atzei levonah*' (literally 'with all the woods of frankincense'). We should not miss the clearly intended wordplay with the '*atzei halevanon*' (the 'woods of Lebanon') in the Solomon interlude in 3.9. Lebanon is linked to the temple and to the lovers. By Lebanon's constant interplay with 'frankincense', we realise that 'frankincense' is more than just another spice and we are invited to share the allusions which the editor clearly wants us to make to its use, not just on the bodies of the lovers, but also its prescription in the tabernacle and omission from the temple.

The Lebanon used in the Solomon interlude becomes the male lover's word as he uses it four times in his first long speech in chapter 4 of the Song of Songs. It is an important part of him 'finding his voice', as it were, given his reticence in the first three chapters of the work. 'Lebanon' makes its next appearance in the female lover's only *wasf*. Here the word's intricate associations reach their culmination. In 5.15, she describes her lover's appearance as like Lebanon and choice as cedars. To the untutored eye, this reference is merely geographical but we have learnt to be sceptical of single-meaning explanations. Lebanon and cedars point not only north but also to the seat of power in Jerusalem where cedars grow[386] in the house of the Lord. Her lover is apparently being likened to both. Within the context of the question she is being asked in 5.9 ('how is your lover better than another lover?') to which this comment is her answer, we realise that 'Lebanon' is in fact a point of comparison which favours the lover over any other lover and, by implication, even over the Lebanon cedars, whether in their original habitat, or in their more familiar environment in Jerusalem.

---

[386] See Psalms 92.13-14 for this image of cedars 'growing' in the temple.

The final reference to Lebanon in 7.5 appears not to be playing on the Lebanon/temple terminology which has had such an important part in the previous references. It occurs at a later stage in the Song of Songs where, within the context of the verse, references are being made to northern Israel and southern Lebanon.

Literary messages by use of word repetition

Segal highlights the number of times a word is used as itself constituting a message from the editor of the text.[387] He stresses that the words 'Solomon', 'daughters of Jerusalem', 'mother' and 'my soul' all appear seven times. To this we can now add the word 'Lebanon' which also appears seven times. Segal argues that repetition in this way is an acknowledged literary technique. Indeed he refers to an article[388] in which the Biblical commentator, Robert Gordis, maintains that, when speaking of the significance of numbers, '[p]re-eminent above all others in Semitic life and thought is the number "seven"'.[389] There are of course many examples of this which Gordis quotes, such as the Sabbath, the seven-yearly Sabbatical year, the Jubilee (7 x 7), the feast of weeks (taking place seven weeks after Passover) and the seven days of Passover. But prime amongst these is the creation story itself.

Gordis' insight may have derived from the work relating to the creation story of the mid-twentieth century commentator Umberto Cassuto. Cassuto analysed the Genesis story and found numerous examples of the text playing with the number 'seven' - i.e. the first verse contains seven words, the second verse fourteen, the words in the paragraph about the creation of the Sabbath contain thirty-five words etc. He also gives numerous examples of individual words appearing seven times.[390]

Both Gordis and Cassuto were considering examples of the appearance of the number seven in literary units considerably shorter than the 117 verses of the Song of Songs. The question which we face is whether the number of occurrences of key words in a longer text such as the Song of Songs retains the meaning which Gordis and Cassuto, in my view, persuasively argue for in the shorter texts which they have analysed. The number 'seven' was associated with perfection precisely *because* it was related to the creation of the world in seven days.

---

[387] Segal, 151-4.

[388] *'The Heptad as an element of Biblical and Rabbinic Style', Robert Gordis.* Journal of Biblical Literature 62 (1943) 17-26.

[389] Ibid 17.

[390] *A Commentary on the Book of Genesis: Part One From Adam to Noah*, Magnes Press, Jerusalem, 1998, 12-15.

I, for one, retain a certain scepticism. It is highly likely that certain words will appear seven times in any text without any forethought on the part of the writer.[391] Yet there are certain critical words where one's scepticism is challenged. Take for instance the key word 'Solomon' which, of course, appears seven times. As we have seen, the word is not just a name; it also means 'perfection'. The word is transformed in the song, as it were, onto the lovers. She uses the language of the temple and palace to describe him in Solomonic terms (5.14-15). He expressly describes her as 'the perfect one' (7.1). They have each become 'Solomon'. Scholars agree that the very final verse to be added to the text was probably the superscription. In other words, the editor was faced with a text with *six* references to Solomon. To render it perfect, another had to be added as part of the superscription; in doing so, it became seven and 'perfect'/'whole'. This literary device appears to have been followed in the other late Biblical work where Solomon appears as a character in the form of Qohelet; in the book of Ecclesaiastes, the word '*Qohelet*' also appears seven times.[392]

Whether such an argument can be sustained in relation to words such as 'Lebanon', 'daughters of Jerusalem', 'mother' and 'my soul' is also a fascinating one given that they all appear seven times. The symbol of 'Lebanon' is tremendously important in the Song of Songs as described above. So is Jerusalem; Lebanon comes to Jerusalem in the Song of Songs much as Birnam Wood comes to Dunsinane.[393] The number of insertions could have been deliberately chosen to reflect their symbolic importance. Perhaps not, though; scepticism rears its rational, ugly head again. All such number links could also be coincidental. Indeed, one can ask similar questions with roots which appear to have great significance. The root '*m-l-ch*' appears seven times, five times in male form meaning 'king' and twice in female form as 'queen[s]'. The relationship with royalty is an important one, discussed above in the commentary and in detail below. Was the number of references to royalty deliberately linked to the perfect number?

I wish we knew the answer, but this is a question where a great deal of doubt must remain. It relates to the intention of the editor concerning the Song's overall structure. In this regard, thankfully, there are certain aspects of the Song's structure which yield much greater clarity and where clearer conclusions can be drawn. It is these which we now consider.

---

[391] For example the word *'yayin'* 'wine' appears seven times (1.2, 1.4, 2.4, 4.11, 5.1, 7.4 and 8.2) but it is difficult to see that this word has any greater significance than others which appear six times (*'yonah'* - 'dove') or eight times (*'re'ach'* - 'smell').

[392] Ecclesiastes 1.1, 1.2, 1.12, 7.27, 12.8, 12.9 and 12.10.

[393] *Macbeth* Shakespeare. Act 4, scene 1

The overall structure of the Song of Songs

The 'Lebanon' motif in the Song of Songs, analysed earlier, highlights a more general issue which is crucial to understanding the whole poem's nature. If, as appears likely, the Song of Songs was, indeed, originally a separate series of poems, there is no doubt that it is their weaving together by the editor which exhibits genius. Words and motifs transcend the original poetry to create a whole out of an apparently disparate set of parts. It is for this reason that the discussion in chapter 5 of this book regarding the analogy made to Schubert's *Schwanengesang* was necessary. At that stage, it was not yet possible to say much more about how the disparate parts of the work fitted in together. Now that we have finished the commentary, we are no longer inhibited in this way. A deliberate choice was made by the editor as to the order in which the poems would be presented to the reader and/or listener. We need therefore to take a broad sweep of the structure of the Song of Songs and examine what that tells us about the editor's literary intent in the use of this structure.

The starting point for any study of the overall structure of the Song of Songs must be an acknowledgment of the difficulty of such a venture. Various attempts by commentators at constructing a 'story' from the poem have mostly failed to persuade readers of their merit. The references to lovers, mothers and weddings suggested to many eighteenth- and nineteenth-century commentators that this was an elaborate wedding ceremony. Yet any such notion fails on the basis that parts of the jigsaw do not fit the purported theme - with the result that the puzzle inevitably remained unsatisfactorily incomplete.

Given that it is the aim of this work to bring the presence of Solomon in the Song of Songs much more to the fore, one ought to consider a fresh overall structure of the work with this new perspective borne in mind. Winston Churchill famously described Russia as 'a riddle wrapped in a mystery inside an enigma'. One sometimes feels the same sentiment when looking at the Song of Songs but, perhaps, this new perspective can open up fresh meaning on the old enigma.

Our starting point is the first verse, discussed previously. By the use of the dual-meaning words 'song of songs', it announces itself as both superlative and a unified collection. We are immediately told that it is about Solomon which, given his relatively rare appearances in the work, surprises us. He makes his second appearance shortly afterwards in 1.5 ('like Solomon's curtains') which seems no more than a passing reference (taken as such by many commentators; amended, almost certainly incorrectly by others, to an entirely different meaning). Having read the whole work, we see that Solomon makes another appearance in a scene almost as similarly distant from the end of the poem as this text is from the beginning. Given that there are other words which occur in both these passages, we realise that Solomon provides an 'inclusio' - a wrapping of the poem, as it were. This technique of the use of the same words to indicate the beginning and end of poems also occurs throughout the Song of Songs in relation to *individual* poems; Solomon therefore provides one of the words for this technique in relation to the meta-poem, the whole of the Song of Songs. It is a strong hint as to his overall importance.

Yet, notwithstanding this, at the beginning of the work, Solomon seems to disappear from the scene as quickly as he was introduced. He makes no further direct appearances in the first two chapters. These chapters contain dialogue between the lovers in which the female lover speaks considerably more than her male lover: four times as much. At one point indeed (2.10-13), he can only speak via her words ('my lover answered and said...'). Their words, through these two chapters, are tender, teasing, erotic and often redolent of other Biblical texts,[394] a reminder to us, if one were needed, that we cannot understand the Song of Songs independently of its context, one important component of which was the other Biblical texts to which the editor had access.

Near the end of chapter 2, there is a hint of a breakdown. At 2.15 is an enigmatic sentence, probably spoken by the female lover, which relates an incident concerning foxes ruining the vineyard. We are left in tantalising suspense by this information which is never fully explained. It does introduce us, though, to the first five verses of chapter 3 which break this rustic image of lovers' delight. The scene now is the female lover's bed in the town. She is alone and gets up to search for her lover. She is clearly speaking of a loss about which we previously had had no idea. Her deepest hope is to find him, the image occurs for the first time in this passage (3.1-5) and will recur at later stages in the Song of Songs, possibly resolved almost at the very end of the work (see commentary on *'kemotzait shalom'* 'like one who finds peace' - the final two words of 8.10).

The Solomon interlude (3.6-11) is crucial. It transforms the dialogue of the parties. It does so in two ways. First, as we will see, the relationship between the two lovers changes utterly after its appearance - their terms of reference are entirely different. Second, its appearance induces new vocabulary such as the *'levanon'/'levonah'* wordplay not used previously. Its significance is perhaps not fully understood except with the benefit of hindsight. We know that, at the end of the Song of Songs,

---

[394] In this regard, see commentary on 1.4, 1.17, 2.5, 2.12.

Solomon is explicitly scorned by the male lover (8.11-12). In that light, the puzzling, ambiguous references to Solomon in this interlude take on a clearer satirical tone with their comments concerning the need for bodyguards and fear of the night. Beds and palanquins which parade around Jerusalem may seem odd at first sight and could, indeed, have an innocuous purpose but, in the context of a king who is ultimately expressly rejected, take on entirely different overtones. The great King Solomon is being ridiculed.

In its aftermath, discourse changes. Prior to the Solomon interlude, the poem consists of short dialogue in which the female lover does the majority of the speaking. Thereafter, each lover speaks much more equally and the male lover has found his voice. The three *wasf*s (4.1-7, 5.10-16 and 7.1-7) all follow the Solomon interlude and all react in one way or another to it. They share common features. They all use the idealised description of the body popular at the time and adapt it to their purpose of showing why the lovers are so much better than Solomon. This is achieved in the first *wasf*, in particular, by the '*levanon*'/'*levonah*' wordplay. In the second *wasf*, the female lover describes her lover in statuesque terms with vocabulary taken from the story of Solomon and the temple, implying that he is better than Solomon, given the nature of the question to which the *wasf* is the answer. In the third *wasf*, the male lover expressly refers to his lover with a pet name - '*hashulamit*' - which has obvious connotations of the female form of Solomon.

In all cases the scene in which the *wasf* occurs does not end with the description. Further material is appended to each, some sort of erotic epilogue to add to the intensity of the physical description. So in the first *wasf*, the male lover, having described to her how beautiful her body is (4.1-7), then invites her to come away and introduces the image of the garden (4.8-16). In the second *wasf*, her description of his body to the daughters of Jerusalem in response to their question (5.10-16) is followed by erotic allusions to 'spice beds' and 'pasturing in the gardens' (6.2-3). By the end of the third *wasf* (7.1-7), he cannot prevent himself adding further bodily images (7.8-10).

In between the first and second *wasf*s is the second, dream-like night scene (5.2-8). As highlighted in the commentary, it has an even more mysterious, frightening aspect than the first night scene (3.1-5). It builds on the vocabulary in the first *wasf*, adapting it to its own purposes. But its structural 'location' is crucial. The first night time scene precedes the fullest description of Solomon in the Song of Songs. The second night time scene precedes the only full description of the male lover in the Song of Songs, inviting the comparison, and contrast, between these two male figures.

We can sum up the structure as far as the end of the second *wasf* as follows:

> Superscription describing the quality and nature of the collection of songs and its connection with King Solomon (1.1).

1. 'Dialogue' between the lovers, led predominantly by the female lover (1.2-2.17).

2. First night time scene (3.1-5).

3. The transformative Solomon interlude (3.6-11).

4. His description of her body 'top down' (the first *wasf*), plus material following it (4.1-5.1).

5. Second night time scene (5.2-8).

6. Her description of his body 'top down' (the second *wasf*) in response to a question, plus material following it (5.9-6.3).

Any structural analysis such as this one is open to objection; for example, the opening two chapters could be subdivided. Yet for our purposes, this division into six parts separates clearly distinct areas comprising one 'dialogue', two night time scenes, one Solomon interlude and two *wasf*s. Each such passage takes up a minimum of five verses and, in three cases, goes into considerably more detail. This is important because thereafter the nature of the structure changes considerably, which is now considered.

The third *wasf* and material following it takes up chapter 7. In itself, this follows the structural format described above. However, immediately prior to it (6.4-12) and following it (the whole of chapter 8) is material which defies easy structural analysis. Some of the material is relatively weak (e.g. 6.5b-7 which is the repetition of a part of the first *wasf*). Some of it is notoriously difficult to understand (e.g. the meaning of *'ami nadiv'* discussed in the commentary to 6.12). Much of it is of the highest quality. What links all of it, however, is its fragmentary nature; each section rarely lasts more than two or three verses. We could add to our structural analysis as follows:

7. Fragmentary material, some new, some a repetition of older material (6.4-12).

8. His description of her body 'down up' (the third *wasf*) plus material following it (7.1-14).

9. Fragmentary new material (8.1-14).[395]

What are we to make of this structural change? On one level, we can explain the apparently weaker material on the basis that a proper editing process had not fully taken place and lines were left in which ought to have been removed. But that cannot explain the whole shift. First, most of the material in chapters 6.4-12 and chapter 8 (to which this structural change refers) is not weak in any way whatsoever. Indeed, it contains some of the most powerful images in the whole of the Song of Songs. Yet it clearly works differently from a structural point of view. It is more aphoristic in nature and its focus is different. What appears to be taking place is a shift from the material to the abstract. That shift seems to occur in the opening (7.1) and closing (7.7) of the third *wasf*. The male lover opens by describing her as the 'Shulamite' implying 'wholeness'. He ends it with a paean to 'love amongst pleasures'. This then allows the poet to address the nature of love and jealousy in 8.6-7 as abstract ideas. These verses do not therefore come out of the blue; they have been prefigured in the structure of the Song of Songs. It is only following the description of the abstract idea of what love is in 8.6-7 that Solomon is scorned in 8.11-12. This may well have been deliberate - locating the act of rejecting Solomon in the aftermath of the Song's depiction of the real nature of true love.

What conclusions can we come to as a result of this structural analysis? Perhaps the clearest is a dichotomy between literary and structural narrative. The Song of Songs defies a clear literary narrative. As discussed above, those who have sought to set out a clear plot have failed. Yet there is a much clearer structural trajectory to the Song of Songs. It is of a woman who instructs her lover at the outset, who expresses her full emotional anxiety when her lover is not there. It encompasses three passionate bodily descriptions and ends by stressing the importance of love and the rejection of Solomon.

---

[395] The commentary analysed chapter 8 into eight distinct sections - 8.1-2, 8.3-4, 8.5a, 8.5b, 8.6-7, 8.8-10, 8.11-12 and 8.13-14.

This structural analysis shows not only the nature of the Song of Songs but it highlights one other aspect of the book. It is radically different - there is no other book like it in the Hebrew Bible, as we are about to see.

SEVEN

An Upturned World

Introduction

While there is broad agreement amongst commentators that the Song of Songs is unique, it is the contention of this book that it is also one of the most radical books in the Hebrew canon. There is much less unanimity on this proposition. However, with the refocus of analysis on the role of King Solomon, the Song of Songs' radicality becomes very clear. It has four aspects which are considered in this chapter.

First, the Song of Songs does not fit the ideology of most other books in the Bible. It has what I term a 'counter-narrative' which is discussed below.   Second, it believes in a more equal and just world. This is certainly not a standard view of commentators but when one's focus is turned to the role of Solomon, one sees that the countryside and nature more generally represent a rejection of the world represented by the town and are linked with the quest for a different, fairer world. Third, the lovers may not be royal but there are frequent references to kings and queens and their entourage. This has a radical message separate from that of the role of nature. Finally, we considered in chapter 3 of the Solomon section of this book the link between the actions of Solomon and the 'law of the king' in the book of Deuteronomy. We saw that Solomon in the book of Kings failed the test set out in Deuteronomy on every count. We now have to consider the degree to which the 'law of the king' can be applied to the Solomon who appears in the Song of Songs. This is not as simple a comparison as the one we undertook between the book of Kings and the book of Deuteronomy because the comparison factors there were express and clear. They are more hidden in the Song of Songs, but the final section of this chapter will consider what conclusions can be drawn. So, we now turn to the first of these areas of radicality: the Song of Songs is a counter-narrative.

1. Radicality - the Song of Songs as counter-narrative

One feature of the reception history of the Song of Songs previously discussed has been the Rabbis' interpretation of the Song as an allegory of God's love for Israel; this involved issues of covenant between God and Israel, repeated failure on the part of Israel, exile as a result of failure and then redemption. Such a Rabbinic reading did not arise in a vacuum but rather flowed naturally from a reading of most other books of the Bible. There is what one might call a meta-narrative which encompasses vast swathes of these Biblical books. They contain a teleological or end purpose.

This involves a narrative of a contingent promise - in the end 'X' will happen if you do 'Y'. We have already seen this in the book of Kings where the promise to Solomon of greatness is couched in the contingency of observing the commandments. We analysed this as a Deuteronomic gloss on the Solomon story in the books of Kings (and indeed in the books of Chronicles). The contingent promise continues, however, after Solomon's death in describing failure on the part of the many kings who 'did evil in the eyes of the Lord' - in other words the covenant could not be fulfilled because of the failure of human beings.

This narrative of contingent promise in Kings and Chronicles is itself merely a continuation of the narrative with which Israel has been most associated throughout the millennia. The exodus from Egypt may have been a physical event (the children of Israel really did leave Egypt according to the book of Exodus) but its spiritual effects were dependent on other factors as well. True departure from Egypt not only involved a journey but was also contingent on an acceptance of the commandments handed to Moses on Mount Sinai. Failure to do so resulted in a 'return to Egypt', most often interpreted not as a physical return but rather as a failure in strength and morale - in other words, the notion that there is a 'slave' mindset which cannot be overcome in the generation which has experienced it even when the actual slavery has ended.

So contingent promise is linked in the Biblical mind with mental strength in the history books but it is not limited to this. This form of meta-narrative appears in the prophets as well. The prophets rail against the injustices which they see in their own society. They do so by creating their own form of this contingency which appeared in the Exodus story. The better society which the Bible seeks to create is, the prophets argue, contingent on a society built on a fairness and justice which their contemporary version of society signally failed to exhibit. The prophets are, in other words, part of the narrative while modifying it by stressing its social justice aspects above that seen in, say, the books of Samuel and Kings.

This narrative of contingent promise is so prevalent, in its various guises, throughout the Bible that it is entirely apposite to term it the Bible's normative view. However,

I have argued elsewhere[396] that a counter-narrative also exists in the Bible and that it is the book of Ecclesiastes which bucks the trend. It shows us what that counter-narrative is. The book of Ecclesiastes simply does not concern itself with the normative contingent promise theory of the history of Israel so prevalent otherwise. It is this lack of contingency which forms the counter-narrative. Ecclesiastes rejects the linear idea of history with its contingent promise of a better future world and suggests, in its stead, a more cyclical view of the way the earth works ('that which was, will be, that which was done, will be done and there is nothing new under the sun').[397] Its message of meaninglessness in an unfair world is forthright and utterly different to any of the world views in the various versions of the meta-narrative.

One can add the Song of Songs to the book of Ecclesiastes when considering the issue of counter-narrative. Clearly the two books are wholly different in nature, style and purpose. The Song of Songs is less cynical (and indeed less cyclical) than Ecclesiastes but they share a very different view of the way the world works. Without any hint of contingency, the Song of Songs presents a radical message which will be set out in the rest of the chapter. In other words, there is no condition imposed upon the better world the Song of Songs seeks.

Of course, the prophets' message of social justice can also, correctly, be described as 'radical' but, unlike that in the Song of Songs, it sets out that message within the normative meta-narrative of contingent promise. What the prophets are seeking to do is to change that promise's terms of reference - in other words, *only if* one acts justly can one truly fulfil God's commandments..

The Song of Songs, like the prophets, represents a radical message. Like Ecclesiastes, however, it also represents a counter-narrative to the prevailing normative view of contingent promise contained in the majority of the rest of the books of the Hebrew Bible. What that radical message in the Song of Songs consists of will form the content of the rest of this chapter.

2. Radicality - comments on issues of equality and justice - an upturned world in nature

At no point does the Song of Songs directly raise the issue of poverty in the powerful way that, say, Isaiah frequently does. Its intent is not the same. The obvious hint though, that the issue of justice is being raised, is near the end when Solomon is

---

[396] *Ecclesiastes and Contemporary Argument:* Andrew Levy, *European Judaism* 17/2, 158-164
[397] Ecclesiastes 1.9.

scorned (8.11-12). But its message of creating a different, more just world is far more covert than that in the prophets which, in turn, is so powerful for its very directness. However, we are told regularly early in the Song of Songs that our lovers are shepherds. She works in the fields and is sun-tanned from all her work. They are not the sort of people about whom history is normally written. The author has created a world where two ordinary young lovers are permitted to do extraordinary things. They see themselves as royal and address each other in regal terms. They dress in the finest jewellery. This is not the normal world. It is also not a fantasy world which could never occur in reality. Rather, it opens up a host of new, real possibilities. This is a different world - a world shaken up and transformed. I will consider how that world appears in the Song of Songs shortly.

We can, however, also see a version of this transformed world in the remarkable reinterpretation of a Talmudic passage by the modern Hebrew poet, Chaim Nachman Bialik (1873-1934). At first, one might think that neither the Talmud passage nor the poem by Bialik has anything to do with the Song of Songs (there are no intertextual links with it); yet they provide a fascinating parallel with themes which emanate from the Song of Songs.

The Talmud, at one point, recounts the following story: 'Joseph, the son of Rabbi Joshua, grew weak and fainted. [He rose from the dead] and his father said to him "what did you see?". He responded: "I saw an *upturned world*. Those who were up had gone down and those who were down had gone up." He replied: "You saw a clear [i.e. rightly-conducted] world"'.[398] (My italics.) The most well-known of all Jewish interpreters, the eleventh century commentator Rabbi Shlomoh ben Yitschak ('*Rashi*'), adds that this last comment is about wealth. The final reply from the father that the upturned world *is* a rightly-conducted world itself constitutes a powerful gloss on the passage and an indication of the transformation which the father believes has occurred in the upturned world of the dead. It is a better world than the one we know on earth.

But such a world of transformation in the next world has been seen by many as a justification (manufactured by religion over the centuries) for the reality of unjust acts in this world - through the promise of something different after death. What, though, of a this-worldly transformation? Initially such transformatory discourse may be the stuff of dreams; visions, however, can become the launchpad for those dreams' ultimate realisation. The Talmudic passage just quoted is clearly the inspiration for one passage near the beginning of *Ha-breichah*, ('The Pool'), a long

---

[398] Baba Batra 10b.

poem by Chaim Nachman Bialik written in Hebrew in 1895.[399]   It is Bialik's reinterpretation of the Talmudic passage in this poem which is fascinating.   The poem commences as follows:

'I know a forest, and in the forest
I know a sheltered pool.
In the thicket of the wood, set apart from the world,
In the shade of a mighty oak, blessed in light and well-versed in storm,
Alone it dreams for itself a dream of an *upturned world*
And it will spawn, in secret, its golden fish
But no-one knows what is in its heart.'

(My italics.)

Bialik is a master of this anthropopathic vision of nature with human emotions.   It is also quite clear that the inspiration for his reference to the 'upturned world' is the passage in the Talmud just quoted.   While a similar idea of transformation is clear from passages in the Bible,[400] the Hebrew two-word phrase which Bialik uses for 'upturned world' (*'olam hafuch'*) appears only in this Talmud passage.   Indeed it could not be Biblical - the word *'olam'* only has the temporal meaning of 'a long period of time' in the Bible and never the spatial meaning of 'the world' which was given to it by the Rabbis.[401]   The word *'hafuch'*, by contrast, has its Biblical roots in the events which occurred at Sodom and Gomorrah,[402] indicating a complete upturning of the town and, by implication, of its values.

Bialik's transformative poem is a slow burner.   He describes the way the pool changes its appearance at various times and seasons - in the morning, on a moonlit night, in a daytime tempest and at dawn, all the time fashioning a sophisticated description of nature in an old-new language that he was, in the process, himself transforming.   At first, the only hint of a Biblical reference is to Samson and Delilah

---

[399] '*Ha-breichah*', Poems Bialik D'vir, Tel Aviv 1966, 361-369. Translated by Ruth Finer Mintz in *Modern Hebrew Poetry: A Bilingual Anthology*, University of California Press, Berkeley and Los Angeles, 1968, 2-19.

[400] See in this regard Isaiah 24.1-2. The sentiment is the same but neither the word *'olam'* nor the word *'hafuch'* is used.

[401] The only apparent exception in Ecclesiastes 3.11 proves the rule. The King James Version translates *gam et ha'olam natan belibam* as 'also he hath set the world in their heart'. Modern commentators largely reject this translation seeing the word *'olam'* as either meaning 'eternity' or being a scribal error where the original version intended *ha'elem* meaning 'the concealed'.

[402] Genesis 19.21 and 19.25. The root of the word *h-f-ch* is used in modern Hebrew for a revolution (*'mahapechah'*), indicating further its radical connotations.

where the golden nets of a tree in sunlight are compared to the voluntary captivity of Samson in the presence of Delilah.

But this nature idyll is deceptive. More than two thirds of the way through the poem, Bialik changes utterly the context of his description. He still depicts the pool but, all of a sudden, his language is seeped in vocabulary and imagery taken straight out of the description of the tabernacle in the book of Leviticus. Remembering his time as a young Yeshiva student, he describes coming upon the pool. He recalls himself wandering alone, uniting his heart with his God until he came 'to the Holy of Holies in the forest - the apple of its eye'. The next line in Mintz's fine translation is 'Within a hanging of leaves'. It cannot here, though, do justice to the imagery of the Hebrew (*'mibait laparochet shel he'alim'*). The first two Hebrew words are used in the tabernacle to describe the location of the inner sanctuary (where they mean 'within the curtain').[403] So this pool has become Bialik's own sacred tabernacle. Here the poet finds himself at a place where there is what he describes as 'another small world, a second world ... and as I sat there at the side of the pool, looking out over the riddle of two worlds, twin worlds, without knowing which of them came first.' Then 'the voice of the concealing God explodes suddenly from the silence: "Where are you?".' This reticent God who now appears quotes to the young Bialik the words of interrogation which were uttered to Adam in the garden of Eden.[404] God then tells the poet to see the divine 'in the tremor of golden wheat, in the pride of mighty cedars, in the rustle of a dove's pure wing and in the eagle wing's sweep'.[405]

The Talmud describes two worlds, our own and the one which is upturned which lies beyond the grave. What Bialik does is to transpose the second world onto the earth. The first world is the one we know and live in. For him, this would have been the town or village in Eastern Europe. It also represented the world of the Yeshiva in which he had been educated and towards which he felt a profound ambivalence. However, it is also the world which speaks throughout the ages to all who live the non-rural life. The second world, as we find out, is the other 'small world' discovered by the pool, the world which teaches the young Bialik to appreciate the God who created nature which is all around him. Bialik's other 'small world' may be of the spirit but it is reflective of a way of thinking about that other, second world which has the power to transform us.

At first sight, this late nineteenth-century poem, written in a rejuvenated Hebrew language, may appear to have little to do with the Song of Songs. Bialik does not

---

[403] See e.g. Leviticus 16.2.

[404] Genesis 3.9. In Hebrew, 'where are you?' is one word: *'ayeka?'*

[405] I have used Mintz's translation for this last quotation from *ha-breichah*

appear to have been inspired by the Song of Songs in writing it. Bialik's poem concerns nature and the joy in solitude, and communion with nature, which the poet describes. Like Bialik's masterpiece, the Song of Songs is obviously also a poem where nature plays an important role. The Song's depiction of nature, like Bialik's, is always in relation, and in contrast, to the town. To use Bialik's terminology, nature in the Song of Songs is the second world which offers a vision of a better, 'upturned world'. Nature therefore has a transformative effect for the lovers as it does for Bialik in his great poem.

In this regard, one of the many aspects of the Song of Songs which goes beyond a simple love song is the desire to escape the town and experience the different world which nature can offer. The reason why Bialik's poem is so apposite is that it mirrors the Song of Songs in two ways. First, as explained above, it seeks solace in nature. This is a standard part of nineteenth-century romantic poetry of which Bialik's poem is an example. But second it does so by reference to religious imagery, as does the Song of Songs. As we saw in the commentary, the Song of Songs explicitly uses religious imagery to describe the lovers and its purpose is to show the deep desire on the part of the lovers (and therefore almost certainly on the part of the editor) to escape the clutches of the city. This again has a Solomonic link. The town is associated with power and a hierarchical system which the lovers eschew. One needs to examine these passages again in the Song of Songs, largely in the order in which they appear, to see how powerful that need to flee is. It is therefore to the role of nature in the Song of Songs which we must now turn.

Radicality - the Song of Songs and its relationship with nature

Near the beginning, the Song of Songs contains the implication that the field is seen by other characters in a negative light. The female lover asks the daughters of Jerusalem *not* to cast negative aspersions on her merely because she is sun-tanned, the fairly obvious hint being that her work in the field was frowned upon. Indeed her brothers were angry with her - whether this is because of this work is not made clear, but the comment comes in the same line as the reference to the sun-darkened skin, so is a possible explanation (1.6).

Immediately thereafter we see that her lover is a shepherd, a role which she sees in the most positive light (1.7-8). The imagery of horses amongst Pharaoh's chariots may also be an image in nature (1.9-11) but the description of her lover as 'in the vineyards of Ein Gedi' (1.13-14) undoubtedly is.

But the clearest example of the use of nature and religious imagery occurs at the end of chapter 1. This was discussed in detail in the commentary but it is worth refocusing on it given the new information which is provided to us through the rest of the Song of Songs. She says that: 'Our couch is luxuriant; the beams of our houses are cedars, our rafters are cypresses' (1.16b-17). This locates the lovers in a forest which we would normally presume must be somewhere nearby. As mentioned in the commentary, this cannot be a real place because cedars did not exist in the countryside surrounding Jerusalem. The lovers are in their literary, fantasy Arcadia. They need no beds, walls or roofs because nature provides all this for them here. And, as in Bialik's masterpiece, the rural idyll is accompanied by imagery originally associated with an entirely different context. Bialik's imagery is taken from a place (the inner sanctuary of the tabernacle and then the temple) for which he clearly still retained a deep affection, notwithstanding his move away from Jewish religious orthodoxy. We see little affection in the Song of Songs for the original places where the cedar and cypress could be seen in Jerusalem but a deep desire to escape to the (non-existent) forest where they could enjoy each other in the infinitely preferable alternative world.

In chapter 2, the lovers compare themselves to nature. She is a 'rose of the forest, a lily of the valleys' (2.1), he is 'an apple in the trees of the forest' (2.3). As we have seen, she swears an oath 'by the gazelles, or by the hinds of the fields' (2.7 and 3.5). The words for the animals, as discussed in the commentary, are homonyms for divine names - the author seeing, like Bialik, the presence of God in nature. Nature, then, is where the lovers experience real joy - away from the prying eyes of their so-called betters in urban, built-up areas. Whilst this may be a commonplace for love poetry, the Song of Songs is unique in the way it attaches that love to a transformation of religious imagery.

So it is in the countryside where the lovers experience their most heightened emotions for each other - e.g. he strides over the mountains and leaps on the hills as she hears him coming (2.8) - but it is also where we hear a jarring tone. First, the elusive reference to the little foxes raiding the vineyard (2.15) but then to the male lover 'turning' (2.17). This would, of itself, probably not strike us but for the fact that, immediately thereafter, the relationship between the lovers itself 'turns'. She is in her bed at night (3.1) and we are told immediately that she must now be in the town because she gets up to search for him there (3.2). So she may have lost her lover in the countryside when he 'turned' but nevertheless she associates this loss with the town. It represents for her all that is negative in this scene. It is natural to jump ahead at this point and consider the second night time scene (5.2-8) because so many similar emotions to the first night time scene (notwithstanding the differences) come to the fore and are indeed heightened. In this second night time scene, he comes to her whilst she is asleep but then disappears. As previously, she goes into the city but, in her search for him, she is found by the watchmen of the city who manhandle her (5.7). Again, an apparent lovers' tiff (if that is what is being described earlier in the scene) becomes transformed into a comment about the dangers lurking in the city for the young woman and the need to get away and escape its clutches.

When we come to the Solomon interlude (3.6-11) we see an immediate reference to the desert[406] from which the mysterious female figure emerges 'more fragrant in myrrh and frankincense than all the power of the merchant' (3.6). This appears to be a highly positive judgement. We discussed in the commentary the dual-identification of this enigmatic woman with the female lover and the Queen of Sheba who hails from the desert. That is highly significant. For the Bible, the desert is 'other'. It is also, of course, seminal to the Israelite narrative. Exodus from Egypt did not involve a direct journey to the promised land; that would have involved God guiding the children of Israel through the land of the Philistines which, in turn, would have led to a fear of war, a downturn in morale and a desire to return to Egypt. So God 'swivelled' them towards the desert by the side of the Red Sea.[407] It is only in the desert that the Children of Israel receive the law; indeed, it is only here that they *can* do so - once they have got rid of the slave mentality which they learnt in Egypt.

The desert therefore may be wasteland but it also represents the ideal. A voice can cry out that in the desert a way should be prepared for the Lord.[408] However, the fact that the desert represents the ideal should not blind us to the fact that the desert is also 'other'. Religious hierarchy did not exist in the same way beyond the boundaries of the town because it lacked any control there. To use imagery from the Song of Songs in relation to the issue of control, there are no 'watchmen of the wall' (5.7) in the desert - *they* belong to the town and all it stands for.

We have therefore reached circumstances where the religious norm had created a paradox. It celebrated the Israelite cult in a temple at the heart of the largest town in Israel while, in theory, extolling the values of the desert. Yet it could not realise

---

[406] The word is repeated at 8.5 but it is here in a fragment from which it is difficult to assert more general explanations.

[407] Exodus 13.17-18. I have chosen to use the word 'swivel' as it seems to me to get the gist of the Hebrew word '*vayaseiv*' (Exodus 13.18), indicating that God controls the children of Israel as if they were puppets on a string.

[408] Isaiah 40.3. In the septuagint (and then in the New Testament), the accentuation of this sentence is subtly different. For these versions, the voice itself cries out *in* the desert. I have read it in accordance with the masoretic accentuation but both readings make my point.

those values, as the lovers knew only too well. It is my contention that the editor of the Song of Songs determined that it was for these lovers to embody the values to which the establishment in Jerusalem paid only lip service.

The four passages referring directly to Solomon (1.1, 1.5, 3.6-11 and 8.11-12) do not expressly set out location.[409] So we do not know whether they take place in the countryside or in the town. But there is nevertheless something of the 'other' about the longer passages or, to use Bialik's terminology, they reveal an 'upturned world'. The 'palanquin' seems to be a parody of the temple (3.9). It has pillars notwithstanding that it is moveable. If this verse is linked to the previous two, then this palanquin has sixty guards surrounding it for fear of the night (3.7-8). This is not the Solomon we encounter in the books of Kings and Chronicles but a parody of him. So whilst no geographical indicators in the passage allow us to understand where it takes place, it is part of the symbol of the countryside in the Song of Songs which represents the other 'upturned' world of which this story of Solomon clearly plays a part. The relationship between the passage relating to Solomon's vineyard (8.11-12) and nature is discussed below.

All the *wasf*s are full of rural imagery. His first description of her in chapter 4 uses similes taken straight out of the vocabulary of a shepherd which, as we understand from chapter 1 of the Song, appears to be his occupation. He even describes her 'mouth' or 'speech' by the word *'midbaraich'* which appears only here in the Bible in such a context. The word is a homonym for 'desert' (discussed previously in relation to 3.6) and so is another subtle reference to nature.

The second *wasf* (5.10-16), comprising her only full description of his body, is noteworthy because it divides into two separate sections. It uses natural similes for his face (5.12-13) but statuesque imagery (which we identified with Solomon) for his torso (5.14-15). The vision she beheld of him was compared to Lebanon and cedars - these have all the ambiguity of both Jerusalem and the geographical area north of Israel which Lebanon and cedars come to represent in the Song of Songs.

His final description of her in the third *wasf* (7.1-7) is full of references to natural phenomena for her neck, head and hair in northern Israel and Lebanon which imply an importance because a 'king is trapped in the curls' (7.6).

---

[409] The final passage refers to a vineyard but does not let us know where the characters are when speaking the lines. The words in 8.13 *'kerem sheli lefanai'* ('my vineyard is before me') *might* indicate location in the vineyard but are more likely, in the context, to be a figure of speech.

His reference to 'Lebanon' at the end of his first *wasf* in 4.8 has been discussed within the context of the discussion in chapter 6 above about Lebanon. Within the context of nature, it also has a role to play. It is quite clear that the northern geographical locations mentioned indicate something rural - they are the site of lions' lairs and leopards' mountains (4.8). The word 'Lebanon', as we know, has an ambiguity to it. When he says: 'With me from Lebanon, bride', this could well be quoting an original Ugaritic source (as discussed in the last chapter) but its other meaning is the need to get away from the 'Lebanon' of the temple in Jerusalem to the countryside.

The 'garden' is a well-discussed part of the natural imagery in the Song of Songs. Commentators have also seen its symbolic value: 'The garden is a cultural form that serves as a microcosm for ideals about the natural world.'[410] It has a sense of the uncontrolled because of the wind referred to in it (4.15-16).[411] Yet there is another important factor to take into account in relation to the garden, given the tenor of this commentary. It does not arrive as a metaphor until halfway through the Song of Songs (4.12).[412] We think of gardens as natural but gardens are of course human creations. They are manufactured nature. That, however, does not make them any less relevant to the town/country dichotomy which is the subject of this discussion. For the purposes of the two lovers, their gardens represent for them their own creation of a natural world separate from, and superior to, the natural world transplanted from Lebanon and imposed on the city of Jerusalem by Solomon which is what has just been described before the garden is introduced into the Song. Linked to the garden are the spices which are referred to in conjunction with the garden more than once (4.14, 6.2 and possibly 8.13-14). And garden imagery provides any number of erotic metaphors which the lovers can use.

When one uses the word 'outside' or 'outdoors' in English, it often comes with the implication of nature as in 'the great outdoors'. It is ironic that its Hebrew equivalent *'chutz'* which appears only once in the Song of Songs (8.1) is clearly associated with the city. But yet again within its context it goes to show the superiority of the values of the countryside to those of the town. Would that her lover were her brother; if that were the case, then she could 'find' him 'outdoors'. The word 'find' immediately links us with the two night scenes which are the only two scenes in which the word for 'find' has previously occurred. On both those occasions, the woman was in a place of fear when she stepped outdoors. This now has the potential to repeat itself because he is not actually her brother and being open about their

---

[410] James, 59.

[411] Ibid, 77.

[412] The middle of the book, in terms of verses, is 4.14.

relationship in the city presents real dangers. Only in the countryside can she be safe with her lover.

The Song of Songs ends with a number of references to nature. Solomon's final scene refers to his vineyard where he is scorned (8.11-12). The reference to the location could well be significant. He might own the vineyard but the rustic associations are incompatible with the acquisitive values which he represents (the location is after all called '*baal hamon*' - 'master of wealth') - values which the lovers eschew.

The final scene of all (8.13-14) refers to the gardens which form the humanly-manufactured symbol of the lovers' rebellion against the world of the town. The female lover invites her beloved to escape - we realise this escape is every bit as much a flight from the clutches of the town as it is from our own clutches as this is how the Song of Songs ends. The escape is to a 'hill of spices' - the lovers' very own upturned world.

The previous section of this chapter considered the radicality of the Song of Songs to be based on its complete silence in relation to the narrative of contingent progress which is at the heart of most of the other books of the Bible. Yet, in relation to its portrayal of nature, it shares many of the themes hinted at in other books of the Bible. For the Song of Songs the town is the norm and the countryside is 'other'. The desert plays a similar role in the Exodus story, and it also does in the book of Isaiah on several occasions. But rarely do those other books focus on the role of nature for individuals who, themselves, are 'other'. They need nature *because* they are 'other'. The lovers are not the heroes of history whose deeds of bravery, or encounters with the divine, are the normal topics of epic stories. They are 'other' because they are ordinary. They need the countryside because they are young and cannot realise themselves in the stifling heat of observation and repression which they experience in the town. There is a reason for that. The next section takes up the theme of their so-called 'ordinariness' and considers that reason. How do the lovers (and thereby the editor of the Song of Songs) relate to royalty specifically, and hierarchy in general?

3. Radicality - the relationship between the Song of Songs and royalty and hierarchy.

We considered early on an important decision we had to take about the meaning of the superscription.[413] Its wording could have indicated that the author was claiming to be King Solomon. That was an analysis we rejected given the pejorative tone of the other references to Solomon contained in the poem. It could only mean that the Song of Songs was about Solomon. We now need to look at the overall relationship which the Song of Songs has with royalty specifically, and hierarchy more generally.

A. Kings and queens

Apart from the reference to Solomon who, as I have said, appears seven times in the Song of Songs, the word *'melech'* ('king') appears five times. We have already closely analysed each reference to Solomon but have not done so systematically for each of the references to the 'king'. Given the opening reference to Solomon, what do the 'king' references add? In chapter 1 of the Song of Songs there are two references to a 'king' (1.4 and 1.12). Both in context are references to the male lover and imply that he is, as it were, the 'king' - an early hint that this is a book where normal roles are challenged. In both cases, they imply a domestic, yet erotically-charged role for him. The 'king' should bring me to his room (1.4), she says, and later adds that her spikenard brought forth its fragrance 'whilst the king [was] on his divan' (1.12).

The references to 'king' with the most obvious direct link to Solomon are the two in the Solomon interlude in 3.9 ('King Solomon made for himself a palanquin') and 3.11 ('..rejoice daughters of Zion, about King Solomon, about the crown with which his mother crowned him'). These are the only two of the seven Solomon references to give him his regal title. The Solomon interlude (3.6-11) has been discussed frequently in this book and it is not necessary to repeat here the points already made. However, one other feature in relation to the royal terminology is worth making. Is the fact that Solomon is being referred to as 'king' intended to heighten the parody by an ironic reference to the regal title? We cannot be sure but that seems on the face of it an eminently plausible reading. We can be assisted in this regard, however, by considering other Biblical regal references.

Use of royal title, or lack thereof, plays an important part in the literary telling of the David story in the books of Samuel. Whether or not David is given the honorific

---

[413] See chapter 1 of this book.

regal title before reference to his name is often highly indicative of a subliminal message which the narrator wishes to convey to the reader at that particular point in the narrative. One example among many will suffice. At no point in the description of David's murder of Uriah the Hittite (II Samuel 11) is David referred to as 'King David' - one might have expected it, at least perhaps for the sake of variety, given the constant references to 'David' which the story requires. But no, it simply does not occur, notwithstanding any number of references to the palace as 'the house of the king' and Uriah's vexed problem of how to deal with David as 'the burden of the king'.[414] The message is clear. David is the king; he has the power to prove it - but the narrator's reluctance to honour him with the title commensurate with that power is a telling pointer to the narrator's scorn for his actions - and a not-so-subtle hint at the sin which will become central to the rest of the David story.

If we now return to the Song of Songs, we should ask to what degree an analogy can be made. In the Solomon interlude (3.6-11), the king is introduced merely as 'Solomon' without further ado (3.7). Thereafter, both references to him acknowledge his royal status. In most circumstances, such an additional soubriquet would be a clear indication of the honour to be given to the person; but we need to look more closely at the context of the Solomon interlude and the order in which Solomon is referred to. We have understood that this is a parody of him. He is first introduced as just 'Solomon' and then, as his self-aggrandising is revealed to us, the ironic use of the royal title is added. It is probably intended as a sarcastic swipe at his reputation.

The final reference to a 'king' is in 7.6 and it is clearly not a reference to Solomon, whatever other ambiguities there may be about it.[415] The context is the male lover's final *wasf* where he is in raptures about her beauty and, just before his peroration, he says that 'a king is bound up in the curls'. This seems to be a reference to any regal figure with the implication that he, the male lover, is that regal figure given how besotted he is with her. The message we are invited to take from this, therefore, is that the male lover, who we know (1.7) is a shepherd, can also be a king - at least in the upturned world which the Song of Songs has created for itself.

There are in fact seven explicit regal references. The five references to a king are accompanied by two to *'melachot'* ('queens') in 6.8 and 6.9. They take on a role with which we are now familiar. Royalty is referred to merely to be scorned and rejected. 6.8 tells us that there are 'sixty queens' (which reminds us immediately of

---

[414] II Samuel 11.8.

[415] See commentary ad loc.

the entirely unnecessary 'sixty heroes' surrounding Solomon's bed (3.7)) together with eighty concubines and maidens without number. They contrast with the one perfect lover (6.9) whom the queens and concubines praise. So in one way, this example relating to the queens is different from the king examples. In 1.4, 1.12 and 7.6, it appears as if the male lover *takes on* the role of king whereas the queens in 6.8 and 6.9 stand *in contrast to* the one perfect female lover. Yet contrast is at the heart of the way in which the lovers view royalty. Real kings *and* queens in the outside world are eschewed; regal qualities can be taken on by the so-called 'ordinary' lovers in the upturned world of the Song of Songs.

Therefore, the comments directly relating to 'kings' and 'queens' show a clear, negative perception of royalty by the lovers. However, it is not only in relation to royalty that the Song of Songs shows clear anti-hierarchical views. Such views are also exhibited in two distinct ways which need to be considered. First, what can we learn from the description of the lovers themselves about hierarchy? Second, there are other characters referred to in the Song of Songs besides the two lovers and King Solomon - their portrayal, too, assists us to an even greater extent to draw certain conclusions in relation to the Song of Songs' view of hierarchy.

B. The lovers and hierarchy

At the outset, we are told that her skin is darkened from the sun (1.5-6) indicating that she works in the field and that he is an ordinary shepherd (1.7), yet that does not prevent them from being described in the most opulent terms. In his longest comment before his first *wasf*, he describes her as being like a 'mare amongst Pharaoh's chariots' (1.9) with jewellery of gold and silver (1.10-11). One highly doubts whether in reality such apparently poor workers at that time could be so conspicuously adorned with items associated with luxury. But the message from the Song of Songs is clear - this is the upturned, preferable world of the lovers. In this world, ornaments, otherwise beyond the reach of the normally downtrodden, become available. Similarly houses of cedar associated with royalty become their natural habitat (1.17). They are no longer the purview only of the wealthy but are accessible also to these lovers.

C. Other characters and hierarchy

One should say, at the outset of an analysis of the other characters in the Song of Songs, that many of the references to such characters are ambiguous. Some have been interpreted in this commentary as in reality references to one or other of the lovers. So, for example, in 8.8, we identified the 'little sister' as a playful reference by the male lover to his beloved. There are many other characters referred to, though, who clearly do not fulfill this ambiguous dual role. They are interesting in that they can broadly be broken down into two types. First, there are those who appear to be part of the societal hierarchy and, in one way or another, are hostile to the lovers and, second, there are those who play a supportive or neutral role. We shall consider each in turn.

C1. Other characters hostile to the lovers

Those characters who are hostile to the lovers cover a broad sweep of functions and, indeed, degree of hostility; but what links all of them is that they are part of the hierarchy in the society in which the lovers live. The most obviously hostile characters are the *'shomrim'* ('guards') (3.3), also described as 'guards who roam in the city' (5.7) or 'guards of the wall' (5.8). These men pose a clear, physical threat to the female lover on her nocturnal perambulations. They seem to have fulfilled the role in ancient times that city policemen in a tyrannical state would perform nowadays. They may not, however, be the only characters who threaten violence. There is a reference to the wrath of 'my mother's sons' (1.6). This could mean full or, possibly, half brothers; in any event they were angry with her and placed her as a 'guard over the vineyards'. Again, we see some indication, if taken literally, of forced labour which the female lover is required to undertake by her (half-)brothers.

But hostility comes in different forms in the Song of Songs and other characters also represent the hegemonic rule without posing a physical threat. So the shields of the mocked 'heroes' protecting Solomon (3.7) become part of the neck of the lover and are therefore brought down to size, as it were. Queens are contrasted to the one perfect lover (6.8) but so, in this verse, are concubines who represent a further part of the hegemonic royal coterie. Ultimately, both queens and concubines can do nothing but praise that perfect female lover (6.9). Finally, a further group of royal flunkeys is scorned. Solomon is rejected in 8.11-12, as discussed previously, but so are the *'notrim'* (the 'guards' of the vineyard). Solomon is given his thousand and the guards have to make do with 'two hundred' (8.12) for guarding his fruit.

This negative picture, especially with our refocus on Solomon, should assist us in realising that one of the prime messages of the Song of Songs is the utter rejection of the society in which the lovers live, in all its aspects. In turn, one strongly suspects that this must be a comment on, and a critique of, the *actual* society which the editor lived in and clearly disdained.

C2. Other characters sympathetic to or neutral to the lovers

The characters who appear most in the Song of Songs apart from the lovers and Solomon are the 'daughters of Jerusalem' who are referred to seven times.[416] We see them three times in the context of the adjuration to the daughters of Jerusalem (2.7, 3.5 and 8.4) and they are the audience for the female lover's only *wasf* about her lover (5.8 and 5.16) and, thereby, form their own inclusio round the *wasf*. Their only other reference is in the Solomon interlude where they are enjoined to go out with the daughters of Zion at King Solomon's coronation (3.11). That apart, they may in 5.9 also have a speaking role in that it is difficult to think within the relevant context that the question which is asked of the female lover in 5.9 ('how is your lover better than another lover?') could be posed by anyone other than the daughters of Jerusalem.

The question as to who the daughters of Jerusalem are, and what role they play, is not an easy one to answer. They seem, however, to be her companions and of a similar age to the lovers. They are advised by the female lover in the adjuration not to arouse love until it is ready, indicating some form of comradeship. This conclusion is enhanced by the question they pose which allows her to describe her lover in the second *wasf*. It is, perhaps, possible to read their question at 5.9 as containing a hint of jealousy but, as there is nothing else supporting this in the rest of the Song of Songs, it is unlikely to have been the editor's intention. Their only other reference (apart from the adjuration and the material surrounding her *wasf*) is in the Solomon interlude (3.6-11). It leads to them being paralleled by the poet with the daughters of Zion.[417] Here their purpose appears to be more of a background role at a wedding or, as discussed in the commentary, a coronation. Whilst their role when they appear with the female lover is anonymous, there is at least a strong hint of friendship. In the Solomon interlude, they seem more functional; they join with the daughters of Zion as cheerleaders at a coronation. They do not speak but merely form part of the crowd - whether voluntarily or otherwise is not revealed to us.

The female lover's brothers (or half-brothers) are described negatively as 'my mother's sons'. Yet the direct references to the 'mother', whom we never actually encounter, are entirely positive. Most of these are in fact to the *female* lover's mother. At the end of the first night scene, the female lover says that she will not let

---

[416] 1.5, 2.7, 3.5, 3.10, 5.8, 5.16, 8.4. Jerusalem is referred to on its own one further time in 6.4. 'Mother' is also referred to seven times but not on each of these occasions as a character - i.e. 'the house of my mother'.

[417] See commentary in relation to 3.11 where the Masoretic text has been amended to achieve this parallel in accordance with most modern and ancient commentators.

her lover go until 'I have brought him to the house of my mother' (3.4). A similar sentiment appears at 8.2. In many ways, these comments are the exception which proves the rule. So much of the message of the Song of Songs is that joy can only be obtained in the countryside, as a result of the stifling mores of the town from which the lovers constantly need to escape. Yet fulfilment can seemingly occur in the mother's house as well which is presumably in the town, though the text is silent on this point. On some level therefore, the mother's house and the countryside are being equated. Perhaps it is that in both places urban values and the hegemonic culture can be ignored.

The male lover also notes his lover's uniqueness as she is 'one to her mother' (6.9) just as much as she is 'one' to him - in contrast to the many queens and concubines. The final reference to the female lover's mother is in the context of her wish that her lover could have been her brother 'sucking from my mother's breasts' (8.1). Here the positive image of the mother relates to her nurturing qualities.

There are two further mother references. The first of these need not detain us long. It refers to the male lover's mother. 8.5 contains a cryptic fragment spoken by the female lover about the apple tree and 'there your mother was in travail for you'.

The only other 'mother' reference is in the Solomon interlude where it is to Solomon's own mother crowning Solomon (3.11). Its implications and link to the Solomon/Bathsheba story were discussed in detail in the commentary but at this stage it is worth noting how positive the images are of both Solomon's mother and the female lover's. In a certain fashion, they appear role models - they are both, in their own ways, the powers behind the throne.

Perhaps the most tantalising reference to another character, positive in tone, is the final one. In 8.13, perhaps in plaintive tone, the male lover addresses his beloved and says: 'O one who dwells in gardens, friends listen to your voice, let me hear it'. We thereby learn that she, or both lovers together, have 'friends'.[418] In some manner, these 'friends' are presumably supportive of the lovers whose message is so different to that which we have otherwise heard from Israelite society. What is it that they shared? Were their values similar? Did they also recognise the upturned world which the lovers sought to inhabit? Of course we are not told. The Song of Songs unfortunately leaves us with more questions than answers.

---

[418] The reference to 'friends' is *'chaverim'* in Hebrew indicating by use of the masculine form that the reference cannot be *only* to the daughters of Jerusalem who would otherwise be the most likely reference point for this statement. They therefore have at least one male friend and possibly many more.

So how can we sum up our analysis of the Song of Songs and its relationship to hierarchy? The book's main focus of attack is King Solomon but, as has been demonstrated, he is by no means the sole one. The examples also reveal a profound mistrust and rejection of the values of the hegemonic hierarchical structures. For this alone, the Song of Songs is profoundly different from any other book in the Bible.

Yet paradoxically the role of a king is a deeply ambivalent one, not just in the Song of Songs but in many other books of the Bible - the Song of Songs differs because it mounts a much broader attack on hierarchical structures generally. We have already seen that Deuteronomy 17.14-20 contains a note of caution about the role of a king which, itself, was linked to events in the life of King Solomon. As we saw in chapter 1 above, the Song of Songs is about Solomon; so we need to examine the extent to which the Song of Songs and Deuteronomy interrelate.

4. The relationship between the Song of Songs and Deuteronomy

In the book of Samuel there is a telling passage about the relationship between the people and their need for a king.[419] The context is that the prophet Samuel is now old and his sons have not followed his ways so will not follow in his footsteps as a prophet of Israel. Seeing that all other peoples have a monarch, the people ask for a king. Samuel approaches God to say that the people have rejected him. God replies that it is God's rule, not Samuel's role, which has been scorned. God invites Samuel to tell the people, who have never had a king of flesh and blood, what havoc such a person would wreak. The picture painted is a detailed one of tyranny, oppression, exploitation and servitude - and of a God who would not answer the people at their time of need because of their unwise choice. Notwithstanding this litany of doom about to descend on any people who makes such a rash decision, the people's response is as follows: 'But the people refused to listen to the voice of Samuel and they said "No, we would rather have a king over us so that we would also be like all the nations and our king would judge us and go out before us and fight our battles".'[420]

The passage is interesting on a number of levels. First, it shows that the human need to be similar to others is based, sometimes, on irrational grounds contrary to people's real economic and social interests. It also exhibits the powerful hold which the concept of monarchy exerted on the human psyche. So an attack on a king is an

---

[419] The following passage summarises I Samuel 8.
[420] I Samuel 8.19-20.

attack, in many ways, on the identity of much of the populace. Therefore the attack by the editor of the Song of Songs on the reputation of King Solomon would have been read, by some, as an attack on their very essence. We cannot be sure how the Song of Songs was received in the immediate aftermath of its being promulgated - after all, attacking the ruler has always held a certain populist appeal. But we cannot discount an element of bravery in the creation of a poem lampooning a figure who was likely to have been revered by many simply *because* he was royal. And the Song's implication is that not only Solomon but *all* kings were to be rejected.

Second, it is crucial to realise that the passage in I Samuel 8, like so many other passages in the book of Kings which appear later in the Saul/David/Solomon narrative, has the hand of the Deuteronomist all over it. It has a constant refrain of 'listening to the voice'. This is a familiar phrase beloved of the Deuteronomist but here used in relation to the 'voice of the people' rather than the 'voice of God'. It is a long passage. Its immediate reference point is Saul who is about to be appointed as the first king of Israel. Yet its ambit is not limited to him and it is probably intended to be read literally as a warning about the dangers inherent in appointing *any* king.

This can perhaps be contrasted with the passage in Deuteronomy 17.14-20, the so-called law of the king which we discussed in detail in chapter 2 and which has reappeared often since. This passage, again, appears at face value to be entirely neutral as to who is being referred to. In other words, a simple reading of the text would allow the reader to imply that its target is all kings. As we saw earlier, that view would be mistaken. The 'law of the king' is much briefer than the passage in the book of Samuel but it is also much more specific. It is clearly written with Solomon in mind because, in the book of Kings, he breached every single one of the four warnings about what a king should not do.[421] Those failings are: a) increasing possession of horses, b) sending his people back to Egypt in order to possess more horses, c) increasing possession of wives and d) increasing possession of gold and silver.

What is fascinating is to see the way in which these failings are, or are not, woven into the Song of Songs. As an overview, it is clear that all these sins share one commonality - the need to exhibit material wealth, and thereby power. Trophy wives come into this category every bit as much as horses, gold and silver. They obviously have nothing to do with love and everything to do with the need to accumulate and

---

[421] But not the book of Chronicles which omits the story of King Solomon's marrying seven hundred women and having three hundred concubines from the narrative.

to manifest strength. That is something which the Song of Songs clearly rejects. However, the way in which it deals with the details is also fascinating.

The failings in relation to wives and to gold and silver are obvious from the text of the Song of Songs. The passage at 6.8-9 contrasts the sixty queens and eighty concubines and maidens without number to the one and only, unique beloved. In the end it is the queens and concubines who praise *her* (6.9). The Song of Songs introduces us to gold and silver on her neck (1.10-11). Let us not forget the 'upturned world' quality of this remark, given that we know she is a field labourer and could not be expected to be able to afford such luxury items. The only other combination of 'gold and silver' is in the 'palanquin' (i.e. temple/palace) parody in the Solomon interlude where the pillars are of silver and the back of gold (3.10). Furthermore, one of the key passages at the end of the Song of Songs also contains a rejection of the 'silver' associated with Solomon (8.11-12).

It is fascinating to consider the other two failings of a king in Deuteronomy. The first involves possession of horses; the second involves sending the people back to Egypt to acquire even more horses.[422] So much of the Song of Songs is taken up with references to the north of Israel that Egypt scarcely makes an appearance, notwithstanding the likelihood that much of the material in the Song of Songs was strongly influenced by earlier love poetry in the whole region, including Egypt. There is, however, only one clear reference to Egypt (though the name itself is never used) in the Song of Songs and remarkably it also includes the only mention of horses. It is spoken by the male lover. Like most other commentators, I have translated it: 'To a mare amongst Pharaoh's chariots, I have compared you, my beloved' (1.9). However, the word 'mare' in the Hebrew is *'susati'*. In most Biblical settings, this would be translated as 'my mare'. Some scholars consider that this may have been an 'old genitive setting'[423] which no longer applied at the time the Song of Songs was edited and so have rejected the 'my' reference. Others have argued against this and retained it.[424]

If the 'my mare' understanding is accepted, this would mean that the image of the female lover amongst Pharaoh's chariots would not be one where the lover is distant and far off but one where both he and she are part of Pharaoh's army (and therefore part of Egypt), with all the erotic connotations involved in the image. No doubt (as Alter points out) there are Egyptian parallels to this image (it would perhaps be surprising if there were not). What is intriguing, though, is why it was chosen in the

---

[422] Deuteronomy 17.16.
[423] Exum, 99.
[424] Bloch 144-5, Alter 2015, 10-11.

Song of Songs. Is it intended as a hint of the failing of the king in sending back more people to Egypt to increase horses? On the face of it, it seems to be yet a further positive, erotically-charged, image of one of the lovers; but does it have that other purpose in mind as well? Is it, in other words, yet another example of the Song of Songs using an old image for its own very different message? One cannot be sure but it cannot be ruled out and therefore remains a possibility.

So we can conclude our analysis of the relationship between the Song of Songs and Deuteronomy by saying that Deuteronomy warns about a king increasing amongst other things wives, gold and silver. The Song of Songs explicitly rejects all of these in the hands of the king. Deuteronomy also however warns against a) the acquisition of horses and b) sending people back to Egypt in order to increase horses - one image in the Song of Songs tantalisingly hints at this. Whether it is linked to the Deuteronomistic law of the king, as the others clearly are, is, it seems to me, more of an open question.

Conclusion

The issues contained in this chapter vary but all point to one theme. The Song of Songs is a radical work seeking to address timeless issues in a way which is unique in Biblical literature. Its counter-narrative exhibits a radicality all of its own. In its relationship with nature and hierarchy, it created a message which has extended its appeal over more than two millennia.

It is time to focus on the real hero of the Song of Songs. That person has been a sideshow until now.

That is all about to change.

EIGHT

In the Time of Tyranny

As we near the completion of our journey, we return to where we began. In chapter 1, we considered the superscription and concluded that the Song of Songs not only *could not* have been written by Solomon but also *was not intended* to be construed as such. The evidence points to a love story assembled by an editor with strongly-held, negative views about Solomon and the society of the time.

One commentary, correctly, describes Solomon as the 'anti-hero'[425] of the Song of Songs. If that is the case, then its editor - the person who fashioned the older material into the great work we read today - is surely a prime candidate to be its 'hero'. Who was that person and what evidence do we have?

Regrettably, as so often, the answer is that we have very little evidence beyond that which we can glean from the Song of Songs itself. The introduction to this book sought to envisage a situation in which the editor crafted the first four words of the Song of Songs (which were almost certainly added in the final editing process). At that stage of this book and, indeed, ever since, one crucial issue concerning the editor has been deliberately withheld from the reader. So far, all references to the editor have been written in gender-neutral language to avoid consideration of the editor's gender.

That will now cease and it will do so for good cause. There is every reason to believe that the Song of Songs was edited by a woman. As ever, with the Song of Songs, one cannot be sure but the evidence to support this view comes mainly from within the work itself.

Let us first examine the counter-evidence. It is based on the premise that women were not literate. Our knowledge of literacy levels in Biblical times is limited. One recent analysis has said that, at best, literacy levels were at fifteen to twenty percent of the population. Those people were disproportionately to be found in the military together with a handful of priests and scribes.[426] Other studies put the figure much lower, at ten percent at the time of the creation of the New Testament and lower still

---

[425] Segal 151.
[426] http://mentalfloss.com/article/78416/more-people-were-literate-ancient-judah-we-knew accessed 07.05.2018.

in earlier periods (i.e. including the time when the Song of Songs was composed). None of this directly addresses the issue of female literacy because the higher figure is based largely on roles in society only open to men. It stands to reason therefore that, whichever figure is accepted, the literacy rate for women is considerably lower than these (already low) figures.

If there were professions in which literacy was common or was seen as an expected part of the role, then one can assume that there must also have been educational structures in place to train such people in reading and/or writing. Given that all the professions mentioned above, in which literacy was more likely, were only those for which men would be permitted to train, one can assume that women were effectively barred from most, if not all, such educational structures.

Yet to raise these issues only goes to highlight how unlikely it was that someone from the male professions most likely to be literate - a soldier, a priest or a scribe in the paid employment of the religious establishment - would have written the Song of Songs. It mocks soldiers (3.7-8), rejects the actual temple and is the most radical book in the Bible for all the reasons described in the previous chapter. Therefore it is highly unlikely that the person who edited the Song of Songs was educated in the accepted manner of the time. That does not, in itself, exclude men but it *does* probably exclude the vast majority of those who were literate. The editor was an outsider. That does not necessarily mean foreign; but it does mean someone who thought entirely differently to the way that the more conventionally literate thought - a cultural outsider, as it were.

Arguments in favour of female editorship

This, of course, does not indicate that the editor was a woman but there are clear signs from the Song of Songs itself that the editor is more likely to have been a woman than a man. Indeed, there are, I would suggest, three arguments which support this theory. Not all of them are of equal strength. We will shortly revisit the structure of the Song of Songs which probably provides the strongest evidence of female editorship, but it is also worth considering two other arguments in this regard; first, the radical nature of the book and second, a comparison of how the Song of Songs treats female characters with their treatment in other Biblical books.

1. Gender and radicality

The radical nature of the Song of Songs is itself an indicator of female editorship. One aspect of this has already been discussed within the context of counter-narrative in the previous chapter. We considered how the Song of Songs is radical. So, too, were most of the prophets. We analysed, however, that there was a crucial difference between the prophets and the Song of Songs. The prophets followed the broad narrative sweep of Israelite history which, for them, led towards a better world. That better world was contingent on a focus on justice and better treatment of the poor. In many ways, in modern times, it has been best encapsulated in Martin Luther King's famous aphorism that 'the arc of the moral universe is long but it bends towards justice'. The prophets would argue that the pitfalls that we constantly see in this moral journey are unfortunately to be expected.

The Song of Songs, like the book of Ecclesiastes, is uninterested in contingency. Ecclesiastes also has its own radical agenda about the nature of the self in an absurd world but it has little to say on issues of social justice. By contrast, however, the editor of the Song of Songs saw social justice as one of the central messages to be conveyed within the framework of the love story. Its message of uncontingent social justice is therefore unique. While this is not the strongest evidence for female editorship, it certainly needs to be taken into account. An educated person who writes in a way so totally different to any other work we have from the time is likely to *be* different. In the case of the author of the book of Ecclesiastes which reflects a totally contrasting outlook to that of the rest of the Bible, it is quite clear that that author was a man. The outlook may be different but it is also very male. As we saw in chapter 1 above, the author of Ecclesiastes created a narrator who uses the first person to identify that narrator almost certainly as Solomon, in his choice of name as Qohelet, son of David, king in Jerusalem (Ecclesiastes 1.1). When it comes to the Song of Songs, there is no first-person narrator. There are, however other clues embodied within the language of the Song of Songs itself which hint at female authorship. They were all considered within the context of the commentary but we now need to revisit them in overview to see how they hint at radicality.

We saw at various points throughout the commentary that the Song of Songs adopts phrases originally occurring in previous books in the Bible but then adapts them to its own requirements (in this regard see commentary on verses 1.4, 1.17, 2.7, 2.13, 7.11 and 7.14). One need not repeat here the detailed comments in the commentary but we can note the following common theme. Each phrase had its own function within the context of the Song of Songs but, on every such occasion, we could see that the editor of the Song of Songs had transformed the original meaning, found in an earlier book of the Bible, into something wholly different to meet the very different purpose for which the Song of Songs was created.

Again, this hints (but no more) at a female editor because of its indication that the educated person writing the great work did so with a completely different mindset to that in which most educated men would have been trained to think. Of course that does not preclude a radical man thinking beyond the limits of his educational training but it opens the pool of possible editors to those without that training and such a pool is likely to have been more evenly spread between men and women.

Much of the evidence for female editorship has already been discussed in detail but without reference to gender. Put simply, the orientation of the text is towards the woman in a way which no other Biblical text is. This has a number of components to it so must be broken down. Before we do so, we will consider briefly how other books in the Bible portray women and then contrast this with how the editor of the Song of Songs depicts the protagonists.

2. Other female Biblical characters

In other works in the Bible, the female character is always the 'other', even if she is a rounded character. Whether or not she is portrayed sympathetically and even whether or not she is the dominant figure, she is still different. She always has to act within the context of a patriarchal society. Consideration of women in the Bible has led to a huge corpus of work and the summary of female characters set out below only scratches the surface of a vastly researched area.[427]

In the book of Genesis, all four matriarchs exhibit cunning to assert themselves in their society. Sarah demands of Abraham that he expel Hagar, her handmaiden and competitor, together with Ishmael, Hagar's son.[428] Rebecca goads her favoured son, Jacob, into stealing the birthright from his elder brother, Esau.[429] Rachel is favoured by Jacob over her elder sister Leah and then Leah decides to take matters into her own hands by using mandrakes to win him back.[430] Rachel, in turn, steals the household idols from her father Laban by sitting on them and then deceiving him when he searches for them by saying that she cannot move because 'the way of women is with me [at the moment]'.[431] Rarely can women achieve anything in the

---

[427] For a comprehensive analysis of the issues and literature on the subject, see: *Reading The Women of the Bible*: Tikva Frymer-Kensky. Schocken, New York, 2002.
[428] Genesis 21.10.
[429] Genesis 27.5-10.
[430] Genesis 30.14-16.
[431] Genesis 31.35.

book of Genesis except by guile. They exhibit what Harold Bloom calls 'American "toughness"'.[432]

The Exodus story revolves around the children of Israel but the human hero is Moses. He has two siblings, Aaron and Miriam. Whilst the portrayal of Miriam is mostly (but not entirely[433]) positive, it is not surprising in a patriarchal society that Miriam's role is significantly more limited than Aaron's. This is not to say, however, that Aaron's role is entirely positive; it is not and he is criticised severely in relation to the episode of the Golden Calf. The point, though, is that his character is more developed. Whilst we find out something about both Moses' siblings, we find out much more about Aaron than we do about Miriam - she has considerably fewer verses devoted to her. Miriam can be described as a prophetess[434] but Aaron is a priest and that is what the Bible focuses on in the Exodus story contained in the final four books of the Pentateuch.

In later books of the Bible, the role of women can be more central, though that is by no means always the case. Two of the later books in the Bible are named after women. In the book of Ruth, Ruth and Naomi, her mother-in-law, are portrayed in more detail and more sympathetically than any of the male characters. But Ruth's role, and how she can act, is ultimately determined for her by her future husband Boaz who tricks her *'go'el'* ('kinsman'/'redeemer') into allowing Boaz to marry her (see Ruth chapter 4). This only goes to highlight the limited power of women and the fact that a woman was still seen by society as part of a complex property transaction. Throughout this whole episode, Ruth stays entirely silent. She has nothing to say because that is not her role when it comes to legal contracts.

In the book of Esther, again the heroine rises above the role for which she would otherwise be destined. However, as one commentator puts it: 'To the extent that she "overcomes" the limitations of those positions of weakness she is heroic, not because she is a "liberated woman" seeking independence and autonomy, but because she moves from a low status to a high status.'[435] In other words, Esther is seen as heroic because of what she does *within* the confines of acceptable behaviour in the Bible. She may do it supremely well but she does it within a society dominated by men.

---

[432] *The Book of J*; Harold Bloom and David Rosenberg; Grove Weidenfeld, New York 1990 at 312. Bloom's assertion of female authorship of the J source in the Pentateuch is interesting but seems more of a supposition and provocation against conventional reading than anything for which he brings in strong evidence. Regardless, his comment shows that 'toughness' is required by a woman in the man's world which the book of J describes.

[433] Numbers 12.1-2.

[434] Exodus 15.20.

[435] *Esther: The JPS Bible Commentary* Adele Berlin, JPS, Philadelphia, 2001: page lvi

We have also had cause to consider another female character, more minor than either of these, outside the Song of Songs. We have seen how, in the book of Kings, Bathsheba was able to manipulate her husband David to ensure that her son became king. We then saw how she manipulated Solomon, now king, to ensure that he killed off his main competitor for the crown (see in this regard chapter 2 above). In so doing, she not only manipulates her husband and son, but also the patriarchal society in which she has to operate.

The lovers in the Song of Songs also lived in a patriarchal society. How they relate to it, in turn, reveals a great deal about the editor. The description of the female lover is entirely different from the depiction of any of the women referred to in other books of the Bible. Yet it is not through the female lover's character by itself that we see the strongest evidence for female editorship of the Song of Songs; it is how that character is manifested within the context of the structure of the Song of Songs. It is to that structure that we now turn.

3. The structure and text of the Song of Songs and issues of gender

First, as almost all commentators note, it is she who speaks more lines in the Song of Songs than he does. How many more is not clear because some of the verses do not give us enough indication as to which of the two lovers is speaking. What has been less commented upon, but which this commentary has stressed, is something more detailed and more significant. What one needs to consider is not just *who* speaks most but also *at what stage* they predominate and what conclusions can be drawn from this. It is *she* who initiates in the early stages of the Song of Songs. Indeed he hardly speaks in the first three chapters. And when he does, she gently encourages with a much greater elaboration of his theme.

An example makes the point. Consider the following to be found at the beginning of chapter 2 of the Song of Songs. She opens with a simple sentence describing herself - she is a rose of the Sharon, a lily of the valleys. He hears her comparison of herself to a lily and uses it to compliment her with his own image - that she is a lily amongst thorns when amongst the daughters. She then takes his comparison, uses it about him but, in so doing, modifies and expands it considerably. So she first says that he is like an apple in the trees of the forest (2.3) but then uses the apple image for her own recreation of the image in erotic terms - she is to be supported with raisin cakes and upheld with apples because she is lovesick (2.5).

Merely to say that she has more lines than he does in the Song of Songs if one adds them all up is somewhat to miss the point. The unevenness of speech between the lovers is itself unevenly distributed throughout the poem. By this I mean that she speaks much more than he does at the beginning but their voices are far more equal by the end. In the latter part of the book, she only describes his body once whereas he is allowed to describe hers twice. As this commentary has said, he finds his voice; but the reason he does so is because she allows him to. Whether she educates him in the ways of love is not revealed to us; it is crystal clear, however, that she teaches him how to give voice to that love verbally in the most subtle of ways.

Yet if the relationship between the young man and young woman is not only one of lovers but also one of teacher and pupil, there is no hint of the power relationship which so often goes hand in hand with such a relationship in the Bible. The book of Proverbs for example is replete with warnings about the father failing to control the child in the process of educating him. The English proverb, 'spare the rod and spoil the child' is clearly taken and adapted from Proverbs 13.24: 'he who spares his stick hates his son and he who loves him takes care to discipline him'. This is as far as one can travel from the role of the female educator in the Song of Songs. The father loves his son by beating him. The female lover loves her lover by teaching him how to express himself.

We find out other features about her beyond her ability to educate her lover. We see her emotions. Her anxiety is revealed to us in all its complexity. Its first obvious appearance is in the night scene (3.1-4) where she seeks but cannot find him. Something similar happens in the second night scene (5.2-8). Of course her anxiety is focused on her relationship with her lover but it mingles with the danger to which she exposes herself by looking for him in the empty night time streets of Jerusalem. Whatever anxiety she may have about how he feels about her is, however, more than matched by her concerns about how their relationship will be publicly perceived in her own society. We find out about her inner mind and what concerns her. The male lover learns how to speak the language of love but the editor allows all the male lover's emotions to be focused on this alone. Where he uses imagery which has a dual meaning (such as 'Lebanon' and 'frankincense' especially in his first *wasf* and speech thereafter - 4.1-5.1), he has normally appropriated that imagery either from her or from the Solomon interlude.

In other words, she is a much more emotionally rounded character than her lover is. We simply know more about who she is and how she 'ticks' than we do about him. As Jill Munro has said in her fine commentary: 'The Song is not a philosophical treatise about love, but rather the experience of love, from the perspective of the woman, which the images seek first and foremost to convey'.[436]

Another fascinating insight into the gender of the author comes from the gender of the other characters in the Song of Songs. In chapter 7 above, we discussed who they were and whether their role was hostile or sympathetic/neutral to the lovers. The hostile characters consist of Solomon, the city guards, her 'mother's sons' and the keepers of the vineyard. If we add to this list those characters who are mocked and therefore seen with an implied hostility, then we also need to take into account the heroes/soldiers guarding King Solomon and his queens. With the exception of the final group, all these characters are male.

If we now consider those characters who are viewed either sympathetically or neutrally, we will see that they consist of the daughters of Jerusalem, the female lover's own mother, the reference to Solomon's mother Bathsheba hinted at in 3.11 and the 'friends' referred to right at the end of the Song in 8.13. With the exception of this final group of 'friends', all these characters are female.

Munro ends her commentary by focusing on the mother figure. She notes that the positive mother figure must be contrasted with the entirely absent father. We are simply told nothing about the fathers of either of our lovers. Munro sees this as further evidence of the hand of a female writer: 'The feminine bias of the Song is enhanced yet further by the positive role played by the woman's mother, in contrast to the negative portrayal of her brothers and the absence of a paternal figure. These indications together strongly suggest female authorship, a suggestion which however must remain an intuition in the absence, up until now, of confirmatory evidence'.[437]

I disagree with Munro's comment about the absence of 'confirmatory evidence'. I see such evidence not only in the other characters as she does but also in the portrayal of the two lovers and the very structure of the Song of Songs which suggest a woman leading a man to self-discovery and fulfillment rather than the other way round. Nevertheless, Munro's caveat on her 'intuition', which implies an element of doubt and therefore caution, is a wise one. Cheryl Exum, who knows her way round the Song of Songs better than most, warns at point number four in an eye-catching article entitled *'Ten Things Every Feminist Should Know About The Song Of Songs'*[438] that

---

[436] Munro, 143.

[437] Munro, 147.

[438] See T*he Song of Songs A Feminist Companion to the Bible (Second Series)* edited by Athalya Brenner and Carole R. Fontaine, Sheffield Academic Press, 2000. Exum's article is at 24-35.

'the woman, or women, in this text may be the creation of male authors'.[439] Is this a female voice, she asks or do we have a male fantasy in which a male author has created his ideal dream woman?

Exum's fly in the ointment of a rush to acceptance of female authorship is well taken and any such note of wariness from a commentator who has written one of the finest comprehensive commentaries in recent years is impossible to ignore. Yet one can, possibly, overcome it.

How strong is the evidence of female editorship?

The issue of female editorship has thus been the subject of some discussion. What conclusions can we draw from this broad analysis? First while there is no certainty, a large amount of evidence, as shown above, supports the view that the editor of the Song of Songs was a woman. What degree of weight ought we to give to that evidence? Does it 'prove' that the editor was a woman?

Perhaps an analogy can be drawn to English court procedure. In an English civil case (i.e. for cases involving contract claims and the like), a judge will decide whether the defendant is liable to the claimant on the basis of 'the balance of probabilities'. In other words, liability is established if it is 'more likely than not' that the defendant committed the wrong or breach of contract of which he or she has been accused by the claimant. On that basis, I would argue that the evidence shows that it is 'more likely than not' that the editor of the Song of Songs was a woman and thereby satisfies the test.

By contrast, if it were a criminal case and the defendant had been accused of a crime, the judge would direct the jury to convict the defendant only if the members of the jury were 'sure' that the defendant had committed the crime. On that basis, if I were a juror, I would not be able to argue that the editor of the Songs was a woman even though I think the counter-evidence is weak. I cannot be 'sure'. The evidence does not support such a rigorous test implying 100% certainty.

Most citizens of the UK will be aware of a test for criminal liability which appears to be subtly different. The phrase they know (which also applies in the USA) is that the defendant is presumed innocent unless the prosecution has proved 'beyond reasonable doubt' that the defendant committed the crime. This was the test which was regularly applied until the last few years when the phrase given to jurors was

---

[439] Ibid at 28-9.

changed to the requirement that they must be 'sure' of the defendant's guilt. It is an oddity of the English legal system that the change of phrasing from 'beyond reasonable doubt' to 'sure' is not seen as an amendment to the law; it is rather that 'sure' is seen as a gloss on, and an explanation of, a longer and perhaps more unwieldy and antiquated phrase.

That is somewhat surprising because, as I have said, I do not think that I (or indeed anyone else) can be *sure* that the editor of the Song of Songs was a woman. I am, however, much more tempted to say that the Song of Songs was edited by a woman 'beyond reasonable doubt' because the longer phrase seems to me to insert a wholly new element into the equation which the concept of 'sure' does not. There are indeed doubts on this issue; they have been raised and certainly lead us to question our understanding. But how reasonable are those doubts?

I think that the evidence is strong enough to pass the test. I find the structural weighting towards the female lover highly persuasive. It is the strongest but not the only evidence supporting the theory of female editorship. On that basis, I will conclude that 'beyond reasonable doubt' I consider that the editor of the Song of Songs was a woman. You are my fellow juror. I hope I have persuaded you as well!

CONCLUSION

CONCLUSION

A Slave of our Passion

Passion lies at the very heart of the Song of Songs. The lovers declare their love for each other in the most passionate of terms. We, in turn, gladly enter into their world and share their passion: we use their words as the basis for our songs and our weddings.

But erotic passion is also the Song of Songs' Achilles' heel. It led some of its earliest readers to worry about the damage it could cause to orthodox thinking and so the Song of Songs was allegorised to mean something never originally intended. A later generation reinstituted the passion between the lovers but, in so doing, failed to understand that there was a third party whose passion was not being properly considered.

That third party was the work's editor. Her passion (and it probably was a woman) involved creating a work of erotic sophistication imbued with layers of extra meaning. We are now more able than ever before to reveal those meanings, through the discovery of parallel ancient near-Eastern literature. Yet still the myth persists that the only passion involved in the Song of Songs is the erotic one between the two lovers. The erotic is a powerfully passionate flame; it is not surprising so many of the Song's readers see it, find themselves caught up and unable to see beyond.

It is not the purpose of this book to pour cold water on that passion in any way whatsoever; indeed, we ought to revel in it and certainly not extinguish it. But we have perhaps been guilty of being blindsided by our passion in failing to see beyond the erotic. To use the Scottish philosopher David Hume's phrase from a different context, we have perhaps become the 'slave of our passions'.

There remains a mystery to the Song of Songs. We cannot unravel all its layers; its enigmatic nature still endures. But the aim of this work has been to show that erotic passion was only one of a number of emotions at the heart of the editor's mind when she edited the Song of Songs. Seeking to unpick as many of those layers as will yield to such a task is, in my view, an immensely fruitful exercise; if this work leads to others investigating only a small part of what remains to be understood, it will have proved successful in its objective.

The Song of Songs is indeed a work of passion - arguably the finest in the whole of the western canon. It comprises passion for the erotic, passion for equality between the sexes and passion for social justice. And all these are enveloped in an all-consuming passion for a different, 'upturned' world. Let us celebrate all those passions and not be slaves to one alone. Love is therefore possible, even in the time of tyranny.

ACKNOWLEDGEMENTS

This book came about as a result of a discussion with my friend Gabriel Josipovici. I had written an article for *The Jewish Quarterly*. It included a few paragraphs outlining the thesis which is at the heart of this book. Gabriel said that each of those paragraphs merited a chapter. To my protestation that I did not have the time to devote to such an undertaking came the withering response that, if I wanted to write the book, I would make the time. I owe him a huge debt for goading me to embark on what has proved to be a labour of love.

Others have given of their own time to look at what I have written. In particular, I wish to thank Jeannie Cohen and Lilian Levy who have looked through every word and saved me from any number of infelicities. I have been lucky enough to receive comments on some or all of the substance of the text from Jan Fokkelman, Harry Freedman, Julian Gilbey, Gabriel Josipovici, Francis Landy, Jeremy Schonfield, Dennis Snower, Rosie Solomon and Jonathan Wittenberg.

The buck stops here though; I am responsible for any unexpunged errors.

BIBLIOGRAPHY

Alter, Robert. *Ancient Israel. The former Prophets: Joshua, Judges, Samuel, and Kings. A translation with commentary.* New York, W.W. Norton, 2013.

Alter, Robert. *Strong as Death is Love. The Song of Songs, Ruth, Esther, Jonah, Daniel. A translation with commentary.* New York, W.W. Norton, 2015.

Bloch, Ariel, and Chana Bloch. *The Song of Songs: A New Translation with an Introduction and Commentary.* Berkeley: University of California Press, 1995.

Brenner, Athalya & Carole R. Fontaine. *The Song of Songs: A Feminist Companion to the Bible (Second Series).* Sheffield, Sheffield Academic Press, 2000.

Chamaish Hamegillot (The Five Scrolls). Jerusalem, Mossad Harav Kook, 1990.

Cogan, Mordechai. *I Kings.* AYB10 New Haven, Yale University Press, 2001.

Exum, J. Cheryl. *Song of Songs: A Commentary.* OTL. Louisville, KY: Westminster John Knox Press, 2005.

Falk, Marcia. *The Song of Songs: A New Translation and Interpretation.* San Francisco: Harper Collins, 1990.

Fishbane, Michael. *The JPS Bible Commentary Song of Songs.* Philadelphia: Jewish Publication Society, 2015.

Fokkelman, Jan. *The Song of Songs: A Mercurial Wonder.* In 'Welcome to the Cavalcade. A Festschrift in honour of Rabbi Professor Jonathan Magonet' pp 12 - 23. Kulmus, 2013.

Fox, Michael V. *The Song of Songs and the Ancient Egyptian Love Songs.* Madison: University of Wisconsin Press, 1985.

Fox, Michael V. *A Time to Tear Down & a Time to Build Up: A Rereading of Ecclesiastes.* Michigan, Eerdmans, 1999.

Fox, Michael V. *Proverbs 1-9.* AB18A. New Haven, Yale University Press, 2000.

Fox, Michael V. *Proverbs 10 - 31.* AB18B. New Haven, Yale University Press, 2009.

Garsiel, Moshe. *Olam hatanach. Melachim alef.* (The Biblical world. I Kings). Biblical commentary. Tel Aviv, Yediot Achronot, 2002.

Goodman, Micha. *Ha-na'um ha-acharon shel Moshe.* (Moses' Final Oration). Or Yehuda, Kinneret, Zmora-Bitan, Dvir, 2014.

Goulder, Michael D. *The Song of Fourteen Songs.* JSOTSup 36. Sheffield, UK: Sheffield Academic Press, 1986.

Gurevitch, Zali. *Qol dodim - al lashon ha'ahavah shel shir hashirim.* (The Sound of Love: On Erotic Language in the Song of Songs.) Tel Aviv, Babel, 2013.

James, Elaine T. *Landscapes of the Song of Songs: Poetry and Place.* Oxford, Oxford University Press, 2017.

Kasher, Menachem M. *Torah shelemah: Megilat shir hashirim.* (The Complete Torah. Talmudic-Midrashic compilation of the Song of Songs). Jerusalem, Noam Aharon, 2010.

Keel, Othmar. *The Song of Songs: A Continental Commentary.* Translated by Frederick J. Gaiser. 1st Fortress Press Edition. Continental Commentaries. Minneapolis: Fortress Press, 1994.

Landy, Francis. *Paradoxes of Paradise: Identity and Difference in the Song of Songs.* BLS7. Sheffield, UK: Almond Press, 1983 (1st Edition). Sheffield Phoenix Press, 2011 (2nd Edition).

Munro, Jill M. *Spikenard and Saffron: The Imagery of the Song of Songs.* JSOTSup 203. Sheffield, UK: Sheffield Academic Press, 1995.

Pope, Marvin H. *Song of Songs.* AB7C. Garden City, NY Doubleday, 1977.

Segal, Benjamin J. *The Song of Songs. A Woman in love.* Jerusalem, Gefen 2009.

Spencer, F. Scott. *Song of Songs: Wisdom Commentary.* Collegeville, Minnesota, Liturgical Press, 2017.

Tanakh: The Holy Scriptures. The New JPS Translation According to the Traditional Hebrew Text. Philadelphia: The Jewish Publication Society of America, 1985.

Watson, Graeme. *The Song of Songs: A Contemplative Guide.* London, UK. SPCK, 2014.

Whedbee, J. William. *The Bible and the Comic Vision.* Minneapolis, Fortress, 2002.

Zakovitch, Yair. *Shir ha-Shirim im Mavo u-Ferush.* (The Song of Songs with Introduction and Commentary). Tel Aviv: Am Oved, 1992.

Printed in Great Britain
by Amazon